Dr. David Young,

Thanks for going the "2nd mile."

Tim Meador

RHYTHMS OF

THE HEART

EDITED BY
SHELLEY CHAPIN

VICTOR BOOKS

A DIVISION OF SCRIPTURE PRESS PUBLICATIONS INC.
USA CANADA ENGLAND

Scripture quotations are from the *Holy Bible, New International Version®*. Copyright © 1973, 1978, 1984 by International Bible Society. Used by permission of Zondervan Publishing House. All rights reserved.

Max Lucado's readings on Compassion, Disappointment, and Significance are adapted from his book *In the Eye of the Storm,* © 1991, Word, Inc., Dallas, Texas. Used with permission.

Max Lucado's readings on Courage and Hope are adapted from his book *And the Angels Were Silent,* © 1992, Questar Publishers, Inc., Sisters, Oregon. Used with permission.

Copy Editor: Greg Clouse
Cover Designer: Joe DeLeon
Cover llustrator: Tom Duckworth

A portion of the royalties from the sale of this book goes to the ministry of Joni & Friends, 28720 Canwood Street, Suite 102, Agoura Hills, California 91301.

Library of Congress Cataloging-in-Publication Data

Rhythms of the heart / edited by Shelley Chapin.
    p.   cm.
  ISBN 1-56476-008-1
  1. Devotional exercises. I. Chapin, Shelley.
  BV4801.R48   1993
  242 — dc20

                                   93-15306
                                       CIP

---

1 2 3 4 5 6 7 8 9 10 Printing/Year 97 96 95 94 93

The rhythms of my own heart were set in motion by the love, the example, the pains, the joys, the struggles, and the dedication of my mom and dad.

To Chape and Melita Chapin I am eternally grateful for the freedom to fail, the confidence to succeed, the security to grow, and the belief that I can be all that God has designed me to be.

A special "thank you" to those of you who took the time to contribute to this ministry. May other hearts find rhythm from the wisdom shared within the pages of this book.

CONTENTS

Foreword	11
How To Use This Book	15
Anger	17
Anguish	33
Belonging	51
Brokenness	67
Comfort	87
Compassion	103
Control	123
Courage	141
Disappointment	157
Endurance	175
Failure	193
Faithfulness	209
Fear	231
Forgiveness	253
Grace	271
Grief	293
Guilt	309
Hope	325
Joy	345
Loneliness	361
Love	375
Obedience	393
Peace	413
Shame	433
Significance	451
Success	469
Suffering	483
Worship	499

ABOUT THE EDITOR

Shelley Chapin is Executive Director of CSC Ministries ("Committed to Sharing Christ"), manager of two Christian radio stations in Tyler, Texas, and a family counselor in Dallas. A graduate of the University of Texas at Dallas and Dallas Theological Seminary, she is currently working on her Ph.D. in Counseling.

Shelley began a journey with cancer in October 1982, and since that time has traveled widely to churches, medical schools, hospitals, and conferences to share the lessons she has learned in the company of suffering. Her love for people has taken her overseas for many short-term missions trips, including more than twenty trips to Poland.

A musician and writer, Shelley has also authored *Within the Shadow* (Victor, 1991), a biblical look at suffering, death, and the process of grieving; and *Counselors, Comforters, and Friends* (Victor, 1992), a book about caregiving in the church.

CONTRIBUTORS

Frank Beaudine
Chairman
Eastman & Beaudine, Inc.
Dallas, Texas

Ken Boa
Eastern Division Director
Search Ministries, Inc.
Alpharetta, Georgia

Buck Buchanan
Pastor of Care & Concern
  Ministries
First Evangelical Free
  Church
Fullerton, California

Marilyn Budde
Wife and Mother
Tyler, Texas

Pam Campbell
Manager of Adult
  Education
Victor Books
Wheaton, Illinois

Mark Cosgrove
Professor of Psychology
Taylor University
Upland, Indiana

John Coulombe
Pastor of Senior Adult
  Ministries & Lion
  Tamers Anonymous

First Evangelical Free
  Church
Fullerton, California

Shelly O. Cunningham
Instructor in Christian
  Education
Talbot School of Theology
La Mirada, California

Sally Dobbs
Artist, Wife, and Mother
Tyler, Texas

Tim Hawks
Pastor
Hill Country Bible Church
Austin, Texas

Mark W. Hoffman
Teaching Assistant
Talbot School of Theology
La Mirada, California

Martha Hook
Author
Henderson, Texas

Phillip Hook
Professor of Bible
LeTourneau University
Longview, Texas

Jay Kesler
President
Taylor University
Upland, Indiana

Marianne Koons
Wife and Mother
Georgetown, Texas

Max Lucado
Pulpit Minister
Oak Hills Church
San Antonio, Texas

A. Boyd Luter
Chair & Associate Professor
   of Bible
Talbot School of Theology
La Mirada, California

David Lynch
Senior Pastor
East Side Church of God
Anderson, Indiana

Chris McCray
Draftsman
Longview, Texas

Carolyn Means
Teacher
Tyler, Texas

Sharon Moss
Supervisor of
   Correspondence
Prison Fellowship
Reston, Virginia

Ellen B. Quarry
Staff Counselor
Granada Heights Friends
   Church
La Mirada, California

Pamela M. Reeves
Medical Missionary
Africa

Gary Richmond
Pastor of Single Parent
   Ministries
First Evangelical Free
   Church
Fullerton, California

Annette Richter
Author
Santa Barbara, California

Marilyn Rhode
Author
Fullerton, California

Bonnie Sloat
Adjunct Faculty
Taylor University
Upland, Indiana
and
Marriage & Family Life
   Counselor
Life Center Counseling
   Center
Marion, Indiana

Joni Eareckson Tada
Founder and President
Joni & Friends
Agoura Hills, California

Mary Dale Thomas
Wife and Mother
Tyler, Texas

FOREWORD

Friday morning comes up singing with sunstreams through your kitchen window, washing the walls in a golden glow. The birds are chirping. The sky is blue. A light breeze through the screen door wafts in the scent of lilacs in bloom by the back steps. Coffee is perking, bread is toasting, and honey and butter are on the table.

Your heart rises easily in praise to God and you find yourself saying out loud, "Lord, what a beautiful day. You are absolutely wonderful!" And He is. After all, there are no disagreements hanging over your head and no pressuring appointments screaming at you from your desk calendar. The kids marched happily off to school and the dog has been fed. All utility bills are paid and all house repairs are finished. Phone calls are up-to-date and your car pool responsibilities are over for the week. Nothing but clear sailing on a glorious Friday morning with a hot cup of coffee, toast and honey, and "Regis and Kathie Lee."

But oh, what a difference a day makes—because twenty-four short little hours later finds you wishing Saturday morning would go away. The car gave out yesterday on the way to the market and your husband has been arguing over estimates for the last hour. One teenager darted out of the house leaving her room a national disaster area while the other child has been whining all morning that you forgot to get Capt'n Crunch at the store. Earlier in the week you failed to drop off your husband's shirts at the laundry and he has to be out of the house to catch a plane by noon. You can see it coming—your husband will head out the door in a huff and at least one child will be sent to his room.

Your heart sinks easily in dismay and you stand slump-shouldered at the kitchen sink saying out loud, "O God . . . where *are* You when I need You?"

It happens all the time to Christians everywhere. We get excited about God when circumstances are delightful. When the weather invigorates us. When the medical checkup goes fine. When nobody is nagging us or expecting us to perform up to some unearthly standard. God seems near and close when the pot roast turns out delicious . . . but He seems far and distant when the casserole turns to charcoal in the oven.

Why is it that when things are good we feel that God is good; and when things are bad, it feels like God is off in Tazmania taking care of little devils or in the Middle East setting the stage for Armageddon?

Perhaps it's because we are so prone to permit our circumstances—whether good or bad—to dictate our view of God. We allow our hormones to set the stage, our emotions to direct our thinking. Moods can shift and swing, and they are influenced by everything from a death in the family to too much sugar from all that cake and ice cream. Feelings can't always be trusted.

That's why time and again the Bible tells us to reach beyond our moods and connect with our God who is faithful. As it says in Deuteronomy 7:9, *"Know therefore that the Lord your God is God; He is the faithful God, keeping His covenant of love to a thousand generations of those who love Him, and keep His commands."*

Did you get that? The Lord is not just *a* faithful God, but *the* faithful God. He is the same steadfast and good God on a sullen Saturday morning that He was on that free-wheeling Friday. Scripture alone must be our frame of reference for who the Lord is . . . circumstances do *not* a good theology make.

Now you can see why I like *Rhythms of the Heart.* It's

a collection of readings that connect your mood to God's Word. Like an anchor, the Word of God holds you fast against the swelling tide of grief or disappointment. Like a bit and bridle, God's Word reins in your anger before it runs away with you. Like a rock-solid foundation, the Scriptures in *Rhythms of the Heart* provide a stable and sure beginning to each day, no matter if it's good or bad.

I should know. There are days when I cry to think how rich and full God's love is. On such days God's tenderness melts my heart and I reach out to Him as my Friend. Then there are days when I'm battling pride or wasting hours in silly daydreams. That's when God's Word slices through my sinfulness. It stings and His hand seems heavy, but it's the Lord's way of reminding me He's my Refiner. There are mornings when I wake up and feel helpless and frightened. It's times like that I hide under the shelter of His wings and snuggle safely in the cleft of my Rock.

Rhythms of the Heart will help you take whatever mood you're in and thumbtack it to the Word of God. With this book, you can know exactly how to relate to your Lord, whether you fall on your knees in awesome respect or climb up in His lap to be held in His arms.

So take a mood. Any mood. If your heart is restless and anxious today, then flip to the readings on "Control." If your blood pressure is skyrocketing from a squabble with your neighbor, try turning to the section on "Forgiveness." If you feel like throwing in the towel and giving up, I suggest you read from "Endurance." And if today is one of those bright shining mornings with clear sailing ahead, then please turn to "Worship" and give God all the praise He's due!

Listen to the rhythms of your heart. What is your soul telling you? Look at the circumstances around you today and ask yourself, "How can I use this to press myself up against my Lord?" And now take a breath, breathe a prayer for guidance, and get your heart beating in tune with today's reading.

Match your rhythm to His . . . and watch this day shine with God's glory!

Joni Eareckson Tada
Spring 1993

How to Use This Book

You've probably used a devotional book at some point in your life. Journals can be helpful in so many ways. They can organize our morning or give direction to the day. They can help us focus on matters of the spirit.

Rhythms of the Heart is intended to do just that — set the heart in forward motion. Instead of reading a thought that's been indexed by the date, this journal guide is indexed by topics of the heart.

If you're working through forgiveness, you can spend anywhere from a day to an entire week examining both the concept and its application. If you're wrestling with anger, you can read insights from those who, like you, have been wandering through anger's expressions and purposes.

It is our intent, through *Rhythms of the Heart*, to link your place in life's journey to the Word of God. We want to help His Word become more real to you. We want to help you connect your mood to God's wisdom in order to bridge that gap between where you are and where you want to be.

How can you use *Rhythms of the Heart* effectively?

• First, take a moment to familiarize yourself with the format of the book. There are twenty-eight emotions or moods covered in the journal with entries from various authors comprising each section. The topics themselves are listed in alphabetical order, making it easier for you to turn to the section you need the most.

• Next, think your way through the list of topics and choose an emotion or mood that best describes your place in the journey right now. Take an entry today and spend some time thinking with that author. Then tomorrow take another contribution and think a bit more on any topic of your choosing.

• Finally, notice the blank page at the end of each of the twenty-eight sections. This page is there for you to record any insights, complaints, questions, prayers, or creative writings which come to you as you work your way through the topic. The page is there solely for you, so use it in a way that is most beneficial.

This book was written with you in mind and is designed to serve your emotional and spiritual needs. Allow God to love you in the rhythms of your heart.

Our Father is intimately acquainted with our ways and feelings, our needs and concerns, our disappointments and longings. Join in a pilgrimage of love as we set our hearts in motion.

ANGER

WHAT, ME ANGRY?

"Rend your hearts and not your garments. Return to the Lord your God, for He is gracious and compassionate, slow to anger and abounding in love, and He relents from sending calamity. Who knows but that He may turn and have pity and leave behind a blessing—grain offerings and drink offerings for the Lord your God."
Joel 2:13-14

I wish I had the proverbial nickel for every time I have said, "I'm not an angry person" or "I don't get angry." Yes, for years I prided myself in insisting that anger and I have never been nor will ever be companions. Somehow it seemed more "noble," more "Christian" to deny the emotion of anger. Perhaps you too have either denied its existence or thought yourself less than "spiritual" in its company.

It is difficult for some of us to understand anger's scope and message. In my case, I learned to associate anger with hurt and misunderstanding. My early experiences with the emotion caused me to hold it suspect. I feared that it could not be expressed in a God-like fashion, so I decided to try to block anger from my development.

I did not realize my fear of anger for many years, but I have since come to see that anger can be helpful, healthy, and quite appropriate. It is part of our God-given repertoire of emotions. It is a means for examining that which we find painful, sinful, or otherwise unjust. It is a means of identifying that which transgresses. Anger is one of our options for sharing that which troubles the soul.

Our Heavenly Father is well-versed in the emotion of anger. He has observed the condition of sin and the pain that grows from it ever since Adam and Eve accepted the enticements of the serpent. We are told in Genesis 6 that God literally grieved when He looked down upon the earth and saw the havoc that His children were reaping.

God has wrestled back and forth with anger through the years. We observe His anger, and then we observe His compassion. We know the reasons for His anger and we can understand, and yet we pray for grace and mercy rather than justice. We pray, Moses prayed, Zipporah prayed, Abram prayed. Deborah, Jeremiah, Amos, Joel, Paul, Stephen, Elizabeth—all prayed for God's compassion. And the answer to our prayers? The death and resurrection of our Lord.

God relents. God forgives. God weeps. God grows angry. God struggles with His wayward children. God hurts for His beloved. And God shows mercy.

We cannot obliterate anger, hard as we might try. And pretend as we will, there are times when all of us experience that emotion. It is just a difficult emotion to take responsibility for, much less express.

The key is to begin at the beginning, acknowledge that which bothers us and then deal with the emotion in a wise and loving manner. Anger is an emotion that need not be feared but awed. It need not be denied but acknowledged. It need not be condemned but examined, sifted, and then wisely expressed.

I lived much of my life afraid of anger. I pray to live the remainder of my days understanding anger and choosing mercy.

██████████████ THOUGHT FOR THE HEART

I feel afraid of anger at times. I would like to learn to examine those times when I feel angry, learn from them, and then express the anger in a way that is helpful for all concerned.

—Shelley Chapin

ANGER

●
SHORT ACCOUNTS

"In your anger do not sin; do not let the sun go down while you are still angry." Ephesians 4:26

When I became a Christian in 1970, I was no stranger to anger. I'd had an angry relationship with my dad for as long as I could remember. I was a master of that mild-mannered exterior until anger turned me into the "incredible hulk."

Soon after becoming a believer I more or less "bottled up" the angry side of my personality. My reasoning went something like this: *Since Christians aren't supposed to be angry people, we should never express anger.*

Though I now realize such an outlook is both illogical and unbiblical, it "made sense" to me at the time. And others seemed to practice the theory. I learned to avoid my anger so rigorously that I buried the ability to recognize even appropriate anger.

Don't be fooled! There was anger (and plenty of it!) hidden inside. As hard as I tried to silence its cries, the anger beat steadily against the door of that high security cell deep in my heart. Finally, anger, worry, and some unresolved choices united in a "power play" against my health, depositing me in a hospital bed with viral pneumonia. During those humble weeks of 1990, there was no place left to turn but honesty.

Learning to release and then control my sheepishly admitted anger is still a difficult process. Sometimes I stifle the embryonic anger because I'm afraid its release will result in a chain reaction of destruction. Sometimes I stifle the anger because of pride. But fortunately, the Lord continues to patiently reprogram me about anger. He continues to help me recognize and appropriately express that which is felt within me.

How can we healthily express an emotion which seems so threatening or destructive?

A key for unlocking the door to healthy anger is "keeping short accounts." Whether our anger is with God (which almost everyone experiences occasionally) or with other people, this key can be the difference between bitterness and resolution.

Keeping short accounts means being as honest as possible about what we are feeling. Keeping short accounts means expressing our feelings in as edifying or graceful a way as possible. And keeping short accounts means releasing the anger once it has been acknowledged and expressed.

The Apostle Paul understood this concept when he wrote to the Ephesian church. Having learned lessons the hard way himself, Paul wanted us to know that anger cannot be avoided and need not be carried forever.

We are not asked to deny our anger. We are asked to keep short accounts and to deal with that anger as considerately and expediently as possible.

Short-term anger is healthy emotional housecleaning, and it won't come back to haunt us later!

THOUGHT FOR THE HEART

I am aware of these areas of my emotional house where anger resides and needs my attention.

—Boyd Luter

●

BEING WISE IN YOUR ANGER

"In your anger, do not sin; when you are on your beds, search your hearts and be silent. Offer right sacrifices and trust in the Lord." Psalm 4:4-5

ANGER

It seems that anger is the story of my life. I can hardly remember a day of my childhood when I was not angry. I'm sure that there were days I felt content, but strangely I remember those that were punctuated by anger. Life seemed (and still often seems) so unfair.

"Why am I a preacher's kid while all my friends are from 'normal' families?" "Why is my father crippled while other fathers are healthy?" "Why do we have to be so poor while others have plenty?" "Why are other kids popular while I am not?" "Why can other kids dance while I am not allowed?" The list could go on.

I remember stepping on every crack in the sidewalk and swearing with each step. Never once did anyone hear me swear, but the words echoed deep in the chambers of my mind. Life was not treating me fairly, and I couldn't seem to just "accept" this reality. Slowly but surely the anger built its house of resentment deep inside until it became the comfortable response to all loss and disappointment.

As I grew up, the anger became quite valuable. I was sure it made me a better competitor. And it worked wonders at home—my mother did not know how to respond to me. My wife now says I once proclaimed, "If I give up my anger, I'll lose what makes me good."

One day I was sitting in the audience at Pine Cove Conference Center in Texas. Just as you might guess, a Bible teacher was giving a message on anger. I had heard countless messages on anger before, but this time I heard something different.

"God is described as angry over 400 times in the Hebrew Scriptures," he said. "We tend to forget that God experiences anger." And suddenly a great light came into my mind.

God feels anger, I thought to myself, not surprised by the fact, but newly aware of the reality.

It is not wrong to be angry. Anger is a normal response in a world where life is unfair. I began to feel a real sense of relief.

Anger is not, in and of itself, wrong. What can be wrong is how we use and express our anger. I had been using mine unhealthily for most of my life, but the anger itself is a God-given response to an unfair world.

I wish I had understood this all-important concept much earlier. While still young, I had learned to use anger as a selfish tool against life's seeming unfairness. I saw it as my protector, my understanding friend, the barrier to separate me from more pain or rejection.

What I didn't understand is how to let others know of my anger. I didn't know how to communicate my pain. I didn't know how to trust and reach out to those who could help.

God acknowledges anger. Such a powerful emotion is no surprise to Him. He acknowledges, accepts, and even expresses anger, but He also asks that we be wise in its release.

Anger plays an important role in our wrestling match with sin and disappointment. Anger says, "I'm hurting, and I need someone to care." But the psalmist has a good idea. When angry, it is best to be silent and think before speaking or releasing the fury.

Allow someone to care about you in your anger. Try not to use the anger to isolate you from the world. And try not to use the anger to separate the world from you.

■■■■■■■■■■ THOUGHT FOR THE HEART

I am aware of feeling angry. I would like to learn to stop and think, and I would like to learn to invite others to walk beside me in my pain.

— Phil Hook

ANGER

●
SLOW TO ANGER

"Everyone should be quick to listen, slow to speak and slow to become angry." James 1:19

Nothing robs us of peace of mind more than unresolved anger. Sometimes we argue in the heat of the moment and then remain cold for days. Sometimes we bear a grudge against a family member and then try to appear "civil" during the holidays. Sometimes we grow discouraged when a coworker seems to foster resentment or jealousy. And some of us are bound by the chains of anger, forged in the yesterdays of our lives. At some point in time, all of us suffer with the burden of anger.

Is it possible to rise above anger and bitterness? Must we allow the habit of anger to define who we are? When we find that we cannot live *with* our angers yet lack the power to live *without* them, how can we seek the kind of healing that is offered us by God?

We are encouraged, in Scripture, to be slow to anger and also to express ourselves healthily. In other words, God understands the emotion of anger and He provides us with a way to both recognize the emotion and yet maintain a healthy posture and attitude.

Being slow to anger does not mean burying our feelings. To the contrary, our reactions to life's hurts are natural. Being slow to anger means controlling the way we express that anger before it's unleashed on the rest of the world. It means not causing harm to others or to our relationships, and committing our hearts and minds to a course of understanding rather than division.

An admirable goal, but we all know that it isn't easy to learn healthier ways of releasing our anger. I've been working for quite some time to express my anger in ways that work toward resolution. While I am certainly no "expert" in anger expression, perhaps these insights will help.

Expressing my anger healthily begins in not delaying the process. Many a time I've allowed resentment to build and build, and the end result is anything but comfortable — for the other person or for me. In fact, I am aware that it often takes time for me to admit my anger, even to myself. It is for our good and our peace of mind that we are urged to repair relationships and live in peace with one another.

Secondly, I've found it is best to identify the person with whom I am angry and why. This step may seem obvious, but there are times I take my anger out on one person when I'm really angry with someone else. It seems that those closest to me are easier targets for the release of my anger, but an easy target is not a deserving target! Our relationships are so important — they are clearly worth the "trouble" of identifying the object and source of our anger before releasing it on whomever is at hand.

Thirdly, I have found that my anger is most bearable when I am actively seeking some form of resolution. I am rarely "happy" when the anger is swept under the table. Resolution isn't always possible between two people, but at least it is possible to work for resolution within our own hearts.

It is a privilege to feel and explore our own emotions — even anger. Learning to recognize the source of the anger and express it healthily is one of the great privileges of knowing and being known by God.

THOUGHT FOR THE HEART

I am aware of feeling angry and needing resolution in these areas or relationships.

— Mark Cosgrove

ANGER

●

HEAD TO HEAD WITH PRIDE

"The Lord is compassionate and gracious, slow to anger, abounding in love; He will not always accuse, nor will He harbor His anger forever; nor does He treat us as our sins deserve or repay us according to our iniquities. For as high as the heavens are above the earth, so great is His love for those who fear Him; as far as the east is from the west, so far has He removed our transgressions from us." Psalm 103:8-12

When they brought her to me she was almost dead. At first glance, toxemia. She was close to delivery and she had a terrible fever. I did not know if I could save her.

I didn't recognize the tribal clothing so I asked for a translator. Such a request can often take hours, if no one in the clinic can speak the specific dialect. I had tried all my words, but no communication took place. I was losing the woman — fast — I found no heartbeat for the baby.

We were specially blessed by God; someone waiting outside in line knew the language of this tribe. I worked to stabilize the patient while I heard her story.

It seemed they had traveled many miles to reach our clinic. The woman had been ill for several weeks and the tribal medicine had failed to make a difference. She needed a physician, so they brought her to "the doctors."

"Are you aware that the baby has no heartbeat?" I asked through my translator. Those with the woman nodded their heads vigorously.

"How long?" I continued to probe.

"Two weeks." This woman was slowly being poisoned by her unborn child. It seemed she had developed a fever several weeks earlier, and no efforts to reduce the fever had proved effective. I knew I had to remove the baby quickly. I ordered the preparations.

ANGER

"No!" A man grabbed my arm. He had been in the back of their group and had spoken not a word. Though he didn't know English, he knew the word *no!*

"I must," I tried to explain, but before I could speak he began to pry the woman from the examining table.

"What are you doing?" I asked. Unfortunately, when we are excited about something we tend to speak in our native tongue. He paid no attention to me.

"Tell him," I said to the interpreter. "Tell him she will die if she leaves." The interpreter obeyed my request, but there was no use trying. The man was her husband, and he was determined to take her back to his village and to his medicine. He did not trust the white doctor nor did he believe my diagnosis.

I wish I could describe how furious I felt. I wanted to tell that husband how terrible I thought he was; how self-ish for letting his pride get in the way of his wife's well-being. But there was nothing I could do. He was in charge.

There are times when others enrage us. Their attitudes and actions are ignorant, if not deliberate, and they refuse to listen to a word we say. Even if our message is one of life or death, there are times people will not hear. (I think it's safe to say that parents feel a bit of this frustration from time to time.)

As I watched that man carry his wife away, I knew that fear, ignorance, or pride stood in the way of her life and death. I knew he would be grieving before long. I knew he would feel that somehow the world had let him down. I knew he would say we hadn't helped and the unnecessary trip had caused her death. And I knew he would go on, both in life and in his ways.

I also knew, just a bit that day, how God must feel each time we fail to listen. From God's perspective, the truth that He shares is life-giving. It is accurate. He knows what He's talking about.

Yet we so often long to hold on to our old and tired ways. We like to see the world the way we've always seen the world. We prefer to nurse the pride, the ignorance, and the fear.

How gracious God is with you and me. He grows angry when we fail to obey His truth, but His love is never far from the anger. Thank You, Father, for working with us.

▬▬▬▬▬▬▬ **T H O U G H T   F O R   T H E   H E A R T**

These situations and these people tend to foster my anger. I am willing to try to work with others the way that God, in His grace and compassion, works with me.

—Pamela M. Reeves

●
EXAMINING ANGER'S SOURCE

"Saul was very angry; this refrain galled him. 'They have credited David with tens of thousands,' he thought, 'but me with only thousands. What more can he get but the kingdom?' And from that time on Saul kept a jealous eye on David." 1 Samuel 18:8-9

The phone rang one day and it was our middle daughter on the other line.

"Dad, something's wrong with the car," she said. She knew what my response would be.

"What's the matter?" I replied rather coldly.

"There is oil all over everywhere," she answered. I could feel my frustration starting to rise.

"Where are you, honey?" I continued, trying to soften the growing edge.

"In a parking lot in town." She knew well what to do. Just give the facts to Dad when he's angry.

"What did you do?" I pressed (notice the accusation!).

"I kept driving until I had a safe place to park," she

said, the defensiveness growing in her voice.

"What color is the oil?" I continued.

"It's pink, Dad," she said.

"Stay where you are."

Angrily I gathered up wrenches, towels, and other paraphernalia. She was driving one of my favorite cars! It was a classic Jeep convertible, and I'd heard there were only seven of them in our part of the country. I considered the car very valuable.

When I reached the parking lot I saw the nightmare immediately. Barbie had been correct. There was oil everywhere! I asked her a series of irrational questions and bad turned to worse.

"Why did you do this?"

She had done nothing.

"Why didn't you stop sooner?"

She had stopped as soon as she could.

"You girls are always messing up *my* cars."

I sent her home in *my* car while I worked to fix the Jeep. It was a long afternoon.

The problem was a simple one. The transmission line to the radiator had slipped off and the repair job only took five minutes. The mess was a different matter.

When the line slipped, the oil sprayed into the fan which, in turn, spread oil everywhere! And while it was a harmless display, the cleanup job was a two-hour ordeal.

By far the longest part of the repair process was my anger. As accurately as I can recall, the recovery took about two days. Imagine! Two days of anger with someone I love—over a car! (Many of you *can* imagine!)

Barbie had done nothing wrong. In fact, she had done everything right. She was the undeserving recipient of an anger that had nothing to do with her. The anger was all about me and my cars and my sense of value.

I've learned, through the years, that Saul and I have

something in common. We have felt anger and then turned that anger toward someone who is neither its cause nor its resolution. I am reminded of my own tendencies each time I read about Saul's anger toward David.

David had done nothing but serve his friend Saul. From the time he was a young boy, David had soothed Saul's pain with his songs and looked for ways to please the king. David loved Saul, and Saul returned that love until David stepped into Saul's arena.

Young David thought he was doing good for his king. Side by side they battled the Philistines and enjoyed great victory. The problem came when people offered David some of the praise that Saul wanted all for himself.

There are times when our anger is really about us, not the other person at all. We feel insecure, exposed, threatened, or vulnerable, and so we attempt to "protect" that which seems important at the time. Saul tried to protect his reputation; I wanted to protect my car.

Examine your anger. See if there is something there which is simply for you to learn. And grant yourself grace in the discovery.

We are human and we do struggle with anger. But learning from anger is one of the great gifts God gives the believer.

▬▬▬▬▬▬ THOUGHT FOR THE HEART

I need to examine my anger with these people or these situations and see what is there for me to learn.

—Phil Hook

RHYTHMS OF MY HEART

ANGUISH

IN SEARCH OF THE GOLDEN THREAD

"I am the man who has seen affliction by the rod of His wrath. He has driven me away and made me walk in darkness rather than light; indeed, He has turned His hand against me again and again, all day long. He has made my skin and my flesh grow old and has broken my bones. He has besieged me and surrounded me with bitterness and hardship." Lamentations 3:1-5

"Since that time I have not believed that God is a good God," she said. Her voice shook slightly and her clear, blue eyes were glazed with pain. Her name is Maria, and she is my friend.

I met Maria on a train in Germany. It was my first time to travel alone overseas, and I had prayed for someone to befriend me on my journey. I was scheduled to speak throughout western Europe for seven weeks, and I literally knew no one. By my first week there I realized I had been a bit optimistic about planning such an excursion. I had no idea I would feel so alone, but I did.

Maria's eyes met mine as I entered the train car, and I immediately knew she was a kind and compassionate woman. Her eyes spoke welcome, and I gratefully accepted.

"I have not spoken English since World War II," she said, "but I will try. I must speak slowly." That was fine with me! I was simply delighted to find someone to talk to.

"Tell me about yourself," I asked. (I am always anxious to know about people, and Maria was no exception to that rule!) "Are you married? Do you have children? Did you experience the war?" It was obvious by the look on her face that my questions were generally reserved for close friendships, not casual meetings on a train.

"I'm sorry," I quickly added. "I'm too curious. I just like

to get to know people and your eyes are kind eyes." She seemed to relax, and she smiled at me.

"It's all right," she assured me. "I'll tell you what you are asking."

Leave it up to a young, curious, American woman to ask the very question that would lead Maria through the most painful time of her life. I listened, I wept, and I still stand in awe.

Maria is a physician and married to a Frenchman. During Hitler's regime, a pairing of two countries did not make an easy marriage. Maria was called upon to work for the Nazi soldiers and her husband went into hiding. They had no idea where each other was, and they had no opportunity to communicate for long periods of time.

Maria was on the last train out of what is now western Poland. She had her firstborn in tow and a new infant daughter as the train pulled out of Breslau. The bombing was so frequent and severe that the train had to stop on many occasions so the occupants could disembark and take cover under the cars. A trip that should have taken hours was taking days.

There was no food on the train and not enough liquid, so children cried while mothers tried desperately to comfort them. Maria's own milk dried up after hours of dehydration and her baby grew hungry, thirsty, and ill. Maria — a doctor — had to sit by helplessly, unable to do anything about the atrocities.

When the train reached its destination a group of nuns took Maria's baby to their hospital. She was told that they would nurse the baby back to health while Maria took care of herself and her young daughter. It seemed like they had been given a reprieve from their pain, until . . .

The following day, when Maria went to get her precious baby, she found that the hospital had been bombed and her baby had not survived. She was given only a flashlight to search through the rubble.

"Since that time I have not believed that God is a good God," she said. I knew no words to contradict her pain.

Anguish runs deep. It grows out of tragedy and confusion, excessive loss and deep disappointment. It grows out of powerlessness and fear. And it is difficult, in the midst of life's pain, to see the goodness of God.

God *is* with us always. And He *does* work for our good. Still, it is hard for us to see that good at times. When the pain seems too difficult to bear, it is hard to find the golden thread of God's purpose.

I had no real wisdom for Maria that day, only love, tears, and a willingness to share in her pain. This is my privilege. This is the privilege of our Lord. He shares in our pain, even when we are unaware of His presence.

▮▮▮▮▮▮ THOUGHT FOR THE HEART

Like Maria, I have trouble seeing God's goodness in the sufferings I've experienced. I am willing to explore that goodness. I am willing to accept the presence of God.

—Shelley Chapin

●

GRIEF THAT DOES NOT KNOW RELIEF

"Oh, my anguish, my anguish! I writhe in pain. Oh, the agony of my heart! My heart pounds within me, I cannot keep silent. For I have heard the sounds of the trumpet; I have heard the battle cry. Disaster follows disaster; the whole land lies in ruins. In an instant my tents are destroyed, my shelter in a moment." Jeremiah 4:19-20

I grew up in the Anglican church. The music was somewhat formal and ethereal, but beautiful all the same. I looked forward each Sunday to the quiet beauty of our worship.

ANGUISH

I was intrigued by stories of church in the United States. We heard everything from tales of church held on the beach to church held in people's homes where blue jeans were the favored attire. We also knew that pastors in the States "scream" from the pulpit.

Samuel was our resident expert on the habits of those "renegades" in the United States, and he said these things were true. He spent summers in Maine with his grandparents and they always took a vacation to California. Samuel was an eighth-grade "man of the world."

I'll never forget the summer Samuel returned from three long months in the U.S.A. He brought back a recording of church music from California and a hymnal of favorite worship songs. Being a lover of music, I immediately listened to the tape and studied the songs. I wanted to learn all that I could about other forms of worship.

While paging through the hymnbook I ran across a story written in handwriting on one of the pages. It was the story of Horatio Gates Spafford.

I cannot imagine anguish much deeper than that experienced by Mr. Spafford. You may not recognize the name, but Horatio and his wife suffered one of the cruelest twists of life: all four of their children were killed on the same day, at the same time, in a tragic accident at sea. After colliding with an English sailing vessel, the *Ville du Havre* passenger ship sank to the ocean floor and with it, 226 lives.

I'm not sure how I would respond to such suffering, but I think the word *anguish* might sum up my response. Anguish means distress, agony, wretchedness, and woe. It is a total deprivation of the soul. Anguish is a grief that does not know relief.

Horatio had lost his business only days before the death of his children. The Chicago fire claimed everything he owned. At least he had his family.

Then came the message: "The ship your wife and children were on has been involved in a tragic accident. Your wife has survived, but the children. . . . " Horatio set sail immediately to be with his wife.

As the story goes, Horatio's ship followed the very same route as the French passenger vessel on which his family had set sail. At the spot where his children died, Horatio penned the words to this song. Though you may know the tune, take a look at the words.

When peace like a river attendeth my way,
When sorrows like sea billows roll;
Whatever my lot Thou hast taught me to say,
"It is well, it is well with my soul."

Though Satan should buffet, though trials should
come,
Let this blessed assurance control,
That Christ has regarded my helpless estate,
And hath shed His own blood for my soul.

It is difficult to imagine the attitude Horatio modeled, but his attitude helped to form mine. I was only a young adolescent, but I knew after reading the words to that song that I wanted to serve God in some way. If Horatio could honor God with his pain, surely I could honor God with my life.

I have since turned to Horatio many a time. In the quiet hours of my own disappointment or pain, I have sung the words of this song over and over in my mind.

Horatio offers us perspective in our anguish. He offers us hope in our suffering. He offers us the reminder that God is in control.

When the stabilities of our lives give way, we can say, "It is well with my soul."

A N G U I S H

I am hurting deeply right now and I'm finding it difficult to say, "It is well." Lord, open my eyes to Your perspective in my pain.

—Pamela M. Reeves

●

PREPARED FOR ADVERSITY

"You, however, know all about my teaching, my way of life, my purpose, faith, patience, love, endurance, persecutions, sufferings — what kinds of things happened to me in Antioch, Iconium, and Lystra, the persecutions I endured. Yet the Lord rescued me from all of them. In fact, everyone who wants to live a godly life in Christ Jesus will be persecuted." 2 Timothy 3:10-12

One of the hardest concepts in Scripture to accept is found in Paul's second letter to Timothy. "All who desire to live godly lives will be persecuted." Such a concept sinks in with a thud.

It is difficult to think of affliction as a gift. It is difficult to appreciate the anguish we feel when suffering. It is difficult to see that in the wisdom of God there is a purpose to our pain.

I confess that when I move through times of conflict and adversity it is all too easy for me to develop a poor attitude toward God. It is not so easy to thank Him for what He can accomplish through the process. In fact, such a response often sounds like a form of denial, as if we are saying, "No problem, God. It doesn't really matter that I'm hurting. I trust You completely!"

One of the reasons that it's difficult for us to accept anguish is that we are rarely prepared for adversities. We are more often taught from those Scripture passages that produce the most agreement or comfort.

ANGUISH

Yet far from promising a life of ease and prosperity, the New Testament actually affirms that those who follow Christ will face a new dimension of obstacles and struggles. Difficulties they did not know before committing their lives to Him will become part of their repertoire.

Take spiritual warfare, for example. Before coming to know the Lord, we aren't even aware that there's a war going on! Then comes the "bad" news. The more intensely we commit our lives to Christ, the more intensely the enemy pursues. Such a battle certainly involves anguish.

The New Testament saints were not unaware of this response we know as anguish. Nor were their Old Testament counterparts. In fact, many of the leaders and teachers even prepared their congregations for the realities of pain and suffering.

You may be experiencing anguish right now, and I certainly don't want to trivialize your position. I just want to encourage you that this heartache we know as anguish is not a "strange" occurrence or one that should not be occurring in the life of the believer.

Affliction is a part of this world's reality, and we do best to accept the anguish, count it joy, and trust God with the healing. When I trust in His sovereignty, love, goodness, and wisdom, I am never let down.

Examine your own life for a moment and I imagine you too will be able to say, "God has not let me down."

THOUGHT FOR THE HEART

It is difficult for me to see good in my anguish, but I am willing to begin to accept the reality of suffering and allow God to teach me in the midst of my pain.

— Ken Boa

ANGUISH

●
THE ANSWER TO OUR ANGST

"As the deer pants for streams of water, so my soul pants for You, O God. My soul thirsts for God, for the living God. When can I go and meet with God? My tears have been my food day and night, while men say to me all day long, 'Where is your God?' These things I remember as I pour out my soul: how I used to go with the multitude, leading the procession to the house of God, with shouts of joy and thanksgiving among the festive throng. Why are you downcast, O my soul? Why so disturbed within me? Put your hope in God, for I will yet praise Him, my Savior and my God." Psalm 42:1-5

The German writers have a word they use quite often; that word is *angst*. Angst. A strange-sounding word, but rich with meaning.

When a German writer speaks of "angst," he speaks of a pain or an anguish that is almost unbearable. He speaks of a despair or depression that grows out of intense suffering. And he speaks of this "angst" as a nearly hopeless condition.

When dealing with anguish I think we have to focus on hope. Certainly there are things with which we deal that seem unbelievably harsh, but for the believer there is hope.

I have a friend who lives in Texas. When I first met her, we shared a common sense of angst. She was newly diagnosed with terminal cancer and my wife had just experienced tragedy in her own family. Immediately we had something to share and our friendship was founded in the shared suffering.

One of the most important lessons I have learned from that friend centers around anguish and hope. She has lived well beyond the initial prognosis, yet she also lives on in pain. And so she has had a choice to make: Do I live in my anguish or do I live in my hope? She has chosen the latter, but the need to balance the anguish and the hope is a daily reality.

Each time I am around a cancer patient or a heart patient or someone else who must live with a daily dose of anguish, I am reminded of my own mortality. The only difference between myself and the person in pain on any given day is that which God allows. Today it is my friend with cancer who must choose hope; tomorrow I shall face my own testing ground.

I don't mean to tread lightly on anguish. It is a very real state of mind for the one whose cup for the day includes suffering. I am well acquainted with its message and have had my own moments of angst.

What I mean to do is shed light on the answer to our anguish: hope. We have blessed hope in Jesus Christ. And that gift is the same gift, no matter who we are or what our circumstances demand.

When we have Jesus Christ, anxiety pales. So hold on to the One you have.

■ THOUGHT FOR THE HEART

I have been struggling recently with this "angst." Lord, help me to see my anguish in light of Your hope.

—*Jay Kesler*

•
WHEN ONLY GOD UNDERSTANDS

"In bitterness of soul Hannah wept much and prayed to the Lord. And she made a vow saying, 'O Lord Almighty, if You will only look upon Your servant's misery and remember me, and not forget Your servant but give her a son, then I will give him to the Lord for all the days of his life." 1 Samuel 1:10-11

Life is never easy. It is even harder when you don't follow the rules.

Elkanah was a Jew who lived in hard times. The nation had sunk to the level of anarchy and idolatry, and Elkanah had taken two wives. Though blessed, he also knew much pain and strife.

Life's triangles are always painful. John says that we're not to love the world because we cannot love the world and love the Father as well. In short, the triangle of man loving God and the world just doesn't work.

James decries spiritual adultery. He says that our allegiance cannot be both to God and man, and we know he speaks truth. Throughout Scripture one of the most obvious conclusions is that those who worship idols cannot fully grasp the worship of the only true God.

It is clear that triangles cause great distress. And one of the most difficult triangles for men and women to manage is the triangle of marriage.

Elkanah had two wives. One wife, Hannah, was the favorite. The other wife, Peninah, had children. Hannah had the love of her husband and Peninah had what her world would have called success. Yet both were jealous and unhappy.

One day, Elkanah asked Hannah an unfortunate question. "Don't IImean more to you than ten sons?" he pried. I think Elkanah regretted asking the question before he even heard the answer.

"No," Hannah replied softly but full of conviction. "I want sons."

A son meant just about everything to a woman in that culture. In giving birth to a boy, a woman fulfilled her purpose in life, perpetuated her husband's name, and provided security for herself in old age. Hannah had none of these things. She had no son. And not even Elkanah's love could console her in her pain.

ANGUISH

One day Hannah went to the temple and in deep anguish and heartfelt pain poured out her longing to God. Eli the priest was there, listening and observing those who came to the temple to pray. He watched Hannah and seemed puzzled by his observation.

"How long will you keep on getting drunk? Get rid of your wine," the priest proclaimed.

"Not so, my lord," Hannah responded. "I am a woman deeply troubled. I am pouring out my soul to God." But Eli did not seem to comprehend her pain.

The priest—the one who should have understood—interpreted Hannah's prayer as the jibberish of a drunk woman. And he chastised her in one of her deepest moments of worship and need.

There are pains in life that are too deep to be expressed in any "ordinary" way. There are prayers that it seems only God can understand. Such is the essence of anguish.

God's answer for Hannah was a double-edged sword. She received her son, but she was asked to give him to the very priest who had not understood her anguish in the first place. Sometimes anguish of one kind begets anguish of another, and that is life.

Samuel . . . "Because I asked the Lord for him . . . " the Lord's response to a woman's plea.

█████████ THOUGHT FOR THE HEART

I have been calling out to the Lord in my anguish. I will listen now for His response.

—Phil Hook

●

AN EMOTIONAL BRUSH WITH REALITY

"The troubles of my heart have multiplied; free me from my anguish." Psalm 25:17

A N G U I S H

Few emotions are more invasive than anguish. There is no place to hide . . . nowhere to run . . . no balm to take away the pain . . . no means by which we can deny its presence. Anguish steps in and permeates our entire being with its cry for help. It is a critical condition of the heart.

What storehouse nurtures this hungry pain and then turns it loose to thrive on our demise?

For some, anguish is born of love, once fresh, grown stale. For some, it is born of a sin which threatens to destroy. For some, it is born in the wake of illness or a loved one's death. For some, it is born of countless disappointments in a troubled world. Even "positive thinkers" have a date with anguish every once in a while.

David was no stranger to this emotion. Relentless enemies pursued him until he had no more energy to run. No matter how hard the young king tried to maintain control of the kingdom, his youthful dreams of harmony and peace were tainted by jealousy and idolatry. He was distraught, confused, and weary to the bone.

God is faithful in our anguish, but His faithfulness doesn't remove the pain. He is there, but His presence does not dim the agony of our loss. There is no way to contain the emotion or pretend that it doesn't matter. It is there to serve its purpose.

Anguish lets us know that we are deeply hurt. It lets us know that we must stop the madness and listen to our hearts. It lets us know that we are real, that we feel, and that we are fragile. Anguish is an emotional brush with reality.

Though it is our tendency to flee, make every effort to live with anguish when it visits. Experience its depth and invite God's fellowship. Though He may not remove today's pain, He does walk before and behind to make clear the path and gird our weakness, one day at a time. His fellowship opens up the door of acceptance and bathes us in light instead of darkness.

My anguish grows out of these relationships or disappointing circumstances. I can allow God to join me in my pain.

— *Shelley Chapin*

•

ALLOWING ANOTHER TO ENTER YOUR PAIN

"Like a shepherd's tent my house has been pulled down and taken from me. Like a weaver I have rolled up my life, and He has cut me off from the loom; day and night You made an end of me. I waited patiently until dawn, but like a lion, He broke all my bones; day and night You made an end of me. I cried like a swift or thrush, I moaned like a mourning dove. My eyes grew weak as I looked to the heavens. I am troubled; O Lord, come to my aid." Isaiah 38:12-14

It was my first journey to the continent of Africa. This large land mass would be my home for at least two years (the length of my contract) and I knew I was taking a big risk. After all, I'd been raised in a very comfortable situation. All my notions about Africa told me I would not be enjoying *all* the comforts of home. I felt as prepared as one might be for the change.

Those of you who have made the journey before know it is a long one. And back in 1962 it was a particularly difficult journey. I traveled much of the way by boat, so there were plenty of hours to think.

I remember writing down all of my preconceptions about Africa. For instance, I wrote down that there are cannibals there and very large snakes. I wrote that everyone is starving and that the big cities are much like our own. I even wrote that the missionaries probably live just like the Africans. I was less than accurate on all counts!

ANGUISH

I arrived safe and sound, and began to settle into my new job. For a while I would be traveling to different clinics which had been established either by missionaries or peace-keeping organizations. I thought this would be a wonderful way to get to know my new homeland. Little did I realize how BIG Africa is and how diverse!

Early on, I met a young African woman who would become my traveling companion. I earned easily enough money to pay her to go with me and help me care for both myself and the details of the journey. She was eager to go.

My friend was a wonderful young woman—bright and anxious to make a difference in the world. She told me little about her family and I didn't probe. All I knew was that they lived in Southern Africa in a place where it was dangerous to be black or white. Every once in a while she would smile, thinking about how her family would react if they knew that she traveled and stayed with a white doctor. She enjoyed the controversy.

One day a young messenger came running up to us in a small village near Zimbabwe. He spoke fast and in a dialect I didn't understand, so I had no idea what was happening. I remember my heart racing—I sensed something terrible had happened.

The next thing I remember is the "thud" of the two of us hitting the ground. My young companion had fainted directly against me, and I had not been quick enough to carry both our weights. We tumbled in a heap in the middle of the street. She didn't blink an eye.

It was almost an hour before I learned what had happened. Several men carried her to our clinic where we revived her and got her settled in, but the tears of anguish flowed. I could not comprehend one word she was saying.

I know of few things more frustrating than the hatred that exists between people. Churches split in two, business partners separate, crime occurs between this group and that. The hatred that exists between people is far more deadly than any disease I've been trained to treat. Hatred kills more than the body.

My young friend suffered for days under the weight of hatred. Her brother's involvement in the fight against apartheid had erupted in a high-scale war. In a matter of moments, nine members of her family had been killed and two more wounded. While sitting at the table in her father's house, they had been murdered.

Vestiges of Job's life rang through my mind as she poured out her body, soul, and mind. All I could think of was her loss and my helplessness. There was nothing to say to make a wrong right; nothing to do except listen and love.

My friend has since told me time and again how much she appreciated those days of shared tears and felt pain. Few times in my life have I felt completely helpless, but that was one. Unable to fix her problem, I put aside all I had read or heard and simply cared. Together we carried the pain for more than a year.

Allow someone to love you today. If you suffer under the weight of tragedy or loneliness, reach out and allow others to enter your pain. Welcome love's warmth.

THOUGHT FOR THE HEART

I am hurting deeply, Lord. Nothing seems to work to remove the pain. Lord, help me to find You in this anguish of my soul. And help me to reach out to a friend.

—Pamela M. Reeves

RHYTHMS OF MY HEART

BELONGING

LIKE A CHILD WITHOUT A HOME

"Hear my cry, O God; listen to my prayer. From the ends of the earth I call to You, I call as my heart grows faint; lead me to the rock that is higher than I. For You have been my refuge, a strong tower against the foe. I long to dwell in Your tent forever and take refuge in the shelter of Your wings." Psalm 61:1-4

At the risk of sounding like an "old woman," I'd like to offer a simple encouragement to those of you who feel as if you don't belong. The simple message? You do belong. Perhaps not to the person or place you'd like to belong, but you do belong to God and, very importantly, you do belong to you.

My mother died when I was barely sixteen. The death certificate says, "natural causes," but I have never understood what that means. Who can I blame? Where does this "natural" live? What kind of a "natural cause" takes away someone's mother?

Our home was very formal even when Mother was alive. I don't recall much laughter or any games we might have played together. We had a very solemn family, and I mostly accepted things just as they were.

My mother was not very verbally expressive, but she was a kind and loving woman. And she was my mother. She knew just what I liked to eat, she knew how I liked my room kept, and which clothes I liked to wear most. She could tell when I needed a nap and she would braid my hair before bedtime. I loved her, and I felt comfortable in her care.

When she died, I felt I had no one. My father was living, it's true; but my father and I have never discussed anything of import. He is a quiet man with a quiet mission, and he likes to keep it that way.

I was at boarding school when Mother died, and I returned there just two days after the funeral. There was no opportunity to grieve, no chance to get my bearings, no time to even say a proper good-bye. By the time the semester was through, my father had sold the big house and moved all our things. I didn't belong anywhere.

I decided on college in London and medical school in the States, and I set my sights on such a course. I went home only on holidays and still did not feel like I belonged. I was a misfit, or so I thought; a child without a family.

Africa became my family after graduation. I decided to be a "tentmaker" missionary and roam the world. And I have done just that. But in looking back, I think I chose this course in part to avoid the feelings of belonging to no one. At least with this course I could say it was my choice to roam.

Can you see the dilemma or feel the pain just a bit? It's not that I would change my life; nor am I sad for the choices I have made. I simply have become aware, in time, that belonging is such an important part of a young man or woman's world.

I've also learned that we can feel as if we don't belong right in the midst of our home. Such was my experience with my father. It was easier, somehow, to be a roaming missionary rather than a present yet unknown daughter. It hurts me now to think of the pain I felt but didn't know how to acknowledge.

If you're feeling like you don't belong, please don't avoid the emotions. You can run for awhile just as I have run, but one day the pain will catch up with you. Better now than later.

If you feel as if you don't belong, talk with God about the struggle. Find some friends and a mentor you can trust. Get to know you. Get to know your pain. And get to know the God who cares about that pain.

BELONGING

You do belong. You belong to God. And, very importantly, you belong to you.

I can tell that I also run away from my pain at times. In fact, I've probably been running for awhile from this pain. Grant me courage, Lord, to belong to You, to belong to me, and to acknowledge my need.

—*Pamela M. Reeves*

●
THE VALUE OF RELATIONSHIPS

"I have no one else like him [Timothy], who takes a genuine interest in your welfare. For everyone looks out for his own interests, not those of Jesus Christ. But you know that Timothy has proved himself, because, as a son with his father, he has served with me in the work of the Gospel." Philippians 2:20-22

We study much about theology in Scripture, but we often forget to study the relationships that are so clearly displayed there. One such relationship is that between Paul and Timothy—a relationship not unique for its theological implications, but for its heart implications.

Paul belonged to Timothy and Timothy belonged to Paul. The relationship is a model of reaching out to both give and receive love. It is a relationship of belonging.

Paul left much behind when he came to know Jesus. From what we read, we know that Paul was a Pharisee of the Pharisees, righteous in every way and faultless in carrying out his mission. He was young to have attained so much. And he had great power over people—even power to order their deaths.

On that day when Paul was blinded by the Lord, he left everything behind . . . family, friends, position, possessions, power, and influence. He left these behind for a much better purpose, but he was still alone on this new road of faith.

Timothy was born into a home of argument and division. His mother and grandmother were Jewess believers, and his father was a Greek. Thus Timothy bore the weight of never quite being able to please either side of his parentage. To his mother's family, he was still an uncircumcised Gentile. To his father's family, he was still a believing Jew.

Timothy was in between two worlds and Paul was without the only world he had known. The stage is set for relationship.

Paul longed for the company of a son, and Timothy more than met the qualifications. Timothy wanted to be like Paul, he wanted to learn from Paul, and he wanted to serve Paul through his faithfulness. Timothy met a big need in Paul.

On the other side of the coin, Timothy longed for an accepting father, and Paul was happy to comply. Paul was proud of Timothy, and he had plenty of praise and encouragement to offer his son in the faith. Paul taught Timothy, and he modeled a life of certitude for this young man. He allowed Timothy to fail, to succeed, to ask for support, to need help, and to struggle. Paul met a big need in Timothy.

I long to belong, as I imagine you do. Belonging feels good and it gives us both strength and purpose. Belonging provides encouragement for the journey. Belonging provides a place where hearts can rest in peace.

Belonging is a safe place to return at the end of the day. It is a safe place to go when we need to be held or heard. Belonging is a place we'll find love, truth, and encouragement.

Who do you belong to? And who belongs to you? Do

your heart and your life have room?

I long to belong, yet at the same time I fear rejection. Lord, help me to learn to belong to others — and to let them belong to me.

— Shelley Chapin

●

ETERNAL LOVE TRIANGLE

"How good and pleasant it is when brothers live together in unity!" Psalm 133:1

That sense of belonging to a significant person or group is a wonderful feeling! But there were many times as a child, teenager, and young adult that I felt like a "square peg in a round hole." I longed to belong, but the "fit" just wasn't right.

In the world's eyes, I wasn't a total "misfit." The notable exceptions to my feelings of insignificance were team athletics and a close, encouraging relationship with my younger brother, Bill. As I have since come to realize, though, the "meshing" was not 100 percent. Bill and I did the best we could — but there was still a hunger to belong which I could not quite fulfill.

After becoming a Christian, it slowly but surely dawned on me that there is a new and better kind of belonging in the body of Christ. You can call it an "eternal love triangle" (not to be confused with the typical soap opera story line). Very different people can be valued and accepted for the unique roles they play and the abilities they bring to the unity of the group.

This means that any relationship we attempt to develop with another believer is already undergirded by the accepting, unconditional love relationship we have with

God through faith in Christ. Christian relationships were designed to be not just two-way streets, but three-sided havens of acceptance and encouragement.

Clearly, this radical (but fully biblical!) approach to belonging in the church of Jesus Christ has not "leaked out" (or maybe it has just not sunk in) to all the troops in God's army. The church still shoots a lot of its wounded.

But, thankfully, Christian relationships — whether corporate, small group, or one-on-one — are still the context in which that supernatural sense of belonging, of being "family," of being accepted, warts and all, can occur. We can belong to one another and watch that belonging provide us with strength, encouragement, purpose, and rest.

It stirs my heart to realize (with every fiber of my being!) that, compared to this never-ending story of relationships, what the unbelieving world has to offer is like a one-night stand. What God has to offer is eternal membership in a family where we truly belong.

██████████ T H O U G H T   F O R   T H E   H E A R T

Try to identify those relationships in your life in which you find a sense of acceptance and belonging.

— Boyd Luter

●
CALLED BY NAME

"To the Lord your God belong the heavens, even the highest heavens, the earth and everything in it. Yet the Lord set His affection on your forefathers and loved them, and He chose you, their descendants, above all the nations, as it is today. Circumcise your hearts, therefore, and do not be stiff-necked any longer. For the Lord your God is God of gods and Lord of lords, the great God, mighty and awesome, who shows no partiality and accepts no bribes." Deuteronomy 10:14-17

BELONGING

When someone calls my name, it gets my attention! And I answer those to whom I belong.

I remember my mother calling me to come home at suppertime. I could tell by the tone in her voice how quickly I needed to respond! There was no doubt in my mind who she was speaking to or what she wanted. I belonged to her! And she knew me well.

When teachers called my name growing up, I responded (sometimes with fear if I wasn't prepared that day!). They knew me and I belonged in their classrooms. They got my attention.

Now I have been married for years, and my wife has a special way of calling my name. She can say "David" in a way that no one else can! And I often know what she wants or what she's thinking simply by the sound of her voice.

One of our greatest needs is to belong. And one of the most amazing truths of Scripture is that God knows us by name! We belong to God. He knows the hairs on our head, our thoughts before we think them, the steps we will take, and the fears we harbor. The God of the universe knows each of us intimately.

How grateful I am that I heard Him say, many years ago, "David, I love you and I sent My Son to die for your sins. I want to forgive you. You belong to Me." He knew me and He sought me out and He gave me life. I belong to my Heavenly Father.

Since that time, He has continued to know and call my name. "David, I know you are hurting." "David, I want you to help this person for Me." "David, take this step of faith and trust Me." "David, My grace is sufficient for you to make it through this valley." I still belong to God, and I always will.

Almighty God knows my name. And He knows your name too. If you listen carefully, you'll hear His voice telling you how much He loves and cares for you.

God knows what you're dealing with. He knows and is aware of your needs. His love can bring courage and forgiveness and a reminder that you too belong.

The Israelites were deeply loved by God, but they often lost sight of His favor. They wanted something from Him but were blind to what He offered, simply because His offerings were not always what they wanted.

Our Lord fought the same battle during His life on this earth. He came to give and to serve and He never tired of showing His love. But some people didn't know they belonged to Him. They didn't accept the love He offered.

We want to belong, but there are so many voices telling us how to live, what to choose, and where to belong that we tend to get confused. We become sidetracked by the priorities and expectations of the world.

Remember that there is only One to whom you truly belong. There is only one voice which speaks the truth and He never leads us astray.

Choose to belong. It is a free gift that is offered to you and to me. And it isn't a temporary condition! We belong to a loving and gracious Heavenly Father for eternity.

Well . . . got to run . . . someone is calling my name!

THOUGHT FOR THE HEART

A close examination of my life would reveal that I belong to these people, these causes, and these situations. I'd like to learn more about belonging to God.

— David Lynch

●

THE GIFT OF BELONGING

"Even though you have ten thousand guardians in Christ, you do not have many fathers, for in Christ Jesus I became your father

through the Gospel. Therefore I urge you to imitate me. For this reason I am sending to you Timothy, my son whom I love, who is faithful in the Lord. He will remind you of my way of life in Christ Jesus, which agrees with what I teach everywhere in every church." 1 Corinthians 4:15-17.

A wise person has said, "You can't do much about your ancestors, but you can influence your descendants enormously." How true that statement is for each of us!

When we hear the word *grandparent*, what usually comes to mind? Elderly? Old? Doesn't it make sense that if life itself is a blessing, then the more we have, the greater the blessing?

The words *grandparent* and *grandchild* do not appear in Scripture — there is no Hebrew word for either of these terms. Instead, the Hebrew descriptions are "father of his father" and "son of his son."

In rabbinical literature, however, a different sort of picture was painted around these concepts. "My grandfather" meant, "my old person, my sage" or, "this older person is mine." To call someone "grandfather" was to tell the world that something special exists between this old person and me. In short, "this older person is mine" meant "we belong to each other."

God's plan of faith works much this way. He encourages us to belong to one another and to call each other "brother" and "sister." Throughout Scripture we are given pictures of men and women of faith who needed one another and openly testified to the importance of the relationship. And we watch as "the old" influence "the young."

I am moved by the connection between Timothy and Paul who "belonged" to each other. Paul called Timothy "my son" and, as a proud father, proclaimed Timothy's strengths to the world.

B E L O N G I N G

"This is my son. There is no one else like him. And his heart is true! He cares about people and people love him in return."

Paul didn't *need* to write to the churches about Timothy. He *wanted* to do so. He was proud of this one who belonged to him and he wanted the world to know. And even more importantly, Paul saw one of his most significant responsibilities as that of preparing Timothy for carrying on the work. There was a bond that existed between the two which gave each of them strength and a sense of value.

We are significant, each of us in our own way. But it is difficult to remember our significance when we do not feel like we belong. I have watched countless grandmothers and grandfathers show pictures of their grandchildren to anyone who is interested. And I have seen weary eyes grow bright when asked to discuss loved ones.

When we belong, life looks much different than when we sense we are alone. "That older person is mine" was Timothy's gift to Paul. "This is my son" was Paul's gift in return. Both Timothy and Paul belonged to one another, and that great bond provided both with the strength and purpose to do the work God had given them to do.

In the midst of a somewhat confusing world, it is a gift to belong to someone and to allow someone to belong in return.

████████████ THOUGHT FOR THE HEART

I belong to these people and these people belong to me.

—John Coulombe

•

"FOREIGN ACCENT"

"But our citizenship is in heaven." Philippians 3:20

BELONGING

As the *Cap Bonavista* sailed into the harbor, my senses were bombarded with unfamiliar sights, smells, and sounds. The famous monument, Christ the Redeemer, arms outstretched, hovered over this city as we disembarked and made our way to immigration. Sugar Loaf Mountain glistened in the sun like a jewel surrounded by sand and surf. Rio de Janeiro was my gateway to life as a foreigner.

I stepped into that role with excitement and anticipation. This moment was a culmination of prayers, preparation, and twenty very turbulent, landless days! Nevertheless, I felt prepared to tackle my lifelong dream of being a missionary.

Naively I assumed that once the preliminaries of language study and culture shock were accounted for, I would find my niche in the Brazilian life flow and feel as one with my adopted land and culture. The niche was not so easy to find.

Food. Brazilians excel in culinary masterpieces and my palate embraced these well-seasoned and carefully prepared dishes with delight. No problem here (except *dobradinha* — translated "cow stomach")! Early morning treks to the street market provided seemingly limitless possibilities for healthy and tasteful dining.

People. Homes and hearts were open without reservation. Brazilians are never too busy for friends. The making and drinking of the strong, sweet black coffee seemed to seal the good times and good talks we shared together.

Language. Oh, yes. I managed to buy rice and beans and take care of ordinary tasks but, alas, the extensive and expressive vocabulary of the Portuguese language as well as all the unaccustomed sounds presented me with the challenge of a lifetime. (Our young daughter mistakenly confused the word *accident* with *accent* one day, noting that a certain person "spoke with an accident.")

BELONGING

Let me assure you that my attempts in Portuguese resembled an accident many times! It was this beautiful and enchanting language that forever silenced my notion of one day being "quasi-Brazilian." Sadly the realization dawned that as much as I loved Brazil and her people, I was a foreigner. Years of determined effort would not erase the fact that I would always be a foreigner. If nothing else, my accent and choice of words betrayed me.

One day I was reading Matthew and a verse jumped out at me. "Those standing there went up to Peter and said, 'Surely you are one of them [Jesus' followers], for your accent gives you away' " (26:73). I knew the context of the verse but it struck a chord deep within me.

My verbal accent in Portuguese gave me away as a native speaker of English. I couldn't help wondering if the accent of my heart marked me as a follower of Christ. From that day forward I have prayed for a heart with His accent.

Paul said that "our citizenship is in heaven." Peter spoke a similar message to people scattered abroad by persecution. He called them "aliens and strangers" in the world. They were to live such good lives among the pagans that, though accused of doing wrong, the pagans would see their good deeds and give glory to God (1 Peter 2:11-12).

Even the heroes of Hebrews 11 "admitted they were aliens and strangers on earth" (11:13). They were longing for a better country—a heavenly one, and they knew this world was not their home.

Do you find yourself experiencing a foreignness here on earth, an inexplicable sense of not being truly at home? Good! The Gospel song is a reminder that "this world is not our home, we're just a passin' through."

To be at home here on earth could spell death. To speak the language with the same accent of those who boast an earthly citizenship could be dangerous. To conform here would be such short-term belonging.

Live life today as a citizen of heaven. There is no other place to truly belong.

███████████████ THOUGHT FOR THE HEART

Lord, let my "accent" give me away as a follower of Christ. I'm grateful that I belong to You.

—*Bonnie Sloat*

● HIS SHEEP AM I

"The Lord is my shepherd, I shall not be in want. He makes me lie down in green pastures, He leads me beside quiet waters, He restores my soul. He guides me in paths of righteousness for His name's sake." Psalm 23:1-3

The moon was high that night—high and very round. He always liked the nights when the moon was full; it made it easier to keep track of his children.

"Let's see . . . one, two, three, and four," he liked to count out loud. "All here, safe and sound. Good night!"

He had twenty-seven children, to be exact. They were his charge, and he was their guardian. He had wanted to be a shepherd for as long as he could remember; and now he finally had a flock of his own. He would have no trouble staying awake. This night was special.

David was the youngest child of Jesse. We know that he was a ruddy, handsome youth. We know that he had a sensitive heart and that he loved music. We know that he was a friend to both Saul and Jonathan, that he was interested in people, and that he was willing to lay aside his needs for the needs of another.

Though all of David's brothers were ready for service,

God chose this young shepherd to be Israel's king. God chose this young man for his sensitive heart—"The Lord does not look at the things man looks at. Man looks at the outward appearance, but the Lord looks at the heart" (1 Samuel 16:7).

Who would you have chosen for king of Israel? If it had been your job to find the new king, what qualifications would you have insisted upon?

Would you have chosen a wealthy man? Someone with experience? A politician or a statesman? Someone older or stronger? Would you have chosen a shepherd?

I think God chose this young shepherd with a big heart because He knows that people need a place to belong. For the professional or the wealthy, the strong or the experienced, priorities are often issues or favors. For the shepherd, priority is each individual sheep.

When David penned the words to Psalm 23, he wrote them from a shepherd's point of view. He wanted us to remember that we belong to God. He wanted to assure us that the Shepherd will indeed care for His sheep.

No matter where we are or what we have done; no matter how we act or what ensnares us, the Shepherd is there. God's priority is to care for His sheep.

THOUGHT FOR THE HEART

I do belong to God. Sometimes I try to align myself with other, less important considerations; but when all is said and done, nothing else offers love and complete security. I belong to God, and I am blessed.

— Shelley Chapin

RHYTHMS OF MY HEART

BROKENNESS

PICKING UP THE PIECES

"I have been very zealous for the Lord God Almighty. The Israelites have rejected Your covenant, broken down Your altars, and put Your prophets to death with the sword. I am the only one left, and now they are trying to kill me too." 1 Kings 19:14

I always thought of myself as sensitive and understanding. After all, I was a believer and a very dedicated one at that. Then came my moment of awakening when the world as I knew it came crashing down at my feet. And for the first time in my life I felt broken, alone, and very, very afraid.

For months I didn't seek the Lord. I prayed quite a bit, but I was somehow too fractured to read His Word. If the truth be known, I think I felt too ashamed of being a failure. I had so wanted to live my life without major "flaws" and now I had a flaw that I considered one of the worst. I was going through divorce.

I remember the day I picked up my Bible again—notes in the margin in just the right color ink. I thumbed through the pages and my eyes were drawn to the story of Elijah. Little did I know I would find a companion in my brokenness.

The story is a great one. Elijah was set apart by God to be the vehicle for one of the greatest miracles in recorded history. He was to represent God on a mountain in a test against the prophets of Baal.

Four hundred and fifty prophets of Baal matched against one lone prophet of the Almighty God, and we know who won. The prophets of Baal called on their god all day long to light the fire they had prepared, but no god responded. Elijah was having a great time.

"Maybe you should shout louder," Elijah called. "I don't know if he can hear you. And I've heard he might be on vacation!" (Sounds a bit like a taunting match between two players on opposing football teams, yes?) The prophets of Baal called louder.

And then it was Elijah's turn. The only true God gave fire, and all the prophets of Baal died in the flurry of their religious activity. God had won, and He had used His servant, Elijah, to defeat the enemy!

We are generally on an emotional and spiritual "high" when things go well, and who can blame us? It feels good to succeed, to work hard and see a job well done. And it feels particularly good when we have watched God work firsthand and benefited from His power.

But with most victories come a moment of defeat . . . another test on the heels of the first that feels too hard to bear. Elijah experienced such defeat, and her name was Jezebel.

Jezebel had a terrible reputation! She was mean. And everyone knew that she meant what she said! Elijah knew about her and he shuddered when he read the note: "May the gods deal with me ever so severely if by this time tomorrow I do not make your life like the prophets you humiliated and killed" (see 1 Kings 19:2). This was Elijah's "last straw."

The prophet ran. And he ran so hard and so far that his own servant could barely keep up with him. And then he ran still more. He finally ended his escape a day's journey into the desert alone. He fell facedown in brokenness and despair, and he cried to the Lord to take his life.

When we feel broken, the pieces seem all out of place. The things that made sense yesterday don't make sense anymore. The good feeling we had or the success we enjoyed seems like it never even happened. And we are left to try and pick up the pieces of our own, miserable existence.

What was wrong with Elijah? He felt all alone. He had

no one "in the flesh" to turn to. He didn't think he could take the pressure anymore.

God's solution? He stepped into the prophet's world and brought acceptance. God didn't chastise, condemn, or otherwise blame Elijah for the despair. He simply accepted and loved His servant.

God sent an angel to cook for Elijah and soothe his soul with bread and water. Then God brought His prophet to the mountain where He could speak to him . . . in a gentle whisper. And, finally, God provided Elijah with other prophets to lighten the load and increase the support. Elijah was back together again.

It took a long time for me to feel "back together again." For what seemed like ages I felt like Humpty Dumpty at the bottom of the wall.

But our God is faithful. He accepts our grief, understands our pain, soothes our wounds, and repairs broken pieces. Oh, yes, we have a God who cares about the brokenhearted.

■■■■■■■■■ THOUGHT FOR THE HEART

If I am honest, I am feeling broken and a bit misunderstood right now. How I long for the rest and understanding Elijah received. Lord, help me to be aware of the angels, of the whispers, of the healing balm You bring my way.

— Shelley Chapin

●
FRACTURED FAMILY

"We are hard pressed on every side, but not crushed; perplexed, but not in despair; persecuted, but not abandoned; struck down, but not destroyed." 2 Corinthians 4:8-9

Sharon Moss was a lovely, young wife and mother when

the world crashed in around her. She had weathered storms before—even the turbulence of cancer, but this storm was far more powerful than anything she had known. Even God would be hard pressed to find good in this pain.

In the dark and lonely hours Sharon Moss lost touch with her friends. She had to pool all resources to fight the looming battle. But when the time was right, she reached out once more. Christmas 1992 found her communicating again with those she holds dear.

> In June of 1990, the last thing I ever thought would happen to our family occurred, leaving in its path deep personal pain and grief. My husband left me and the boys to pursue life on his own. He has not been interested in working toward reconciliation and has filed for divorce.
>
> I still wake up some mornings and wonder if it is all a bad dream, only to discover the ever-present reality. We're each left with unanswered questions that need to be put into the hands of our loving, sovereign God.

Sharon's storm is feared by every mother, father, wife, husband, and child. The fracturing of the family unit, the loss of a love once trusted, are some of the most desperate storms that can invade our world. And so often the tempests arise before we have time to flee or seek support.

> There is a sense in which a darkened overlay has fallen across the pages of my life—tainting all that was beautiful from twenty-four years and casting a gray shadow over those chapters not yet written.

I can almost hear Job's despair in the midst of Sharon's

words. How do we reconcile the happiness of yesterday with the sorrow of today? How do we envision a bright tomorrow when this day's pain is gray?

When our security and dreams are broken apart, we are locked in a shroud that seems impenetrable. But that darkness is not complete, nor does it last forever.

By God's grace, our pain can also point us toward the only One who can heal the dreadful wounds. Our brokenness can lead us to the Master. Sharon and her boys have found solace there. Even in the eye of the hurricane they have found God. And, miracle of miracles, they have found Him to be sufficient.

> Over time the boys and I have experienced a measure of healing as we have placed ourselves directly under the care and provision of our Heavenly Father. Adversity has knit us into a close unit. Family and friends have blessed us over and over again as they have been sensitive to the wide spectrum of needs in our lives. The precious promises of God's Word and His unchanging character have become our source of security and strength.

In our brokenness, it is hard to hold on to the peace that passes all understanding. We long for the security of days gone by. But God's peace is real. Even in the wake of our greatest sorrows, God works His good.

Learn with Sharon and the millions like her — those who have known the void of brokenness and the presence of God. Learn about the hope that offers a rainbow. Learn about the love that puts the pieces together again.

> There is a far deeper sense in which God has been showing me how His gifts, especially His love, kindness, and compassion, can bring joy to the present

and hope for the future. Such joy and hope go beyond all disappointments and shattered dreams. Certainly this is the message of love for those who know the pain of living in a fallen world.

Like Sharon, I am broken, Lord. I am not sure where to turn or what to say to You. I cry out, but at times I'm not sure that You hear. Help me to begin to embrace Your love. Help me to begin to accept Your peace.

— Shelley Chapin & Sharon Moss

THE REST JESUS OFFERS

"Come to Me, all you who are weary and burdened, and I will give you rest. Take My yoke upon you and learn from Me, for I am gentle and humble in heart, and you will find rest for your souls. For My yoke is easy and My burden is light." Matthew 11:28-30

Weary . . . burdened . . . broken. Can you identify with those terms? Most of us can at one time or another. In fact, even as I write I can think of friends who are carrying a load that is heavy right now.

I think of Greg who spent many, many days at the hospital by his wife's side. They faced one battle after another, away from home and tired. How broken they must have felt in the turmoil.

I think of some dear friends in Cleveland. My wife and I have shared wonderful times of fellowship with them over the years. They are like family. We have laughed and cried, prayed and planned together.

A massive stroke changed everything. The husband entered a nursing home, no longer able to speak or respond to his dear wife. And no longer can we laugh or cry or pray or plan in the manner we had depended on for years. What anguish the family has suffered! How weary and burdened his wife has felt. The life that they knew was broken apart.

I think of my own daughter and son-in-law. They had been married only a short time when the plant where Norman worked began to strike. Possible unemployment. Time running out. Anxiety and fear gripped this young couple who had planned on something very different.

I think of children who struggle with the pain of divorce. I think of wives who suffer the agony of abuse. I think of lives enslaved to alcohol or drugs. I think of homeless families. I think of the people uprooted by wars and internal strife in their neighborhoods or countries.

Yes, there are many broken and weary people in our world. Some of them occupy the seats right next to you or me on Sunday morning. Sometimes *we* are the brokenhearted in need of understanding and hope.

Is there hope? Can we do anything to make the world better? Where can people turn for the mending of wounded hearts and broken spirits?

"Come to Me, all who are heavy laden, and I will give you rest."

I love those words spoken by Jesus. Rest. Such a wonderful prospect in the midst of our pain.

The rest Jesus offers is not necessarily the removal of the problem. The rest is not always a quick solution. The rest is not always the physical healing we desire or the removal of the source of our pain.

Rest is there for our weary spirits. I cannot tell you exactly when or how our Lord gives this rest, I simply know that He does — in His own time and in His own way. Right in the midst of our personal storm, the Father brings comfort.

BROKENNESS

I am so thankful that our Lord understands our weariness. He was weary too. He experienced rejection, loneliness, abuse, unreliable friends, and the myriad of other pains we undergo. Jesus knew what it was to be weary and to need some kind of renewal and communion.

Our Lord sees when we are weary. He knows the ache in our heart and the pain of the struggle. He understands what makes us anxious and burdened. He says, "Bring it to Me! Cry it out. Tell Me exactly how you feel. Let go and express your emotions — you can be honest with Me. Then, let Me take you in My arms and give you rest!"

THOUGHT FOR THE HEART

I feel broken and weary from these circumstances. I would like the rest that Jesus has to offer.

— David Lynch

●
EMBRACING THE CRACKS IN YOUR ARMOR

"The sacrifices of God are a broken spirit; a broken and contrite heart, O God, You will not despise." Psalm 51:17

Let me come and sit down.
Let me take tea with you and share our dreams.
O, that I were like a butterfly again and could brighten your day with color.
You would point as I flew here and there;
You would smile at me and pleasure would abound.

Let me come and sit awhile.
Let me eat cakes with you and share our dreams.
O, that I were like the owl again and could lighten your load with wisdom.
You would hear as I spoke gently and with Truth;

You would smile at me and pleasure would abound.

Let me come and sit awhile.
Let me cry your tears and share our dreams.
O, that I were like the Savior again and could offer
     love to guild your season.
You would weep as I spilled water on your feet;
You would smile at me and pleasure would abound.

Maurice and I worked side by side through years of service to our Lord. Sometimes God would lead us to separate parts of the globe, but always He would bring us back together again. We were close friends and heart-companions in our work and in our love for the Savior.

It was Maurice who penned the above prose for me. His body was weary from years of serving in places where malaria, TB, and dysentery were like the common cold. We had both lived through this and that over the years. This time, Maurice would not recover.

My friend had cancer, and we often laughed at the strangeness of his death. He contracted a type of leukemia that is quite rare—as if we had not had enough of odd illnesses and strange symptoms. He elected to remain in Africa for his final months.

Maurice was a deeply committed follower of Jesus. He loved the Lord and he knew that the Lord loved him. But Maurice could never quite shake the sense that he, somehow, had not given enough to the Lord or to this world. From my point of view, Maurice had given more than anyone I've ever known.

Finally, as the days grew short and few, Maurice read his prose. He read it as almost an apology to me for his brokenness, his humanity, his inability to fight off death and enter life for one more round with the devil.

Dear friends, we need not despise our brokenness. God's

love is not linked to our performance nor is His pleasure with us linked to some denial of this world's realities.

We are all broken, and thus the privilege of Christ's incredible gift to mankind. He is the toy maker, the one who made and the one who can repair. He is the one who takes joy in loving His children and, one day, bringing them home.

Maurice sees the portrait now. He knows that he was a bright and shining light in a world that can be so gray. Maurice knows now that he was a ray of hope to all who were loved and served by him.

Learn from Maurice. Learn the lessons before you leave behind those who love you so. Learn to embrace your brokenness. It is the crack in the armor that makes us real.

THOUGHT FOR THE HEART

It is difficult for me to accept my own brokenness. I somehow find myself covering the cracks and pretending they do not exist. I would like to grow comfortable in my own reality. I would like to accept and to offer the love of a God who knows us through and through.

— Pamela M. Reeves

●
FROM HUM TO HUSH

"Let us then approach the throne of grace with confidence, so that we may receive mercy and find grace to help us in our time of need." Hebrews 4:16

I was busy and proud of it! Rare was the evening you would find me at home. My theme song was, "Things to do, places to go, people to see."

I seemed to be addicted to activity and thrived on a

hectic pace. Although I would often moan to others of "my busy schedule," in the next breath I was accepting another engagement. In the back of my mind I had a gnawing sense I should be practicing more of the command to "be still and know that I am God," but I was afraid of stopping.

For me, my identity and sense of value were proportional to the amount of "doing" I could log on my "things I did today" list. "Besides," I reasoned, "the Lord has gifted me with an incredible measure of emotional and physical energy!" I convinced myself I was only being a good steward of my gifts. Look at all the ministry I was getting done for Him!

I thought my investments were secure, but my personal stock market crashed in 1989. My physical, emotional, and spiritual income were wiped out, leaving me depleted. My journal entries of activity dwindled from several pages to a few lines; from a few lines to an entry every now and then; from an entry every now and then to writing nothing for months in a row.

I was devastated, but too wiped out to care. I had nothing left to give. It was a good Sunday when I could drag myself to church, but I was unable to do anything beyond that.

Stripped of my activity, I also felt stripped of my identity. I had no energy or even desire to read my Bible. I wanted to hide from God. How could He accept me now that I was doing nothing for Him?

For the first time in my life I had no choice but to be the sheep in need of the Shepherd's arms. I had nothing to bring to Him but my weakness, and in the hush of the stilled life, I felt His grace touching me in my time of need.

I experienced the acceptance of God going deeper than any earning power I might have had. He loves me just because I am His. And His love is secured with grace, not my acceptability or activity.

I was broken. I slowly opened my hands to receive His comfort and I found His grace . . . sufficient.

█████████████ T H O U G H T   F O R   T H E   H E A R T

God's throne is a throne of grace. He longs for us to come to Him with nothing more than ourselves. Are you broken? His grace is sufficient.

— *Shelly Cunningham*

•

WHEN THERE'S NOWHERE ELSE TO RUN

"The Lord is close to the brokenhearted and saves those who are crushed in spirit." Psalm 34:18

Home wasn't a happy place for me. I don't blame my parents. They did and taught what they felt was right, but their rules were difficult for me to understand, much less obey. I was hurting, and I chose to rebel.

It wasn't easy to act out my frustration at home, so school became the primary place for my rebellion. I was so regularly "invited" to leave class that the principal barely looked up when I entered his office. When the time came to leave for college, I felt ready.

For me, relief was spelled "California." It was as far away from home as I could get and still abide by the rules my parents established for attending school. And it was exciting to get to the campus. Imagine a farm boy attending a school that overlooked the Pacific Ocean! I was sure I'd be happy in my new environment.

The only problem was . . . I got kicked out of orientation week on the second day. That wasn't all a mistake. After all, everyone in school knew who I was after such a stunt. I had an identity! I was the one who'd been kicked out of orientation. Dilemma: I also felt uneasy.

I went back to class the next day, but the professor in charge met me at the door and said, "When I kicked you out, it was for good." I was gone. I was not acceptable. And for three days I had nothing to do while everyone else experienced the first week at college.

Those three days were long, painful days for me. In the loneliness of my new surroundings I realized I'd made a terrible mistake: I had taken myself along with me to school.

I had finally gotten away from home, but my rebellion was no better. I had escaped the church. I had escaped the rules. I had escaped the frustration. But I couldn't escape "me." The realization felt overwhelming. I was isolated from everyone, including myself; and I was left alone to ponder my failure.

On Friday of orientation week, I received a note to go to the office of the Dean. True to form, I did not go. I never did things like obey the notes I received from authorities. Then, late on Friday afternoon, there was a knock on the door where I lived.

"Hello," I heard as the Dean walked into the room. "I'm looking for Phil Hook."

"That would be me," I replied with a cautious tone of curiosity.

"I'm glad to know you and I'm glad you're here."

I have never forgotten those two sentences. It seemed like no one was ever glad to know me, much less have me around. And for some reason, that Dean chose to readmit me to the school rather than send me back home. This was the beginning of a whole new pattern for the weeks that followed.

I would get in trouble, the Dean would find me, he would talk with me and encourage me and never condemn or punish. I'd start out in trouble and end up feeling understood. This was a new phenomenon.

Several months later, the Dean invited me to his home. I have often thought that I should have refused the invitation, but I did go. I was systematically breaking all of my own rules of protection. I was only halfway down my list of things I needed to do to prove my rebellion, and here was someone willing to believe in me.

On Saturday morning we sat down to talk and he asked me a question that has altered the course of my life.

"When are you going to stop fighting?" he asked.

"Fighting?" I said, pretending to be confused.

"Yes, when are you going to stop fighting God?" He stuck fast to his intended confrontation.

My mind swirled. I thought I was fighting my home . . . the rules . . . I never realized before that moment that I was fighting God.

When the conversation was finished, I had made a decision. I would not fight God anymore. It is a decision I have not always kept, but it's a decision I've always come back to.

It is hard for us to allow brokenness, particularly when we've been taught by life not to trust and not to allow anyone "in." God is trustworthy, though. And I have found Him always willing to be there.

God does not condemn, blame, shame, or otherwise punish those He loves; instead, He heals the brokenness. It is hard to accept His love, I know. But we have only to let Him into our world. He will do the rest.

THOUGHT FOR THE HEART

I am aware that I resist brokenness, and that I am afraid to let others in. I am willing to begin to trust God with my struggle.

—Phil Hook

B R O K E N N E S S

●
THE TENDER TAMING OF OUR EGOS

"If anyone thinks he has reasons to put confidence in the flesh, I have more: circumcised on the eighth day, of the people of Israel, of the tribe of Benjamin, a Hebrew of Hebrews; in regard to the law, a Pharisee; as for zeal, persecuting the church; as for legalistic righteousness, faultless. But whatever was to my profit I now consider loss for the sake of Christ. What is more, I consider everything a loss compared to the surpassing greatness of knowing Christ Jesus my Lord, for whose sake I have lost all things. I consider them rubbish that I may gain Christ and be found in Him, not having a righteousness of my own which comes from the law, but that which is through faith in Christ — the righteousness that comes from God and is by faith." Philippians 3:4-9

Fred Smith is a successful Christian businessman who has spent years of his life as a consultant to many of the top corporations in our nation. Someone asked him once how he goes in to such corporate giants as General Motors or IBM and discovers the problem.

"That's easy," he replied. "I just look for the ego. When I find the ego, I know where the problem lies."

When I stopped to ponder Mr. Smith's response, I realized that the same thing can be said about any company, regardless of size. This can also be said of churches, school systems, sports teams, marriages, and almost any relationship!

At the crux of most of our problems lies the simple statement (usually unspoken), "I want my way." The desire is at the very core of our human, carnal nature. It is a reality known to us all.

I would like to say that becoming a Christian automatically removes the carnality and ego-battles, but I have been in the church too long to be so naive! When we come to Christ, our sins are forgiven and we begin the process of growth. But that process is one which continues throughout our Christian life; it is not a transformation that is instant and complete.

The Holy Spirit is constantly at work in the life of the believer, breaking down all of those barriers to maturity. If we allow Him entrance and cooperate with Him, He works to cleanse us of the effects of sin and give us victory over the ego we are generally so comfortable protecting.

Like Mr. Smith, the Holy Spirit knows He has to go to the source of our problem — the ego. Even the Apostle Paul had to deal with that issue. He confessed that he had to die to himself daily. He had to experience crucifixion of his own ambitions and self-sufficiency. The Paul-life had to gradually give way to the Christ-life.

Am I demanding my own way? Am I expecting others to change in ways that I am unwilling to change or compromise? Have I developed blind spots that will not allow me to see my own areas of need? Do I think I am so spiritual that I no longer need accountability? Am I willing to take responsibility for my actions and humbly say, "I'm sorry. I've been wrong. Please forgive me"?

These are tough questions, I know. And it is tough to answer them honestly! But the answers just might help us to discover where we need that tender taming of our own wills.

Allow the Holy Spirit the privilege of gently yet persistently breaking you of the ego-controls. Those who are broken and humble make such a difference in the world around them.

Marriages and families are healthier, relationships at work are more gratifying and, in general, life as a believer is far more satisfying and whole when we allow ourselves to be broken and open to maturity.

The ego is quite a large obstacle! And it certainly can be

stubborn. Yet think about the growth that is available to every believer through the ministry of the Spirit.

████████████ THOUGHT FOR THE HEART

I think my ego is "getting in the way" in these relationships or situations. I invite the Holy Spirit to do His work in these areas.

—David Lynch

RHYTHMS OF MY HEART

COMFORT

WHEN WE REFUSE THE GIFT OF COMFORT

"O Jerusalem, Jerusalem, you who kill the prophets and stone those sent to you, how often I have longed to gather your children together, as a hen gathers her chicks under her wings, but you were not willing." Matthew 23:37

My mother passed away when I was thirty-four. She died a slow, painful death from cancer. In the final months, my father and sister took care of her with occasional visits from my brother and me to relieve their tension. It was a difficult time for us all.

After Mom was gone, my father grieved deeply. His depression lasted for months and he would not be relieved. We sought to offer comfort, but it seemed impossible to reach him in that world. He had never prepared himself for her death and thus his grief was intense.

They had shared in the ministry for some thirty-five years—he the pastor and she the partner. They shared in Scripture regularly. They prayed every day for and with one another. They shared in work, they shared in dreams, they shared in disappointments and trials. And for some reason, my father always thought that he would die first. Even when Mom's death was eminent, Dad didn't prepare for the stark reality of living alone.

In the months that followed Mom's death, Dad would talk, but he would never give up the grief or sorrow. I believe he was disappointed not to be the first to arrive at heaven's door. He did not want to live—or die alone.

We tried just about everything to brighten Dad's world. My wife and I invited him to live in Texas with us for the winter. My brother and sister offered encouragement and love. He would visit, he would participate, but he thought of little else than Mom—and going home. All in all, Dad would not be comforted.

COMFORT

Jesus stood on the mountain beside Jerusalem and looked down. His people were enslaved again. This had been a pattern down through history — Egyptians, Assyrians, Babylonians, and Philistines had all reared their powerful heads.

How many times God would have helped, but they would not respond. How many times God would have rescued and healed, but they refused to receive His care. God tried to love His people, but they would not be comforted.

Jesus gazed at Jerusalem. He looked down upon a city which would crucify Him in a matter of days. He longed to forgive their pain and remove their sin, but they would not see. They would not accept His offerings.

Comfort is a gift that is needed by all. At various times in our lives it is the only balm for our wounds. But it is a balm we must receive in order to bask in its healing. Comfort is a powerful gift of the heart.

THOUGHT FOR THE HEART

There are times I refuse Your comfort, Lord. Yet I long for Your balm. Help me to accept the gracious offerings from Your heart to mine.

—Phil Hook

●

THE URGE TO "FIX"

"God is our refuge and strength, an ever present help in trouble. Therefore we will not fear, though the earth give way and the mountains fall into the heart of the sea, though its waters roar and foam and the mountains quake with their surging." Psalm 46:1-3

We try so hard to comfort those in need. A telephone call says Jessie is ill. The pastor reports from the pulpit that

COMFORT

Susan's mom has just died. The prayer chain calls to report that young Johnny Mayberry was hurt today and is having stitches. Graham comes by to say that his wife has just miscarried.

How do you respond? What can you say? Where do you put those uncomfortable feelings of your own? When do you spring into action, when do you wait, when do you pray?

I think one thing that is difficult for us in the arena of offering comfort lies in our propensity to "fix" that which is broken. We are fixers! We feel more comfortable when we can act upon our sorrow. It is hard for us to allow another to hurt and to simply share that person's pain.

One of the tender moments in Scripture can be found in our Lord's response to three dear friends, Mary, Martha, and Lazarus. They were each close to Jesus, and had opened their hearts to Him. They were not just takers; they were friends.

We don't know much about Mary, Martha, and Lazarus, but what we do know helps us to grasp the depth of their relationship with the Messiah.

Martha was the "mother" of the three. She was the older sister, the one in charge, the one who took responsibility for the things that needed to be done. Martha loved Jesus and was very committed to spiritual things. She was also very busy and controlled.

Mary, on the other hand, was, in many respects, Martha's opposite! Mary was the younger of the two sisters, and the one who chose to listen rather than do when Jesus was around. While Martha prepared dinner, Mary sat at the feet of our Lord.

Lazarus lived a relatively unknown existence before his death. As far as we can tell, he was the "little brother" with two very capable sisters! I doubt Lazarus had to do very much at all when Martha and Mary were around.

C O M F O R T

One day, Jesus and His disciples received a message that grieved them deeply. Lazarus was ill, and the sisters wanted the Lord to come immediately. They needed Him.

The disciples expected Jesus to go to the family right away, but He did not. Jesus told the disciples that the sickness would not end in death and He stayed two more days away from the family. During those two days, Lazarus died. (See John 11:1-44.)

When Martha and Mary heard that Jesus at last was approaching their village of Bethany, they desired to be with Him. Martha came first—alone, and then Mary.

"O Lord, this would not have happened if You had been here," each woman spoke to Him privately. Deeply troubled by the loss of their brother, they were hurt that Jesus had not responded to their call. Jesus heard their pain and comforted the women as each had need.

Jesus comforted Martha by talking with her about faith and hope, and by inviting her to reaffirm her commitment. To comfort Martha was to talk with her and share her spiritual pilgrimage.

Jesus comforted Mary by crying with her. We are told that He was so moved by her pain and by the pain of friends who gathered to share her grief that He began to weep. Mary didn't need a theological discussion or an affirmation of her faith. She needed someone to share her emotional suffering.

I also believe that Jesus comforted Lazarus. He comforted this young man by allowing him to die in the first place. Think about it! The death gave a certain significance to Lazarus which we had not seen before. Lazarus became a person with a life and a spirituality all his own.

This story is an important one from many different perspectives. Certainly it teaches us about friendship and love. It teaches us about the power of our Lord and the everyday effort of His followers to trust in that power. The story also teaches us about comfort.

Jesus had the power to fix His friend's pain. He could have prevented the illness before it even began. He could have healed His friend from afar. He could have told both Martha and Mary about His plan to raise Lazarus and, in so doing, spared their grief.

Our Lord could have "fixed" the pain, but He did not. He loved Mary, Martha, and Lazarus and He comforted them through sharing in their anguish.

It is our temptation to "fix" one another's difficulties. It is hard to imagine that suffering can be valuable, so we tend to try to put an end to its discomfort. Yet we learn, through Jesus' ministry and through a myriad of examples in both Old and New Testaments, that God allows pain. God uses our sufferings to "grow us up," to deepen our faith, to show us His love. It is a difficult yet faithful offering to embrace one another's burdens and offer comfort.

THOUGHT FOR THE HEART

I do want to "fix" the pain of those I love. Lord, teach me about comfort instead. Teach me to reach out and offer Your comfort to others in need.

— Shelley Chapin

●
HEALING THE HEART

"Comfort, comfort My people, says your God. Speak tenderly to Jerusalem, and proclaim to her that her hard service has been completed, that her sin has been paid for, that she has received from the Lord's hand double for all her sins. A voice of one calling: 'In the desert prepare the way for the Lord; make straight in the wilderness a highway for our God. Every valley shall be raised up, every mountain and hill made low; the rough ground shall become level, the rugged places a plain. And the glory of the Lord will be re-

vealed, and all mankind together will see it, for the mouth of the Lord has spoken.' " Isaiah 40:1-5

I think one of my hardest tasks as a physician in Third World countries has been to learn the meaning of comfort.

I was born and raised in England and educated in both London and the United States, so my point of reference for "doctoring" has been the more sophisticated parts of the globe. In short, if there is some new technique or some better piece of machinery, my training has been to use what is available! After all, we are to heal the body, or so I've been taught.

When I first began my medical career on the African continent, things were suddenly very different. I saw people die daily from diseases which were easily treatable "back home." I saw people suffer from ills we would not even see in other parts of the world. I found myself quite helpless to respond in areas where I am otherwise confident or skilled. My point of view had to "grow" a little, or I knew I would never be able to maintain my position in such a setting.

God is gracious. Just when we think we have nothing more to learn in an area, He gives us opportunity. One such opportunity came for me when I saw the work of one of our modern-day "saints," Mother Teresa.

I visited India with several things in mind, not the least of which was to learn how this woman could survive with so little medical hope. I had heard of her and read a few articles, but my journey to observe was long before Mother Teresa was a household name.

I entered one of her hospice sites and was immediately taken aback. Where our work in Africa would be considered professionally "behind," this work would be considered extinct. Why, they weren't even treating all of the "patients." Many were simply lying down, receiving comfort from loving hands and cool water.

I addressed one of the helpers who looked the most experienced.

"Are these people waiting to be admitted to the hospital?" I asked. She looked a bit puzzled. I decided to try again.

"I am a physician and I can tell that most of these people need immediate medical care." I tried to sound important in case she was unimpressed.

"This is all the treatment we have available," she spoke kindly to me. "These men and women are waiting to die, and we are offering them love and comfort." I could hardly believe my ears. She excused herself to get back to the job of loving these lovely people.

I had only a few days to stay, but I learned more in those few days than I've learned in other decades of my life. I learned much about love, about comfort and, frankly, about what people really need in life.

In my early years as a physician I thought that comforting came in the form of easing the physical burdens. I thought it my job to remove the physical pain and, if I could, to end the control of the disease. I have since learned that other things are even more important.

Offering comfort means that we move past the physical to the heart and soul of that individual or family. Offering comfort means that we become willing to encounter pain and to walk through that pain with those afflicted. Offering comfort means that we not label death "the failure" but that we label loving "the success."

I think God showed me the difference because He knew that I would need more than a bag full of physical skills. God knew I would need a heart full of love and compassion, and so He taught me about comfort.

C O M F O R T

I too find it easier to try to meet the physical needs of those around me. I would like to become more aware of how to reach out with my heart.

— Pamela M. Reeves

●
COMFORT CLOSING IN

"Praise be to the God and Father of our Lord Jesus Christ, the Father of compassion and the God of all comfort, who comforts us in all our troubles, so that we can comfort those in any trouble with the comfort we ourselves have received from God. For just as the sufferings of Christ flow over into our lives, so also through Christ our comfort overflows." 2 Corinthians 1:3-5

In 1982, at age twenty-eight, I heard the chilling words, "You have cancer. We expect you will live about nine months."

What? I thought. *This can't be. I'm too young. I'm too healthy. Please, God, not this . . .*

I well remember the emptiness of those first weeks with cancer. I was overwhelmed by the news, and the feelings of despair grew with each passing day. I felt more alone in those weeks than I had ever felt before, and I was at a loss for where to turn to find comfort. I wanted someone to step in and erase the circumstances. I wanted someone to take me back to the security of days gone by.

Though the realization was gradual, I began to see God's comfort closing in around me. He didn't remove the circumstances, though that continued to be my prayer for a time. Instead, God began to reach into my heart and bathe me with love. He opened my eyes to the real essence of comfort.

I found that God weeps with my tears. He is present in my prayers and in my longings. He sends friends to soothe, to hold, and to walk with me in the pain. He increases my compassion for the hurts of others. He allows me to question and to cry out in anger. He opens His Word for healing from the inside out.

I found out that God pushes me a little bit farther than I thought I could go. He allows my faith to be tested and proved genuine. He gives me responsibility when I'm certain I cannot rise to the occasion. He withholds all judgment and condemnation. He frees me to be who I am — no more and no less.

We rarely consider the nature of comfort until we are in need of its secrets. We are far more comfortable in the "fixing" mode, but agony cannot be "fixed" — it can only be shared in an atmosphere of love, acceptance, and compassion.

Explore the ways that God comforts you so that your comfort can overflow to those in need around you. Give yourself permission to explore the fearful, the painful, the unthinkable. Invite God's comfort to overflow so that you too have gifts to bear.

God allows no pain without comfort, but the comfort takes time and patience to recognize. God's comfort is eternal, internal, and full of the kind of love that cares more about who we become than what we want.

▬▬▬▬▬▬ T H O U G H T   F O R   T H E   H E A R T

I am aware that God has comforted me in these very personal ways.

— Shelley Chapin

●
RELYING ON OUR FATHER

"Give me a sign of Your goodness, that my enemies may see it and

be put to shame, for You, O Lord, have helped me and comforted me." Psalm 86:17

I have known the Lord for a long time now, but there are times I still wrestle with the "whys" of our existence. Currently, my husband and I are struggling with elderly parents as well as personal physical needs. One of our loved ones is legally blind. Her husband has just gone to be with the Lord. And our own bodies are aging, showing signs of wear and tear.

Our energy sometimes feels drained, as I am sure you also experience. And when I am drained, I discover, anew, a secret. When "forced" to rely on God, I find His comfort sweet. This is what I am learning yet again. My comfort comes when I rely on my Heavenly Father.

Whenever things really get tough, I back up and seek God's eternal perspective. When I can no longer make sense out of life, I trust that He will weave even these circumstances into His tapestry. The only turmoil is that it's difficult to see what God is doing when we are in the midst of the suffering.

God never promises that we will live pain-free. In fact, He promises that we will endure suffering! But He also promises that He will take care of us through each and every storm. God promises to provide all of our needs.

The key to receiving God's comfort does not lie in my circumstances, though I might want Him to bring the relief I have planned. The key to receiving His comfort lies in my own attitude . . . my willingness to apply what I know to be true in one more step of the process.

I am speaking to myself as I offer these thoughts to you. I simply know that in the midst of the storm it is easier to try to fix the problems than it is to relax and accept God's comfort. I don't know how He will bring relief to my family, I only know that He will.

COMFORT

God's comfort, His faithfulness, His purposes become clear as we take each step with Him. As hard as it may be, I will trust the One who cares for me.

God, open my eyes to Your comfort. I want to receive Your offerings.

— Marilyn Budde

●
COMING ALONGSIDE

"So then, those who suffer according to God's will should commit themselves to their faithful Creator and continue to do good."
1 Peter 4:19

It has been said that, "to have suffered much is like knowing many languages: it gives the sufferer access to many more people." Likewise, Paul states that we are able to comfort others from the same comfort we receive in our suffering. While this message is accurate, it is also difficult to embrace. Accepting the reality of suffering is a complicated matter.

Which one of us fails to cry, "Why me, Lord? Why are You allowing this to happen?" In the unfolding of pain, which one of us is not tempted to withdraw from those around us and live in a world of our own?

While we do need "alone" time to reflect, it is often in our withdrawal that pain can turn into bitterness and discontent. In our contact with others, however, God can turn the pain into great benefit for ourselves and worthwhile compassion for our fellow sufferers. One of the greatest gifts we have in our suffering is friendship and support.

The New Testament word for "encouragement" literally

means, "to call someone alongside." This is the same concept used by our Lord to describe the ministry of the Holy Spirit. Truly, we can call one another alongside for help and support when suffering from life's many trials. And we will be greatly blessed as we come alongside others in their time of need.

None of us need "go it alone" in our pain. One of the greatest privileges of being part of God's family lies in encouraging one another. As believers, we stand firmly on the reminder that nothing can separate us from the love of God. And we stand on the reminder that we are part of a large family where support is steadily available.

What about the hard times? We all need encouragement. Try to remember to ask. There are people around you who long to reach out to you in your pain, if only they know they'll be welcome.

And don't forget to share your comfort with others in need. The family of comfort is large.

THOUGHT FOR THE HEART

Suffering is more easily borne by many than one. I can both receive these comforts from others and give these comforts away.

—Mark Hoffman

●
WILLING TO TOUCH

"Though You have made me see troubles, many and bitter, You will restore my life again; from the depths of the earth You will again bring me up. You will increase my honor and comfort me once again. I will praise You with the harp for Your faithfulness, O my God; I will sing praise to You with the lyre, O Holy One of Israel. My lips will shout for joy when I sing praise to You—I whom You have redeemed." Psalm 71:20-23

It has been so long since anyone has touched me, she thought to herself. She was standing in the shadow, listening to the noise of the excited crowd as it approached.

If only I could get a glimpse of the visitor. Perhaps . . . but her thoughts stopped there. *No. I cannot allow these dreams to continue. I won't make that mistake again.* And a faint tear made its way down her hollow cheek.

Abigail's mind was suddenly filled with a hundred images, converging all at once on her furrowed brow. She had trusted people before, but they had let her down. Doctors had promised cures but not delivered, the church had promised visits but not followed through. Abigail was alone in this world, and even more so since the progression of her illness.

Suddenly Abigail's thoughts were interrupted as a large throng of people turned the corner and came her way. She scanned to and fro from one face to another but saw nothing different until . . . yes, there He was. That must be Him.

I've never seen anything like those eyes. Perhaps I can trust this man. Maybe if I just reach out and touch the edge of His robe. Please, Lord, have mercy on me.

Before she realized what she was doing, Abigail stepped into the crowd and lost herself among those who were following. She was slight and quick, and she carefully made her way toward the One whose eyes were fixed firmly in her mind.

There it is, she thought. *There is His robe. I think I can reach . . . yes . . . oh, my!*

In an instant of hope, Abigail's body was renewed and she knew the power of that instant as if it were a long, lost relative. Then He stopped and turned and fixed those eyes on her.

The story is a familiar one, though we are not told the woman's name. She had a problem with bleeding which left her untouchable in the world of the New Testament. She had heard of Jesus' powers, but she had no idea that His love and comfort would set her free.

We tend to offer advice when approached by a friend or relative in pain — whether that pain be the struggles of a marriage or the loss of a job or the suffering inherent in illness.

Yet the greatest gift of comfort Jesus offered this woman was simply His willingness to touch and accept. He comforted her by not being ashamed of her grasp. He comforted her by listening. He comforted her through the care and concern that clearly marked His face and filled His eyes.

We all need comfort for we all face pains and disappointments that must be grieved to be understood. Maybe you are grieving today, or maybe you know someone who hungers for relief from the suffering.

Consider the gift of comfort today. It is a gift generously offered by our Lord, and it comes in all shapes and sizes to fit our pain.

Perhaps touch is needed. Perhaps a listening ear. Or perhaps a gentle reminder that we are loved.

Though sometimes comfort advises, the greatest gift is that of God's love, wrapped in a package that can be seen and felt and digested. Accept that package today. Be that package.

THOUGHT FOR THE HEART

The comfort I long for looks like this. I am willing to seek comfort and I am willing to offer its divine love to others I meet.

— Shelley Chapin

RHYTHMS OF MY HEART

COMPASSION

A HEART LIKE JESUS'

"I will give you a new heart and put a new spirit in you; I will remove from you a heart of stone and give you a heart of flesh."
Ezekiel 36:26

I always thought I had a spirit of compassion, a soft heart. Why? Because friends came to me with their problems, coworkers stopped by my office to ask advice, students from the church youth group I sponsor called me about family troubles . . . the list could go on.

On the exterior, I was always calm, pragmatic, seemingly sympathetic, able to suggest possible ways to deal with problems. Basically, I appeared to have my act together!

I'd love to accept the accolade, but in reality I was as far from compassionate as a person could be. I didn't have a clue how to guide people. Grasping at straws, I hoped I would say something to help alleviate others' pain; but in truth, I always felt drained after the encounters.

I wish I could describe the energy it took for me to make sure I did *not* relate to other people's pain. I had to protect my heart of stone so that I wouldn't feel the anguish. In fact, the pain others expressed only caused me anger and discomfort. I couldn't begin to respond with *real* compassion when I was so busy avoiding my own suffering.

What was wrong with me? What kept me from expressing true compassion toward others?

The answer is very complex, but suffice it to say that I was starved for compassion myself. While I was moved by other people's pain, I couldn't let myself fully respond for fear I might suffer as well. And even though I knew that my friends, coworkers, and youth group members cared about me, their sensitivity to my hurt and pain never seemed to be "enough."

I began to realize that I could depend on no human to give me the compassion I long for. Only the "Wonderful Counselor" who can be "deeply moved in spirit and troubled" is able to fully alleviate the pain of my past, present, and future (John 11:32-44). I need not fear my own suffering when the compassionate One is by my side.

I've always been stirred by the sensitivity Jesus exhibited toward Mary and Martha. I love the part where He was so touched by their grief that He wept openly.

I'm also moved by the depth of remorse shown by our Lord at Lazarus' death. Perhaps agonizing over Lazarus caused Jesus even more sorrow as He looked ahead to His own impending death.

In short, Jesus is not afraid to connect with our anguish and express His own sadness in response to our pain. At the same time, He challenges us to a deeper, more intimate level of vulnerability.

When others turn to us for compassion, do they sense that we are deeply moved? Are we connecting with their pain? If not, then perhaps we're having trouble experiencing Jesus' compassion toward us. I know I have trouble grasping the depth of His concern.

Do you hunger for compassion? Is your heart made of stone as mine sometimes feels? Then let's pray together that God will chisel out change in our lives—change that will enable us to sense Jesus' compassion for us.

May He give us tender new hearts that are dependent on Him so that we can, in turn, be deeply moved to both receive and extend compassion toward those around us.

THOUGHT FOR THE HEART

As God's chosen person, holy and dearly loved, I would like to be clothed with compassion and kindness.

—Pam Campbell

●

WHERE COMPASSION GROWS

"So they went away by themselves in a boat to a solitary place. But many who saw them leaving recognized them and ran on foot from all the towns and got there ahead of them. When Jesus landed and saw a large crowd, He had compassion on them, because they were like sheep without a shepherd. So He began teaching them many things." Mark 6:32-34

There is a little known woman who lives in a village in northern Haiti. Just over the ridge lies the ocean, clear and blue; and La Pointe is surrounded by rolling hills. It is a lovely place to see and a heartrending place to visit.

Like most villages in Haiti, there is a great amount of suffering in La Pointe. People are poor, unemployment is greater than 80 percent, and both men and women live discouraged by their situations. Their lives have little hope, little light, little meaning. Tucked away in the darkness and despair is a place called "House of Hope."

Few have ever heard of "House of Hope," fewer still have visited there. But I entertained such a privilege back in 1989, when I traveled to Haiti with a physician-friend for a short-term missions trip. What I saw I will never forget.

The makeshift clinic in La Pointe is staffed with physicians, nurses, physician's aides, teachers, and administrative personnel. The people who serve there are missionaries—men and women who sense that God has led them to Haiti to use their gifts. I found the people to be honest, loving, a bit tired, and ever so committed. They welcomed us with open hearts.

As our first day dawned in Haiti we dressed, ate breakfast, and headed to the clinic. A line had already formed that would take all morning to service and still more would arrive throughout the day. I quickly learned how important the work of the clinic is—they serve as a literal lifeline for people needing everything from medication for worms to surgery.

Brenda and I worked there for several hours and then we were taken on a tour of the clinic grounds during an extended break for lunch. It was then that we laid eyes upon "House of Hope."

Imagine twenty-plus children running around with smiles on their faces and you begin to get the picture. Now imagine some in wheelchairs, some using crutches, and some dragging themselves along the ground and you begin to see more of the reality there. Now imagine an atmosphere of love, and you have "House of Hope."

The children who live at "House of Hope" have been rejected by their families for the most part. They are victims of diseases such as tuberculosis or malaria, which have often gone untreated too long. Most were so ill by the time they received hospital care that no one expected them to live.

Brenda and I were inundated with children just wanting to be held. She held, I held, until our strength was fading; then we held some more.

I have never seen such joy on the faces of children who have so little, so I began to search for the secret. I found the secret easily in the love of their "mother"—the director of "House of Hope"—Linda.

During our stay in Haiti we learned that this young woman was herself a "graduate" of the program. Linda was grown now, as grown as the early twenties and much pain can make someone. She could have gone somewhere else to start a life or a family, but Linda chose to stay right there in La Pointe. She chose the same four walls, the same small courtyard, the same mission, and the same God. She chose to love the children who must walk the path she once walked. Linda is a woman of compassion.

Compassion grows out of a sensitive heart. Jesus had been working for hours when the crowds came to Him again. He had just learned of John's death and He wanted to spend some time alone. But the people had needs— needs they didn't even understand. Jesus looked at them and saw sheep without a shepherd. Tell me, what shepherd can walk away from a lost lamb?

Jesus had compassion for people. In fact, one of the things that disturbed Him most about the Pharisees was their lack of compassion. They would use a person's pain to try to trick our Lord into healing on the Sabbath. Such insensitivity broke the Savior's heart.

Jesus cared about the needy person, and He made it His mission to reach out to His children. He stepped into the midst of our pain with love and forgiveness, patience and hope.

I watched as Linda loved her sheep. She had time and a special love for each one. They know they are loved by her, they know she will not abandon them. She is a woman of compassion.

Oh, that we all could visit "House of Hope" and see the love that's exhibited there. For now, just imagine and let God fill your mind with the possibilities of compassion. There is no end to what love can do for a needy heart.

███████████ THOUGHT FOR THE HEART

I want to learn to show Your compassion, Lord. There are people around me each day who need a reminder of Your love and their worth. Help me to be that reminder.

—Shelley Chapin

C O M P A S S I O N

●
ENTRUSTED "CARGO"

"Therefore, as God's chosen people, holy and dearly loved, clothe yourselves with compassion, kindness, humility, gentleness, and patience." Colossians 3:12

Clovis Chappell, a minister from a century back, used to tell the story of two paddle boats that left Memphis about the same time. Both were carrying cargo entrusted to their care and both were traveling down the Mississippi toward New Orleans.

As the two boats traveled side by side down the river, sailors from one vessel began to make remarks about the snail's pace of the other. Maybe the remarks sounded something like this.

"Hey there, can't you go any faster?"

"I think your boat's out of fuel!"

"Are you on a sightseeing tour or are you trying to work?"

As you might imagine, such remarks were not appreciated! Words were exchanged, challenges were made, and before they knew it the race was on!

The competition became vicious as the two boats roared through the Deep South. Each team was certain they would win and each captain was intent on proving the superiority of his crew. Then something happened! One boat began losing ground for lack of fuel. They had loaded plenty of coal for a normal trip, but not nearly enough for a race.

As the boat began falling further and further behind, an enterprising young sailor took charge. He found some of the ship's cargo and tossed it in the ovens — and it worked! When the sailors saw that the supplies burned as well as the coal, they began using all the materials they were carrying to aid them in their struggle to "win."

This vessel won the race in the end, but they destroyed their cargo. They failed at the mission they had been assigned to complete. And they failed because they changed their course in midstream. "Winning a race" became more important than completing the mission.

God has entrusted cargo to us as well. Children, spouses, friends, and neighbors have all been given to us to nurture and support. Our job is to do our part in seeing that this cargo reaches the destination.

The struggle we face is this. When the program takes priority over people, people usually suffer. So to be compassionate people we often have to lay aside our own races.

It isn't always easy to be compassionate. It wasn't always easy for our Lord. There were countless people to help, needs to meet, and jobs to do, but He kept giving. He only "rested" from His job to spend time with His Father and replenish His own strength.

How much cargo should we sacrifice in order to achieve the number-one slot of our dreams? How many people in our care will never reach the destination? Are we often aggressive and competitive captains? Do we know how to show compassion?

Let's pray to be aware of the need for compassion. Let's pray to pay attention to our cargo.

■ THOUGHT FOR THE HEART

I am aware that my "cargo" gets lost, at times, in the urgency of my own dreams or goals. I will pray for a compassionate heart—a heart that helps others reach the destination.

—Max Lucado

C O M P A S S I O N

●
A SELF FOR OTHERS

"I think it is necessary to send back to you Epaphroditus, my broth-er, fellow worker, and fellow soldier, who is also your messenger, whom you sent to take care of my needs. For he longs for all of you and is distressed because he was ill. Indeed he was ill, and almost died. But God had mercy on him and not on him only but also on me, to spare me sorrow upon sorrow. Therefore I am all the more eager to send him, so that when you see him again you may be glad and I may have less anxiety. Welcome him in the Lord with great joy, and honor men like him, because he almost died for the work of Christ, risking his life to make up for the help you could not give me." Philippians 2:25-30

The mark of a compassionate person lies in this simple distinction: the compassionate person learns to be a self for others rather than a self for self. Let me see if I can explain.

Epaphroditus was relatively unknown outside his circle of friends some 2,000 years ago. He was probably an ordi-nary person, hard-working and dedicated to family and friends — and then he met Paul.

Paul described Epaphroditus as a "brother" and a "fel-low worker." Epaphroditus was Paul's kinsman in Christ, an associate in the furtherance of the Gospel. He was someone who took hold of the Gospel as quickly as the Good News took hold of him. And he served Paul and the church well in those years following the ascension of our Lord.

Epaphroditus was one of those people who learned to be a self for others rather than a self for self. And he learned and practiced this gift of compassion throughout his days of ministry.

We would not know a lot about this servant of Christ if

it weren't for a few verses in Philippians. Yet through these six verses he has become a cameo of the thousands of unsung heroes who had the courage to trust Christ enough to put the needs of others above their own.

Two things stand out for me as I learn about compassion from Epaphroditus. First, he was willing to care for his mentor and teacher, Paul, even though the care cost him a great deal. In other words, compassion involves sacrifice.

When Paul was placed under house arrest, Epaphroditus cared for him and literally became his "feet." Epaphroditus made the long journey from Philippi to Rome to bring financial help to Paul. And he reached out as Paul's messenger to the church. The end result? Epaphroditus nearly lost his life seeking to serve.

Secondly, I learn that compassion involves seeing the world through the eyes of the person you're caring for. Even though Epaphroditus had been ill himself, he wanted to visit the Philippians personally when he learned they were worried about him. Compassion calls us to see the world through another person's eyes and respond as we are able. For Epaphroditus that meant a visit to the believers who cared so much about him.

Compassion is a gift from one heart to another. And it is a gift we all long for as we journey through this world.

There were many theological issues which caught Paul's attention, but in this passage to the Philippians he was caught by the compassion of one simple servant: Epaphroditus.

THOUGHT FOR THE HEART

I can think of several people who need a compassionate friend right now. Lord, help me to be that compassionate friend to those You send my way.

— Ken Boa

C O M P A S S I O N

●
CONCERN IN ACTION

"Praise the Lord, O my soul; all my inmost being, praise His Holy Name. Praise the Lord, O my soul, and forget not all His benefits. He forgives all my sins and heals all my diseases; He redeems my life from the pit and crowns me with love and compassion. He satisfies my desires with good things, so that my youth is renewed like the eagle's." Psalm 103:1-5

One of the most significant books I have ever read is called *Fearfully and Wonderfully Made,* by Paul Brand and Philip Yancey. It is a book about touch . . . about the human body . . . about compassion.

I was first introduced to the book while recovering from surgery in October 1983. I could not read on my own as the pain was too distracting, so friends read to me. And as the words of the book unfolded, I felt the compassion of its authors. I felt they cared literally about me, for they reminded me that I am significant to my Lord.

When I think of compassion I think of one simple word: *concern.* And I think of that word applied—in action, changing someone else's life, if only for a moment of time.

The Pharisees were angry with Jesus. He would not do what they wanted Him to do. They met a few times here and there to discuss this new hero who was sweeping their world with a popularity unprecedented, but they did not know what to do to stop Him. How could they put a halt to His ministry? How could they convince the people that He was dangerous?

They assembled a few ideas, but none that looked too promising. Still, they had to try, so Plan #1 was put into action. They would put a "decoy" at the temple on the Sabbath—a man with a withered hand—to see if Jesus would help him. After all, everyone knows that you don't heal on the Sabbath.

The Sabbath Day arrived and everything was moving along like clockwork. Old "George" was in his place with the crippled man, "Tom" was posted in the doorway as a sentry, and everyone else was scattered around, trying to look inconspicuous.

"Here He comes," whispered Tom. "Everyone ready?"

"We're ready," confirmed George. And he reminded the crippled man again that there would be money in the deal if he begged well.

Jesus entered . . . He and His disciples, ready to worship and share the Word. But just as George was about to shove the man with the shriveled hand toward Jesus, Jesus looked their way. He gazed long into the eyes of the Pharisee and then He looked at the man. And His voice rang out with authority.

"Stand up in front of everyone," He said. The man responded without delay. "Now, which is lawful on the Sabbath, to do good or to do evil, to save life or to kill?" (See Mark 3:3-4.) And all the world stood still.

Compassion is all about concern put into action. The very people who should have cared about the man didn't care at all. The real leader stood out strong and tall because He was willing to care, and He backed up that willingness with specific measures.

As you might imagine, the man found healing that day. And he found that healing because of a compassionate Lord who cared more about helping one, solitary man than pleasing a horde of Pharisees.

They tried to kill Him for His concern, but love cannot be silenced. And the world still sings His song, loud and clear.

"Stretch out your hand, your heart, your life and allow the Man of Compassion to enter in." Remember, you are fearfully and wonderfully made.

C O M P A S S I O N

I long to accept the compassion of my Lord and to recognize His gentle concern. At times I forget just how much He cares. Lord, help me to care for others as You care for me.

— *Shelley Chapin*

●

NELLIE

"In that day I will make a covenant for them with the beasts of the field and the birds of the air and the creatures that move along the ground. Bow and sword and battle I will abolish from the land, so that all may lie down in safety. I will betroth you to Me forever; I will betroth you in righteousness and justice, in love and compassion. I will betroth you in faithfulness, and you will acknowledge the Lord." Hosea 2:18-20

I never knew how to say her name, so I just called her "Nellie." She didn't seem to mind. She flashed a toothless grin each time I entered her village and she walked with me, offering her help to anyone in need.

Nellie was a woman of compassion. She felt deeply for the people of her village and she allowed that concern to show. I never once entered her domain to find her shirking the duties. She was the "mother" of anyone in need.

As I began to learn the tribal language, Nellie was right there to help me. She knew a smattering of English (the British version!), and she smiled each time I learned a word and pronounced it in such a way that I could be understood! She would praise me and pat me on the back and bow her head over and over. There are few people in the world more compassionate than Nellie.

One thing I have learned from watching Nellie at work: compassion is not an "at the moment" decision. If we wait for the situation to choose, there is a distinct possibility we will be too busy or too tired. Rarely do people need us at a convenient time!

Nellie has taught me that a compassionate person is one who is available. Whether the need comes late at night or early in the morning; whether the individual in need is appreciative or not, Nellie is there to lend a piece of her heart. In short, compassion and Nellie are synonymous in my experience.

It takes time to be trusted in the African culture, so time passed before I was told much about Nellie or any of the others in her village. I knew their medical histories and their physical conditions, but I only gained entrance into their personal worlds one moment at a time.

Finally, one day as Nellie and I were caring for a dying friend of hers, she opened up a bit. It seems that Nellie had once been a young and vibrant member of her tribe. She had married a choice young man and had two lovely sons and they had even learned to love one another. Arranged marriages do not always hold such a privilege.

Nellie says that she was not so compassionate then. She says that her sights were set on building her own dreams and that she rarely invested in others. All that changed one terrible day.

Many of the men were out of the village hunting when a young man returned with panic in his voice. Some of the hunters had been killed by animals. They were bringing back the bodies now. There was nothing to do but wait.

As you might guess, one of Nellie's young sons was killed by an angry lioness. Apparently he had approached a cub and the lioness responded as any mother would. Nellie sobbed as she watched her young and innocent son prepared for burial.

Nellie told me that she felt all alone in the days and

weeks that followed his death. No one knew what to say and suddenly the reality of pain set in. She decided then and there to be a lover of people.

Compassion is a matter of the heart. Few of us know how to live compassionately, but most who have experienced pain can testify that a compassionate friend is a healing balm to an otherwise parched soul. Nellie is that healing balm.

Our God is a compassionate God. He never leaves or forsakes and He always loves and soothes us in our pain. He also equips us to be people of compassion. Consider the privilege.

THOUGHT FOR THE HEART

I remember how much I've needed compassion in my own pain. Lord, help me to accept this challenge. Help me to make compassion a matter of my heart.

— *Pamela M. Reeves*

COMPASSIONATE HANDS

"Though He brings grief, He will show compassion, so great is His unfailing love. For He does not willingly bring affliction or grief to the children of men." Lamentations 3:32-33

For over a decade I have been sharing with people about pain. Though I never intended this to happen, it seems that suffering has become almost a "specialty" for me. I have known pain myself, and I have shared with thousands who, themselves, are in anguish. Whether from illness or divorce, financial difficulty or marital problems, suffering is a reality which touches all of our lives.

When I first started speaking on the topic, it was my

own pain which served as the inspiration. That reality soon changed. The opportunity of walking for awhile in someone else's shoes has taught me the most about compassion and provided me with the greatest opportunity to stretch my own heart.

Our plane was met as usual by a missionary. Otis has lived in Belize for years and is well-acquainted with the customs. He has also seen many a missionary pass through the line at customs. He is a seasoned veteran.

Otis was giving us the schedule before our luggage even hit the back of his well-worn van. He does not mince words and there was much to be done. Some of us would go to Punta Gorda, some to Bermudian Landing, some to the churches on the outskirts of Belize City, some to Belmopan. And all of us would have adventures galore. Belize is one of my favorite places to experience God's handiwork in the hearts of men and women.

Almost in passing, Otis told me about a young girl they wanted me to visit in the hospital. I had been there before so I knew what "hospital" meant in the Belizian world. He said we might have time that day or the next, but that the young woman he wanted me to see was not long for this world. I tucked the information in my mind as we drove into this world I have grown to love.

The time came for my hospital visit and I was eager to go. I walked up a few stairs and around a corridor until I entered the main room where the patients lived and died.

The hospital is large like a gymnasium with beds lined up along the wall. In the center sits an old gray metal desk or two, used by the nurses as their resting place. I approached the nurse there and presented my request.

"I am here to see a young woman with lung cancer," I explained. "She is about sixteen years old and isn't doing very well." The nurse nodded and pointed toward the far wall.

COMPASSION

"She's over there," I was told. "And she is very ill."

"What about her family?" I asked, wanting to gather some information before stepping into this young girl's pain. "Where are they?"

"She's been alone for over a month," was the reply. "Her family does not want to see her this way, and so they come to visit no more." I couldn't believe my ears.

When I reached the bed I knew instantly that this young woman was in great pain. I could hear the fluid rumble in her chest as she labored to take each breath. She was a pretty little girl, but her lips were now swollen and cracked and she weighed less than seventy-five pounds. My heart broke to think of her loneliness at this, one of the most crucial moments in her short life.

I started to touch the young woman but drew my hand back as I noticed something I hadn't seen at first glance. The skin on her arms and legs was literally peeling off and laying in clumps around her on the bed.

I can't touch her, I thought to myself. *I don't know what she has, but something is definitely wrong.* I did not want to "catch" whatever disease was causing the skin to separate from her thin frame. *I'll just lean over and talk,* I justified. *That will be enough.*

Well, I tried to just lean over and talk, but I got nowhere. The poor young girl was barely able to breathe, much less carry on a conversation. And I knew she sensed my nervousness. After all, I had felt the fear of hundreds of people in the days of my own struggle with cancer.

A battle raged in my mind as I tried to decide what compassion would do. In all honesty, I knew what to do; I was simply afraid and I let the fear roll around in my mind for what seemed an eternity.

Finally, with the help of God's grace and reminders of my own need, I carefully and gently placed that young girl in my arms and we rocked. The moment my skin touched hers, her eyes met mine.

I only had a few eternal moments with my young friend. She was lovely and so deserving of compassion and kindness. And I was so grateful to grant her that desire.

We talked about pain. We talked about Jesus. And I told her about a mutual friend and Savior who would wipe away every tear and grant us His love for eternity. She wanted to know Him too.

This young girl remains one of the most important people in my life, though she died less than twenty-four hours after I left her side. She is important to me because she taught me about compassion—about stepping alongside someone else in pain and gently easing the load just a bit.

Compassion is caring more about that other person than you do about your comfort—at least for a moment or two in time. Compassion is reaching deep into the heart of someone else's pain and loving them there.

Thank you, young friend, who lives now in the presence of our Lord. Thank you for teaching me about compassion.

■■■■■■■■■ **THOUGHT FOR THE HEART**

I would like to extend compassion today to people in need of love, acceptance, mercy. Lord, show me where to place compassionate hands.

—Shelley Chapin

RHYTHMS OF MY HEART

CONTROL

DEPENDING ON GOD, NOT ABILITIES

" 'For I know the plans I have for you,' declares the Lord, 'plans to prosper you and not to harm you, plans to give you hope and a future.' " Jeremiah 29:11

My greatest joy as a boy growing up was pitching baseball. I worked and worked and pitched and dreamed until I could play. And God granted me ample opportunities to live out my dream.

Being a pitcher was always one of my definitions of myself. I started pitching as I entered my teen years, and it was both a source of much joy and income for me. Looking back, I can say that my pride was also rooted in my pitching ability. I felt confident in the control I earned over my body and over the game. I felt better about "me" when pitching.

As I aged, pitching became a great way to get attention. When invited to speak at retreats or youth meetings, I would challenge the young people that they couldn't hit a fair ball off of me before I could strike them out! I was usually successful in the challenge and in gaining their confidence.

One evening I was pitching for our church. I had not taken things very seriously that night so I neglected the warmup and was really not prepared for the stress that pitching places on the shoulder and arm.

Early in the game I decided to snap off a curve ball and it landed at my feet, never even reaching the plate. There was silence in the crowd.

I felt a tremendous pain in my shoulder and I sensed it was something very serious, but I'm not very good at admitting to weakness or need. To make a long story short, I went to the hospital the following day, only to discover I had torn the long head of the bicep muscle in my right arm. My beautiful pitching arm was damaged beyond repair!

The surgeon said he could fix my arm sufficiently for "normal" use, but he assured me that I would never pitch again. I still remember the weight of those words. And as I lay in the hospital bed waiting for surgery, I felt extreme anger with God.

I told God how much my pitching had accomplished for Him and for me, and I told Him what an effective tool it was in working with young people. Strangely, God never answered that day. He let me unload my anger.

I went through the surgery and it was successful in a limited way. Gradually the Lord seemed to say, "It's time to grow up, Phil. It's time to say good-bye to sports as an active part of your life. It's time to stop defining yourself by pitching. It's time to devote that part of your life to another part of ministry."

A few months ago I walked out on the mound again. No one was there but a friend as I felt the familiar shape of the rubber beneath my feet. Although I did not have a ball, I could feel one in my hand.

It's been many years since I had to say good-bye, but the feel of the ball, the shape of the mound, and the strategy of the game are still woven into my head. But something else is woven there as well.

My ministry did not diminish with the end of pitching. If anything, my abilities and confidence increased beyond my belief. The opportunities to affect young people did not end with the surgery. In fact, for years my primary job was educating or ministering to those under twenty-two.

God is in control, though it is difficult for us to remember that truth at times. He is in control and He desires life and peace for you and for me.

You may have a pitching arm or two of your own—gifts or abilities that you hold onto as if they define who you are. Try to look at yourself through the eyes of God for a moment. He doesn't need the talents you and I depend on; He simply asks that you and I depend on Him.

━━━━━━━━━ THOUGHT FOR THE HEART

It is difficult for me to trust God right now in this particular area. I still want to hold on to control.

— *Phil Hook*

●
IN HIS STEPS

"If anyone would come after Me, he must deny himself and take up his cross and follow Me." Matthew 16:24

As a small girl, I used to delight in dancing with my father. As we whirled around the room, my tiny feet securely on his, I would imagine myself on top of the world. Nothing could harm me when safe in my father's arms.

Then I began to grow older, and I insisted on testing my own "dancing feet." I longed to lead life my way, and I became more and more convinced of my own invincibility. I had lessons to learn, and my father graciously allowed me the experience.

Without warning, I can so quickly get out of step with God. Even with the best of intentions, I often find myself charging down my own path . . . barely realizing that I stopped consulting the Wise One several days before. Oops. Giving God control is not a state that comes naturally to me. I would much rather be "at the helm," making sure things are done my way, following the plans I've laid.

Why do I insist on leading the dance? Is it that I don't trust God to lead me well? No. I am aware of His infinite wisdom and care for me. Is it that I like my own way better? Not really. God's ways always prove better in time.

I think I just get carried away with myself. I get an idea of some great possibility, and I guess I am afraid to turn loose my plans and see what God has in store for me. It is difficult to exchange my selfish nature for one that resembles His selfless one.

I am much older now, and dancing with my father is not quite as smooth as it used to be. My feet seem so clumsy next to his smooth, artful steps. Though I want to follow his lead, I tend to do little better than stumble after him.

Yet God knows how to lead us in the dance of His making! My Heavenly Father's steps are always ones I can follow with grace. When I can just grant God permission to take the lead, I am never disappointed.

THOUGHT FOR THE HEART

It is difficult for me to let God take the lead in these areas of my life.

— *Marianne Koons*

●
SUPERNATURAL POWER

"Now to Him who is able to do immeasurably more than all we ask or imagine, according to His power that is at work within us, to Him be glory in the church and in Christ Jesus throughout all generations, for ever and ever! Amen." Ephesians 3:20-21

Once, after I had preached a message on prayer, a university student wrote, "I just wanted to let you know that your statement, 'prayer can do anything God can do,' has made a tremendous impact on my life. Somehow I always thought that prayer shared my limitations instead of God's power."

This honest individual is not the only one who comes to

God more aware of human limitations than of God's power. For many of us, relationship with God often becomes a matter of human effort. We find ourselves saying, "Maybe if I pray long enough or hard enough, God will answer." We struggle with who's in charge. And we often attempt to take control.

The truth is, we could pray for two hours and work up a "holy sweat" and be no closer to experiencing God's power than before. The focus of power and control is the One to whom we pray and on whom we depend. It is not the effort itself that gets results. It is the response of the Heavenly Father to the simple, childlike trust of a Christian who believes that God can do anything.

I don't know about you, but when I look at the needs around me—the decaying society in which we live and the awesome mission to which God has called us—I feel terribly inadequate. I am out of control, but God is not.

How thankful I am that the results of life in this world are not dependent on my skills and abilities. How grateful I am for the promises of Scripture that enable me to come to the Father knowing that He hears me and is able to do far more than I can even think or ask. What a blessed relief to know that the outcome is in His hands.

Good news, friend! God is in control, so you can resign. It is not by might or by power or human effort, but by the Spirit of the living God that prayer becomes effective. God is in control.

▬▬▬▬▬▬ THOUGHT FOR THE HEART

I would like to acknowledge God's control in these difficult areas of my life.

—*David Lynch*

●
DIOTREPHES

"I wrote to the church, but Diotrephes, who loves to be first, will have nothing to do with us. So if I come, I will call attention to what he is doing, gossiping maliciously about us. Not satisfied with that, he refuses to welcome the brothers. He also stops those who want to do so and puts them out of the church. Dear friend, do not imitate what is evil but what is good. Anyone who does what is good is from God. Anyone who does what is evil has not seen God."
3 John 9-11

We were always grappling for control in our neighborhood. Each of us wanted to be chosen first for the game, to have everyone come to *my* house, to have everyone play with *my* toys, to watch the television program *I* want to watch or play the game *I* want to play. Before long, a natural "pecking order" developed and we knew just how to get what *we* wanted.

Some children simply changed the rules in their minds: "I didn't want them to come to my house anyway!" Some used feminine charm (or if that didn't work, tears!) to accomplish the purpose. Some used brute strength to persuade the crowd. And some used the definite advantage of "better toys" or "higher trees" to climb.

We had great fun in our neighborhood, once the power structure was established. We all learned when to push, when to pull, when to give in, and when to put up a good fight. We all wanted control in our own little worlds, and we got that control in one way or another and at one time or another.

Our childhood world was really just a microcosm of the world at large. I have seen the same scenario time and again in all kinds of settings. Each of us enters this life wanting certain attentions or privileges, and we learn how to get those attentions or privileges — or die trying! There is nothing unusual about a struggle for control.

What is unusual is the way our Lord taught us to deal with control. While we long to hold on to that which makes us feel comfortable, happy, or otherwise fulfilled, He taught us to turn those things loose. He urged us to release the controls we usually vie for and to accept the new rules for the better game.

We can talk about releasing control, but it's hard for us to actually let go. Even the most committed believers have a hard time turning loose those things which we deem necessary or "rightfully ours."

Diotrephes was no exception to this rule. He was the leader of a group of believers and he loved control. In fact, he loved control so much that he began to believe in his own wisdom rather than in God's. He forgot who is really in charge.

We don't know much about Diotrephes, but I'll try to be fair as I make assumptions about his life and where he went wrong.

Diotrephes must have had an experience in which he came to know the risen Lord enough to commit his life. It wasn't easy to be one of the first generation Christians, so I don't believe he would have claimed Christ as Savior without believing in Him.

I imagine that Diotrephes' story looked an awful lot like yours or mine. My guess is that he was quite talented and, therefore, was called upon by the church for his leadership abilities. My guess is that he felt quite valuable in his new position and probably a bit indispensable. And thus began his downfall.

John wanted to come into Diotrephes' church and teach the believers about the Lord. Diotrephes, for whatever reasons, did not want this visit to occur. At first he probably spoke a cool "no thank you" in an attempt to dismiss

John. But the tactic wasn't enough. The people wanted John to come, and Diotrephes was losing control.

By the time we read about his reaction in 3 John, Diotrephes had usurped authority that wasn't his and resorted to punishing those who dared to disagree. John and his believing friends had become threats, somehow, so Diotrephes fought for *his* power.

When we sense we are losing ground we often fight hard, mean, and unscrupulously until, sadly, no one is left but a few who aren't sure where to turn. Then we take stock, look around, and wonder where we've gone wrong.

Mothers and fathers, husbands and wives, employers, employees, friends and family members, beware of that need to grasp control. And above all else, guard against destroying those whom you love in the endless war for power.

The victory isn't sweet when we resort to slander, gossip, belittling, punishment, or shame. The victory isn't sweet when we hold on so tight to a semblance of control that we miss the joy of love and relationship.

Look around at your "neighborhood" and make a choice to release, to love, to live.

████████ THOUGHT FOR THE HEART

Sometimes I act like Diotrephes to my spouse or my children, to my friends or to members of the church family where I belong. It's hard to release control. But I want to learn, Lord, that You are in control. You need me to be a humble servant, not a bitter critic.

— Shelley Chapin

●

HEALTHY CONTROL

"Jesus answered: 'Watch out that no one deceives you.'" Matthew 24:4

CONTROL

When we hear the word *control* today, it often triggers an uncomfortable response within us. We think of overly controlling parents, demanding spouses, uncooperative children, or our own compulsions. But control doesn't have to yield that uncomfortable response. In fact, Scripture records that Jesus instructed His disciples to take control—healthy control over their lives.

What is healthy control and why do we struggle so to live with a helpful balance?

There are several kinds of control which are good for us and for those around us. Self-control over our own actions is important. Self-control for our part in relationships is vital. And control over our words and attitudes makes all the difference in the world to our ability to live supportively with one another.

The struggle we face in sorting through the control issue lies in a simple observation. We don't know much about healthy control. Most of us have not been taught about healthy control. And many of us have seen few examples of people who practice "good" control. The disciples seemed to encounter this same lack.

The followers of Jesus had questions about their futures. They had expectations about life. And they lived in the midst of a contest between legalism and freedom. Such tensions thrust them into battles of the will. Jesus understood.

Instead of reminding the disciples of their ignorance or inability, Jesus encouraged and instructed them to take healthy control of their lives. He taught them to take responsibility. He encouraged them to act on their gifts. He provided them with opportunity to act upon the truth. And, most importantly, He modeled healthy control in His personal life and relationships.

Jesus wasn't afraid to allow His disciples to choose. He wasn't afraid of their inevitable failures. He didn't seem to need to control their every thought and action.

Jesus didn't say that He would protect His disciples from all who might lead them astray. He didn't promise to correct the tainted messages or sift the world's words. He didn't vow to alleviate their stress or negate their consequences.

What Jesus did was offer His support, and provide the disciples with all the tools they would need to learn and to live. He laid the foundation for His followers to observe His teachings. He gave us truth, He gave us guidelines, and He set us free to practice healthy self-control.

"See to it that no one leads you astray," Jesus offered. And such advice is just as important for us today as it was for Peter or James or John.

Many of us have come from environments which crippled our abilities to practice healthy control. Perhaps we weren't allowed to choose or we felt afraid to fail. Whatever the deficiency, our Lord makes up the difference. He helps us to learn. He equips us to choose. And He allows us to fail in our quest for maturity.

▬▬▬▬▬▬ T H O U G H T   F O R   T H E   H E A R T

I can hear Jesus giving me the same advice He offered the disciples — advice that yields both freedom and responsibility.

— Ellen Quarry

●
IT TAKES EFFORT

"Do you not know that in a race all the runners run, but only one gets the prize? Run in such a way as to get the prize. Everyone who competes in the games goes into strict training. They do it to get a crown that will not last; but we do it to get a crown that will last forever. Therefore, I do not run like a man running aimlessly; I do not fight like a man beating the air. No, I beat my body and make it

my slave so that after I have preached to others, I myself will not be disqualified for the prize." 1 Corinthians 9:24-27

We moved to a new town when I was twelve years old. We didn't know anyone. There were very few children in the neighborhood, but nearby was a ballpark with games each weekday night. From the start, I knew this ballpark would be my haven.

The pitchers in the ballpark became my heroes. I watched them every chance I got and imagined myself in their places someday. You can imagine how good I felt when my parents gave me my first ball and glove.

I began to throw the ball against the garage in our backyard. The more I practiced the harder I threw, and the harder I threw every board in the garage gave way! My father replaced the boards for a time, but finally had to devise another plan. He attached a box spring to the side of the garage so that I could pitch hard and still leave the building intact.

I gradually increased in confidence. No one could catch the balls I pitched. I threw so hard that no one knew where the ball was going (frankly, neither did I!) and after two years, I was ready to pitch my first game. I knew I'd be great that day. My confidence was high! But in reality, I walked so many people that we lost the game.

After my first failure, I worked and worked and applied myself as much as possible. Though the task was hard, within four years I was considered one of the best pitchers in the area. I could pitch three balls out of four in an area the size of a dinner plate! I had finally gained control of my arm *and* of my dream.

God used my ability to pay for my education. Game after game in town after town I would pitch, collect my earnings, and pay for the classes that would lead to my degree. It was a joyful celebration for me each time I picked up a ball and watched it curve.

We all have dreams and places we want to go, but we are rarely taught to discern those dreams and then work toward them in a systematic way. I had to practice in order to pitch. And I had to pay the price of pain in order to reach the goal.

From the time I began watching to the time I actually pitched my first game I experienced many days of hurt and agony. I had to work hard to bring the motion under control. And my arm did not automatically stay in shape throughout the year! The goal was accomplished by pain and by discipline, over and over again.

I know that you have some dreams of your own, some very important goals that you long to fulfill. It isn't that working toward our goals always leads us to the end we had in mind (I am now old and certainly no longer able to pitch a ball game!), but I believe it can be said that we do not reach our goals without real effort and determination.

Be involved with your own life and future! Work with God and work hard on whatever He gives you to do. And I believe you will learn and grow as a result of your efforts.

THOUGHT FOR THE HEART

I am aware that I'd like to work on these goals or dreams in my own life.

—Phil Hook

●

GOD OF THE IMPOSSIBLE

"We do not want you to be uninformed, brothers, about the hardships we suffered in the province of Asia. We were under great pressure, far beyond our ability to endure, so that we despaired even of life. Indeed, in our hearts we felt the sentence of death. But

this happened that we might not rely on ourselves but on God, who raises the dead." 2 Corinthians 1:8-9

Pressures. Stress. Burnout. Frustration. Despair. Fear. All of these are realities that we live with daily. And these realities are quite frequently beyond our control, though try to control them we will!

Do you know anyone who doesn't battle with these enemies of emotional and physical health? And which one of us doesn't become spiritually weary under undue stress and pressure?

We like to think of the Apostle Paul as that unbeatable servant of God, impossible to stop and positive beyond reproach. Paul was, indeed, God's servant. But Paul wasn't protected from the stresses and strains which face us all during our time in this world.

We need only to examine Paul's letters to the Corinthians to remember he knew more than his share of stress and despair. He wrote that "we despaired even of life" and "our hearts felt the sentence of death." Paul knew pain, and he shared his pain openly.

How can we deal with the stresses of life? When we feel out of control, what can we do to regain composure? What can become our help in those times when we seem overwhelmed?

The answer is simple, but certainly not easy to pursue. It seems that Paul's answer to despair was to go to God. The impossible situations he and his friends faced led them into the presence of the One who can do the impossible. And God rescued them, as only He can do, from the need to control what wasn't under their dominion.

I remember a story by Corrie ten Boom. She'd been taught by a friend a secret for handling despair. "When you face a problem that seems impossible, go to a mirror, gaze at yourself, and say, 'Lord Jesus, I've a problem that

You cannot handle. It is way too big for You.' Then wait and see what happens."

Corrie's response was usually a laugh. Realizing her desire to control the uncomfortable, she would laugh, commit the need to God, and receive His rest. Simple, but not always easy.

When we turn to God with our needs, stresses, fears, and feelings of despair, He steps in and takes control. He delivered Paul from the need to worry, and He'll do the same for you and for me.

Perhaps you're facing stress beyond your ability to endure. Perhaps you're feeling out of control from all life's pressures.

Try what Corrie suggested. Try what seemed to work for Paul and his friends. Turn to God, and let Him take the lead.

THOUGHT FOR THE HEART

I can see myself standing before the mirror, telling God, "This is too difficult for You!" I would like to release control over these specific stresses and needs in my life.

— *David Lynch*

●

THE PRAYER OF A YIELDED HEART

"Those who live according to the sinful nature have their minds set on what that nature desires; but those who live in accordance with the Spirit have their minds set on what the Spirit desires. The mind of sinful man is death, but the mind controlled by the Spirit is life and peace." Romans 8:5-6

I was introduced to a prayer not long ago that has impacted my life on several levels. Perhaps it will mean something to you as well.

CONTROL

It was penned by Francois de la Mothe Fenelon, Archbishop of Cabrai, sometime in the early 1700s. The language betrays both the age and the wisdom of the author.

O Lord, I know not what I ought to ask of Thee. Thou only knowest what I need; Thou lovest me better than I know how to love myself. O Father, give to Thy child that which he himself knows not how to ask. I dare not ask either for crosses or consolations; I simply present myself before Thee, I open my heart to Thee. Behold my needs which I know not myself; see and do according to Thy mercy. Smite or heal, depress me or raise me up; I adore all Thy purposes without knowing them. I am silent. I offer myself in sacrifice; I yield myself to Thee; I would have no other desire than to accomplish Thy will. Teach me to pray. Pray Thyself in me.

I know that the words may sound a bit funny to the twentieth-century ear, but I was touched by the utter simplicity of the prayer. I was moved by the author's willingness to relinquish control. I was impressed by the wisdom of one who would say, "Smite or heal, depress or raise up."

It is not always easy for us to entrust ourselves to God. Of course, there are some areas in which we trust with ease. There are times in life in which we find it more natural to grant God His power.

But there are also times in which we clasp our bare hands around all that we hold dear and say, "Not this! You cannot have this! No, Lord. Do something else, but not this."

I will not interpret the prayer anymore. I will simply acknowledge that I have much to learn about releasing control. About the time I think I have my fist relaxed, some situation arises and I find myself grasping once again.

Lord, grant us the courage to let go and follow Your lead.

THOUGHT FOR THE HEART

I will pen my own simple prayer today. Help me, Lord, to unlock the grip and allow You to lead.

— Shelley Chapin

RHYTHMS OF MY HEART

COURAGE

LOVE TOO BIG TO HIDE

"They mounted up to the heavens and went down to the depths; in their peril their courage melted away. They reeled and staggered like drunken men; they were at their wits' end. Then they cried out to the Lord in their trouble, and He brought them out of their distress." Psalm 107:26-28

It was my privilege, many years ago, to be one of the first Americans to travel into Poland for the purpose of teaching the Bible. Everyone, including myself, thought the opportunity exciting and the "danger" of going into an Eastern Bloc country piqued my interest.

Though I had no idea what awaited me, I spoke for nearly two weeks in the mountains of southern Poland to a group of very eager college students. The opportunity was rare in a world that constricted the freedoms of its people.

When I first arrived at my destination in Poland, I was not permitted to talk with anyone. Strangers could not be trusted in those days, and I was certainly an unknown. I prayed, talked with the leadership, and then spoke in increments until finally I was cleared to teach three hours per day.

The three hours went quickly each morning. And though my teaching ended by noon, the opportunities did not. Students were eager to sit and ask their questions. They were ready to hear more. Though they risked much to meet together, the students didn't seem to mind.

Lest I present only part of my journey, I must tell you that the trip was as difficult as it was fun. While the students were anxious to learn, my stomach was anxious for familiar food and clean water! The conditions under which we lived and ate were not what I was accustomed to. And most days I was unable to be away from a bathroom longer than the hours I taught. I loved the teaching and hated the living situation—all at the same time.

When the two weeks were over I could not wait to get home! It's exciting to test your courage and go in to a situation like that, but it takes a rare person to want to stay for any length of time! I loved the people, but I was ready to leave the oppression and lifestyle by the end of my stay.

The first leg of my journey was to be by bus, but I learned that the bus did not always stop at the station nearest our conference. Not wanting to miss my only ride, I asked to be taken to a stop where the bus would be more dependable.

To assuage my anxiety, I was delivered to the beginning of the bus line several hours ahead of schedule! I had my ticket and luggage ready to go, and I literally planted myself right next to the parked bus. I was ready for U.S. soil.

As we were preparing to board the bus I heard a noise behind me. Turning, I found that about twenty-five students had walked the eight or ten miles to the station simply to keep me company and bid me farewell. Next thing I knew, I was surrounded by loving believers who began to sing Christian choruses. They sang heartily and they sang loud. And though I should have felt honored, I found myself feeling fear and a twinge of anger.

What if we get arrested and I have to stay in Poland? I thought to myself. *Don't they realize they're creating a spectacle? Why couldn't they have just let the earlier good-byes suffice?*

Outwardly I smiled and tried to look comfortable, but inwardly I grew more nervous as each chorus resounded. Finally, the bus was ready to leave and the students lined up in a row to give me a hug and the customary kisses. The ceremony had passed without any complications, yet I boarded the bus with an anxiety I could not arrest.

I can't explain my mixed emotions as the bus pulled away from the station. Overwhelmed, I sat silently and wept and thought about the gift I had just been given.

I discovered a true sense of courage that day — people whose desire to express love is more important than safety or physical freedom. The danger was real, but to say "I love you" was the higher priority.

The students had much to fear in their world, but they were not rendered helpless by that fear. They didn't even try to conceal a faith or a friendship for which they could be imprisoned or condemned. Instead, the students spoke and sang with an openness and a confidence that I'd rarely experienced before.

I knew as I took my bus ride back to comfort that I had a few lessons yet to learn. In that bus station in Poland, I experienced the kind of courage that sets people free to love and to be all that God has designed us to be.

■■■■■■■■■■■ THOUGHT FOR THE HEART

I would like to have courage in these particular relationships or situations. I would like to feel free to be all that God has designed me to be.

— *Phil Hook*

●
"I'VE FALLEN, BUT I CAN GET UP!"

"Have I not commanded you? Be strong and courageous. Do not be terrified; do not be discouraged, for the Lord your God will be with you wherever you go." Joshua 1:9

We've all seen the television commercial that made an unknown elderly woman famous! She is lying on the floor saying the well-remembered line, "I've fallen and I can't get up!"

The thing that makes the commercial humorous is the fact that it is so obviously staged! We all know the woman didn't really fall, and so we laugh. But if this were a real-life situation, we would not be laughing at all.

For many people the cry, "I've fallen and I can't get up" is a brutal reality. They have not physically fallen, but the sense of not being able to get up out of the circumstance that holds them down is very real.

Some have fallen beneath a load of sin. It was a gradual fall. Everything seemed so innocent in the beginning. But the wages of sin is always death of some kind. They now sit down to a banquet of consequences and life looks hopeless.

Some have fallen into habits that destroy and degrade. They find themselves trapped in a lifestyle of compulsive behavior over which they no longer have control. They never thought it could happen to them, but it *has* happened. And there seems to be no way out.

Some have fallen financially. The job that once held so much promise is gone. Or habits of spending have gotten out of hand. Bills are piling up. Self-esteem is at an all-time low. They're sure if they see any light at the end of the tunnel it will be a train.

Still others have fallen beneath the load of failure, broken relationships, abuse, rejection—you name it. Regardless of the specifics, all share the same desperate feeling, "I've fallen and I can't get up."

I have some good news for you and for me. God says that we *can* get up. As bad as the situation looks right now, God's grace is greater than our need. Christ came to break the power of sin and suffering so that no matter how far we have fallen, He can lift us up, transform our lives, and give us a new start. It simply takes a little bit of courage on our part to reach out and grasp hold of His grace.

COURAGE

If you find yourself under the weight of unemployment or divorce, disability or grief, you are not alone. If you find yourself single with no change in sight or discouraged about school or a job, you are not alone.

Jesus said, "I will never leave you or forsake you!" He taught us that we can have courage. He lived a life of mercy, transformation, love, and acceptance.

It is the enemy who whispers in your ear, "You can't get up. Just accept defeat."

It is Jesus who says, "You can get up! You can do all things through the strength I will give you." Failure is never the last word. Financial problems do have solutions. Broken relationships can end up in healing or understanding. And you are already forgiven, reconciled, and adopted as children into God's family.

I am not saying that the pain will end or that you'll no longer feel discouraged. I'm not trying to downplay the reality of our suffering. What I *am* saying is that Jesus helps us in everything. There is no problem or habit, no sin or suffering that goes beyond His commitment to help.

You may have fallen—we all do. But you can get up! Simply reach out, take a step, call for help. God will grant you courage—the strength and grace sufficient for the journey.

▬▬▬▬▬▬▬ THOUGHT FOR THE HEART

I am having a hard time not seeing myself through eyes of failure or discouragement. I would like to accept the courage God is offering me. I'd like to believe that I can get up.

— David Lynch

●
INSIDE THE CHILDREN'S WARD

"I am confident of this: I will see the goodness of the Lord in the

COURAGE

land of the living. Wait for the Lord; be strong and take heart and wait for the Lord." Psalm 27:13-14

It takes courage to live. If you have ever traveled through the corridors of a children's hospital ward, you know that this is so. I learned this lesson from Rebecca.

When I was in high school we were given a job to do for our senior project. The job sounded easy enough: we were to volunteer our time on several Saturdays to a worthy organization. The goal was to involve us in the wider community — to expand our horizons, so to speak.

I have always been involved in the lives of children, so I chose to volunteer at the Children's Medical Center in Dallas, Texas. I was to be an aid to the social workers there and read stories or play games with the children. I felt certain I would enjoy my volunteer work.

Saturday came and I pulled myself a bit begrudgingly out of bed (after all, what seventeen-year-old wants to rise early on Saturday morning!). And as I drove to the hospital I remember feeling a bit nervous and then telling myself, "You'll do fine! Kids love you!" For the moment, at least, the reassurance soothed my anxiety.

It only took a few moments for the workers to give me something to do. I read stories and more stories to children in a play room. They had all been quite ill but were doing better, and they could play again! I still recall how good it felt to have the children crawl up in my lap and listen as I read.

After the reading time, a kind, older woman said she would give me a tour of the hospital. "Great," I said, and off we went. I had not even stopped to consider what I would see, but my world was about to change. I was about to be introduced, for the very first time, to intense suffering.

As we entered the burn unit, my stomach turned. There

147

were smells in there I couldn't even begin to identify and quiet tears from weary eyes. I can still experience the eerie silence in that room.

There was no laughter without pain and no joy without sorrow as the children lived moment by moment. Special lights, changed dressings, and sterile masks defined the world they knew. They could not stand and I could not help. I was on the outside looking in.

A sweet, young girl caught my eye and I was allowed to stand fairly close. We talked for a few minutes, and I tried not to show my horror at her pain. Her name was Rebecca, and she had gotten too close to the gas heater. She had already been in the hospital five weeks.

Rebecca told me a bit about her family, her school, and her pets. She talked about the hospital and how nice all the doctors, nurses, and volunteers had been. I was struck by her candor and by her lack of complaint. When I told her I was impressed, she placed the credit on God. "God is with me," she said. And she believed He was there.

When it was time for me to leave, Rebecca asked one simple favor that ended up teaching me quite a bit.

"Please come back to see me," she said. I looked her in the eyes and nodded my commitment to do just that. Then she added a "footnote." "If it isn't too hard for you, please come again." And with that parting remark my hospital tour continued.

Too hard for me? What was Rebecca thinking? My life knew no difficulty compared with hers. There she was— burned beyond recognition in many areas of her body. And yet she had courage—courage enough to wake up and to smile and to allow the doctors to help her. She had courage enough to dream. She had courage enough to love. And she had courage enough to invite a stranger to love her in return.

Rebecca had discovered an adult secret at the ripe old

age of ten. Most of us find it too difficult to live with the pain in this world, so we avoid it. Most of us would not go back and watch a child like Rebecca suffer. What we seem to forget is that God supplies the courage. Rebecca has enough for what she must face, and you and I have enough for that which God allows in our lives.

It takes courage for us to gaze upon the painful. It takes courage for us to live with the sufferings of this world. Sometimes our problems, not to mention those of the wider community, seem just too complex to handle.

Lest we forget and turn away from Rebecca or from life, remember that God gives courage. All the ingredients it takes to survive in this world, He provides. And courage is a big ingredient.

Rebecca is "fine" now. Seven years of therapy and surgery were involved before she could play freely with her friends or walk carefree in the park. Her life has not been that "dream life" of which our fantasies are made.

Rebecca knows about LIFE, though, more so than many who are older than she. She has courage. She takes one day at a time and she lives life to its fullest. She is older now, and even wiser.

God equips us with courage, no matter how difficult or painstaking the growth will be. God grants us courage enough for the day and enough to meet any challenge before us.

■ THOUGHT FOR THE HEART

Lord, I need courage right now. I am facing the pains of life and I need to be prepared for the path that lies ahead. Lord, help me to live with courage.

—*Shelley Chapin*

COURAGE

●
DARE TO DREAM

"Act with courage, and may the Lord be with those who do well."
2 *Chronicles* 19:11.

Hans Babblinger of Ulm, Germany wanted to fly. He wanted to soar like a bird. He wanted to break the bond of gravity and breathe the high air of freedom. There was only one problem. Hans lived in the 16th century where there were no planes, no helicopters, no flying machines. Hans was a dreamer born too soon and what he desired seemed impossible.

Though Hans could not achieve his impassioned dream, he decided there was something he could do that had great significance to the world around him. Hans dedicated himself to making artificial limbs.

In the 16th century, amputation was a common cure for disease and injury, so Hans kept busy. His task was to help those with special circumstances overcome their limitations. And he was well qualified! Babblinger could relate to those he served, for he longed to do the same.

Time passed, and Babblinger learned from those whose lives he touched. As he watched the amputees overcome their obstacles, he began to dream his dream again. And at last he stood in the foothills of the Bavarian Alps, ready to test his first set of wings!

On a memorable day, with friends watching and sun shining, Hans Babblinger jumped off an embankment and soared! His heart raced, God rejoiced, and his friends applauded as he glided safely down. His dream was a reality! He had flown!

How do I know that God rejoiced with Hans' successful adventure? Because God always rejoices with us as we dare to dream. In fact, we are much like God when we dream. The Master masters in newness. He delights in stretching the old. He wrote the book on making the impossible possible. And He grows weary with earthbound realists who clip the wings of dreamers.

Unfortunately, Hans' joy was short-lived. His dreaming wings were clipped one day while entertaining a visiting king with his flying ease. Hans failed to calculate the updraft in the hills, and when he jumped he fell like a rock, straight into the Danube River.

Everyone was horrified at the fall, and the Bishop quickly reached a conclusion. "Man is not meant to fly," the Bishop proclaimed at the service next Sunday, and such marked the end of Hans Babblinger's dream. Never again did Hans try to fly. And he died soon after, gripped by gravity and buried with his dreams.

The church which stilled the dreams of Hans Babblinger of Ulm is no longer occupied by saints. Today, the church is visited only by tourists—most of whom come by plane.

THOUGHT FOR THE HEART

It is hard for me to dream dreams, particularly when I fear failure. But I'd like to keep dreaming these dreams.

—Max Lucado

THE COURAGE TO GET WELL

"Christ is faithful as a Son over God's house. And we are His house, if we hold on to our courage and the hope of which we boast."
Hebrews 3:6

It had been awhile since anyone asked him a question. In fact, it had been so long that he didn't see a reason to answer. No one really cared. Why should he give someone the time of day? He turned apathetic eyes toward the face of a man he'd never seen before.

I wonder what he wants, he thought. He knew all about hustlers. *You never look them in the eye.* His thoughts continued. *He's probably trying to sell something or make a buck off my problems.* The man shifted nervously in his seat. The silence was uncomfortable.

"Do you want to get well?" the stranger repeated.

The man snapped to attention with the voice of the stranger. *There was that word again.* "Well." *What did that mean?* He mentally considered his options.

It could be another gimmick, he mused, *or maybe a cruel joke.* The man could not stop fidgeting. He felt genuinely confused, but he ventured a response.

"Sir, I have no one to help me." He heard his voice and it sounded shaky and unsure. *Maybe that was a good thing. Maybe the stranger would feel sorry for him.* He continued.

"I've been sick for thirty-eight years." He thought his voice sounded dispassionate so he added a bit more feeling. "Every time I try to make it down to the water, someone else gets in before me." He carefully eyed the stranger now, trying to guess what this visitor would say.

The stranger mumbled something under His breath and extended a hand toward the invalid. Next, the stranger spoke with calm authority.

"Get up! Pick up your mat and walk!"

"Wha . . . ?"

The invalid started to object, but before the words could leave his mouth he was up! Mat tucked neatly beneath his arm, he was standing for the first time in decades. And his legs weren't even weak!

I remember the first time I read this story. I thought how wonderful it must have been for the man to receive such a gift. I imagined his joy and the celebration he would hold with his friends—until I read the rest of the story.

C O U R A G E

Jesus healed the man physically, but emotionally and spiritually this man remained an invalid. He didn't want to be well. He probably didn't even know what "well" meant. He had lived with the attentions and excuses that his illness provided, and he wasn't prepared for "well."

During the hours that followed, the man remained a "victim." Instead of spreading the good news, he complained. Instead of leaping, he barely moved. Instead of honoring God, he cursed the One who had made him well. The body looked fine, but the soul was fractured. He even blamed Jesus for making him carry his mat on a Sabbath.

So often we see miracles in terms of physical changes. And physical changes do feel good. But the tougher miracle is that of the soul. It takes courage to embrace "wellness." It takes courage to say "yes" to an invitation for life.

Perhaps you've been feeling a bit unwell lately. You want God to reach down and touch your wounded soul, but you're a bit afraid to let go of the excuses. At least you know how it feels to be broken.

Take courage as your gift today. Anyone who has taken the slow road to spiritual and emotional health can attest to the fact that the journey is well worth the effort. And it only takes a little bit of courage to begin. It only takes an outstretched heart, willing to offer "yes" to the question.

I grieve for our friend in John 5. He didn't quite grasp what our Lord was offering. And he didn't embrace his new outlook on life.

Jesus offers true wellness, though at times this is hard to receive. Our Lord offers health from the inside out.

■ T H O U G H T F O R T H E H E A R T

I would like to embrace well-being and health in my life. Lord, grant me the courage to say "yes" to Your offer.

—Shelley Chapin

COURAGE

●

GIVE ME COURAGE

"I eagerly expect and hope that I will in no way be ashamed, but will have sufficient courage so that now, as always, Christ will be exalted in my body, whether by life or by death." Philippians 1:20

It is difficult to be a man or a woman of courage. We can feel courageous from time to time, but true courage is a daily decision, an act of faith, a gift to the world.

I heard a young woman speak in March of 1992, and the word *courage* kept ringing through my mind. She had faced so many sufferings and yet she seemed content. She had faced so many losses but her purpose seemed clear.

It is difficult for all of us to find courage when we are afraid or weary or overwhelmed or discouraged. Regardless of the circumstance, God promises courage. It is there for the asking. Yet at times we forget that the gift awaits us.

"Where do I find courage, Lord, courage to be who I am? How do I find out who I am? Must I be stripped of my health to realize that, without You, I am but dust? Must I be stripped of my wealth to realize that all things come from Your hand? Must I be stripped of my power to rely on You for my worth?

"Why is it, Lord, that I have so much and appreciate so little? Why do I continually see the negative and the flaws of what I do instead of the positive and the good? Why do I measure myself by the world's standards that fluctuate and vacillate according to the times?

"Why am I so afraid to just be me? Why do I run incessantly, putting out small fires while the forest burns and threatens to engulf? Why can't I give You my burdens, letting go to victoriously live the life You have ordained in spite of my circumstances?

COURAGE

"Give me the courage to love, to let go, and to give You my burdens. Give me the courage to be what You desire — a witness to this world of Your glory, faithfulness, and forgiveness. Give me courage to leave resentment and anger at the altar and, in turn, accept forgiveness for myself and, thus, for others.

"Give me courage to believe that each day of my life can be a blessing, even if I am sick or in excruciating pain. Give me courage to allow You to teach me Your ways in life as well as in death. Allow Your Spirit to cover me, granting the grace to suffer with meaning and purpose.

"Give me courage to change what I can and accept what I cannot change. Give me courage to sort out my thoughts and feelings through Your Word, through prayer, through reflection and writing. Give me courage to accept my lot and confront it with You as Redeemer and Guide.

"Give me courage to place my life in Your hands for Your purpose. Be to me what I need for the moment, nothing more and nothing less. Allow me to be a light in this dark world, a beacon that shines, illuminating Your glory and truth.

"Give me courage to speak boldly, spreading seeds that will germinate and flower into eternal fruit.

"Courage, Lord, that comes from You. I bow and ask, believing I have received."

THOUGHT FOR THE HEART

I ask for courage in these relationships, in these decisions, and in these particular pains of my life.

—Marilyn Rhode

RHYTHMS OF MY HEART

DISAPPOINT-
MENT

COPING WITH LIFE'S UNFAIRNESS

"He has broken my teeth with gravel; He has trampled me in the dust. I have been deprived of peace; I have forgotten what prosperity is. So I say, 'My splendor is gone, and all that I had hoped from the Lord.' " Lamentations 3:16-18

I'll never forget one particular meal. I was seated at a nice restaurant eating my broiled fish like a good cholesterol watcher, when I noticed a man at the table next to me. He was older than me, much heavier, and he was wolfing down clam chowder, fried fish, fried shrimp, French fries, and chocolate cake!

That just isn't fair, I thought. *I am hungry and this guy gets to eat all the food!*

In case you haven't noticed, life isn't fair. And the Bible never promises that life will be fair. Our problem is that sometimes we confuse life with God and we accuse Him of being unfair.

It helps to remember that life is not God. Simply because life deals us tragedy, affliction, or problems we can't handle, it does not mean that God is picking on us or is uninterested in our well-being.

Still, in the midst of our sufferings we certainly feel disappointment. And we are in good company. Job, Jeremiah, and Jonah were all disappointed in life and they spoke openly to God about their frustration.

I too have felt disappointed with God in a very personal area. For a period of time my wife was a cancer patient. She suffered from cancer of the liver, and I don't need to tell you how difficult it was for me to stand by and not be able to fix her pain.

Many people who face debilitating illnesses like cancer grow weary and angry with God. Though anger did not pose a problem for Wanda, she did wrestle with some very real fears in the course of her illness. She lived one day at a time, praying to trust God's love and power, even in the midst of her sorrow.

Jesus said that in this world we will have trouble, and He was right! Why some bad things happen to some good people I do not know.

What I do know is that God has promised never to forsake us. Even through our disappointments, we have the guarantee of God's sufficient grace.

There is a wonderful old hymn that has ministered to me over and over again, so perhaps it will encourage you as well. It goes something like this.

> He gives more grace when the burdens grow greater,
> He sends more strength when the labors increase;
> To added afflictions He adds His mercy,
> To multiplied trials, His multiplies grace.
>
> When we have exhausted our store of endurance,
> When our strength has failed though the day is half
>   done;
> When we reach the end of our hoarded resources,
> Our Father's full giving is only begun.

When faced with disappointment, hold on to God's unchanging hand. He is there, and He will provide the strength, the mercy, and the grace to grow through the suffering.

THOUGHT FOR THE HEART

I am aware of feeling disappointed with God in these areas right now. I am willing to talk openly with Him about my disappointment.

—David Lynch

●
SEASONS OF DOUBT

"When John heard in prison what Christ was doing, he sent his disciples to ask Him, 'Are You the One who was to come, or should we expect someone else?' " Matthew 11:2-3

It is said that great expectations lead to great disappointments. I can certainly attest to that statement! No matter how well we prepare ourselves, it is impossible to guard against disappointments in life. We dream, we expect, we desire, and we all face the pain of disappointment—even when we "know better."

Zechariah and his wife, Elizabeth, had prayed for a child throughout the years of their marriage. Like most couples they longed to share their love with a little boy or girl, but Elizabeth was barren. No matter how much this couple petitioned God for a child, no child came—at least not in their timing.

It was years before an angel appeared and announced the birth of John. Zechariah and Elizabeth were far past the child-rearing age. They had long since ceased praying for a baby. Yet God's time came and John was born—born to prepare the way for the most important Man of all time.

When John came into this world, he found love and support. He found parents who understood his special calling. John found dreams to dream, plans to make, and a future to behold. He had his own set of expectations, and he would feel his own set of disappointments.

John stepped into his role of prophet almost as if he'd rehearsed the lines. He knew where to go and how to act, and his message was both consistent and sincere. I have so often wondered how he kept from giving up or becoming jealous of Jesus' following. I have often wondered how he maintained his enthusiasm even in prison. Yet John stayed true to his God and to his vision.

John the Baptist seems almost beyond the scope of our humanity until God cracks the door of John's expectations and allows us to peer inside. Even if only for a moment, God permits us entrance into the expectations and disappointments of one of the most influential servants in history.

The setting was prison. John had been detained because of the truth he spoke. He had friends — followers who had helped through the years of his ministry. They were hurting for him, and they were all confused.

"If Jesus is really the Messiah, why is John out of the picture?" "If Jesus is the one John prepared the world for, then why isn't John on His team?" "Why is John imprisoned for the very life he'd been destined to lead?" Unanswered questions raced through their minds.

I imagine John entertained the very same questions and doubts. And I suspect that this tireless prophet tried to quiet those distractions. Perhaps he sought solace in his memories of days gone by. Perhaps he found solace in remembering that day when he heard the words from heaven, "This is My beloved Son," as he baptized Jesus in the Jordan River.

As he strained to remain true to his own commitment, I believe John made every effort not to succumb to doubt or discouragement. Yet even a prophet has his moments of despair. While Jesus and His disciples were out changing the world, John's prison cell seemed smaller with each passing day.

"Could I have made a mistake?" the prophet pondered. "Have I misjudged this man, Jesus?" "Have I truly found the anticipated One?"

Even the most faithful entertain disappointments. We become confused and uncertain about things which, yesterday, seemed to be the bedrock of our faith. We feel as though we've been abandoned, and we don't know where to turn. John the Baptist was no exception to the battles we face on our journey.

Our Lord heard the pain in His prophet's soul. He heard John's disappointment. And Jesus sent a simple reassurance to His servant.

With a reminder of His love and purpose, Jesus soothed John's disappointment. With a living example of how to keep on keeping on, Jesus stepped into John's pain and reaffirmed His beloved. With hope in His message, Jesus helped John to focus on the reason they were both alive.

John was not chastised for doubting, nor did Jesus ignore the needs of His prophet. Neither did Jesus remove John's pain.

When we feel discouraged, we want God to take away the doubts and fears and replace them with assurances and comforts. Jesus listens to our longings. He hears our disappointment. And He responds with greater encouragement than we have sought.

Jesus offers His children a constant reminder of truth, of belonging, and of purpose. He offers us a steady reminder of His commitment to our lives.

When you grow disappointed, try to remember that disappointments are a normal response to the conditions of this world. When you grow disappointed, try to look for the encouragement He offers.

Jesus gently reminds us that we are loved . . . today, tomorrow, and every day. Try not to lose sight of His love.

███████████ **T H O U G H T   F O R   T H E   H E A R T**

I have been disappointed lately with these people or these situations. Sometimes I think that God is doing one thing when He ends up doing another. I'd like to learn to focus on what He desires. I'd like to be aware of His encouragement and love.

—*Shelley Chapin*

DISAPPOINTMENT

●

SEEING GOOD IN THE SMALL

"Who despises the day of small things?" Zechariah 4:10

Such an interesting question tucked away in the midst of a prophetic work that is read by few and understood by fewer still. The setting is Israel's return from captivity and the description is one of a people who are disappointed in their new surroundings.

Can you imagine how it must have felt to return to Jerusalem only to see it destroyed? Can you imagine gazing upon the sight of a temple that had once been one of the wonders of the world and finding, in its place, scattered stones? Can you imagine trying to dream dreams in the midst of rubble?

The Jews worked hard to lay the foundation for a new temple, but the result was nothing compared to the temple Solomon built. The joy and the weeping were intermingled. Yes, God's people were thankful to be home, but their efforts seemed futile. The result seemed so small.

So God sent the Prophet Zechariah into the midst of the people, and one of the first questions God placed on his heart was, "Who despises the day of small things?"

I remember a Christmas in our house growing up when my gift was a tractor. It had rubber treads like a Caterpillar and a small wind-up motor. In my mind it was a great tractor, but in actuality the treads wouldn't stay in place and the wind-up motor quickly broke the way Christmas morning toys often do.

So many times, the great expectations of our childhood and our youth end up with treads that won't stay on the wheels and motors that just won't work. And yet God uses the disappointments and the small things to strengthen and provide.

That small temple which the people struggled to build and accept became the foundation of a temple where someday Jesus would stand and pronounce salvation. The small thing made way for the Greatest, and thus our blessing.

Yet the Jews of Jesus' day were also disappointed. They expected someone much "bigger"—a conquerer who was glorious and powerful and majestic in build and ability. "Small" is very much in the eyes of the beholder.

Those who search for the greatness of this world find that it disappears almost as quickly as it comes. It is the small things—the gifts of God's grace—that remain and bring us life.

███████████ THOUGHT FOR THE HEART

I have been disappointed in small things, but I think I can begin to see what God is doing in my life.

— Phil Hook

●
IF ANOTHER CHANCE NEVER COMES

"My God, my God, why have You forsaken me? Why are You so far from saving me, so far from the words of my groaning? O my God, I cry out by day, but You do not answer, by night, and am not silent." Psalm 22:1-2

Phil first met our young friend in about 1977. The telephone rang and worried parents said that their daughter had run away. She was threatening suicide, and they wanted to know if Phil would be willing to help if or when they found her.

Several days passed and a call came again. "We've found her. Will you see her if we bring her right to your office?" Phil immediately agreed.

DISAPPOINTMENT

When she entered his office Phil found a beautiful young girl who was deeply depressed. She had earned every honor in high school. She was a cheerleader and the center of attention. But the world—and the future—changed the day she became pregnant. Early in her senior year, she made a choice that altered her life.

Over the next seven years both of us befriended this talented young woman. The years were turbulent ones. Married at seventeen, she felt cheated by life. She loved her son, but she just couldn't resolve her feelings of disappointment. She had planned on having a very different life, and she fought her reality day in and day out.

We tried to offer wisdom and encouragement, but our friend would not be comforted. She wanted a different life. She wanted a new chance. She wanted something other than what she had.

We all have plans and dreams. We all envision a tomorrow that grows out of our imaginings. Just ask a group of children, "What do you want to be when you grow up?" and the answers are as varied as their imaginations. Yet our dreams rarely include failure or suffering.

It is difficult for us to accept our place in life when the expectations lead to disappointment. We fight what is real. We try to pretend that the situation will end. We want to believe that our plans will, indeed, come to pass. We want to avoid the pain.

Sometimes our plans can be reclaimed. Sometimes the failures or choices only involve a detour before we're back on the road that we planned again.

Other times in life, we are asked to accept what God allows and adjust our disappointment to contentment. When we are successful at this transformation, we gain a sense of peace and renewed purpose. When we hold on to the old way of thinking, the result is generally discouragement or despair. Our young friend chose to hold on to the old dreams. She thought being single would make her happy again. She thought that peace was one step beyond her current reach. She never found that peace in this world.

Our friend took her life one day, and we will never forget the pain. She dressed in white, curled her hair, put on makeup, and ended her existence in this world. Perhaps she thought the only cure for disappointment was death. We continue to grieve her loss.

It is difficult to accept our disappointments, but acceptance is the only way to make peace with our tomorrow. Though hard at times, we must recall that God is always at work, even when the path changes before our very eyes.

God is at work for good in the lives of those He loves— He is at work in your life and in mine. Hold on to the truth. Hold on to His peace. Allow Him to work in your heart.

THOUGHT FOR THE HEART

I'm having a difficult time accepting this change in my life. Perhaps I can learn a little bit more today about contentment, about purpose, about trusting God with my disappointment.

—Phil Hook & Shelley Chapin

WHEN GOD SAYS "NO"

"For God did not appoint us to suffer wrath but to receive salvation through our Lord Jesus Christ." 1 Thessalonians 5:9

Can you imagine the outcome if a parent honored the requests of each child on a vacation? The family would inch their bloated bellies from one ice cream store to the next. The priority would be popcorn and candy and the itinerary would read like a fast-food menu!

"Go straight to the cherry malt and make a right. Head north until you find the chili cheeseburger. Stay north for 1,300 calories and bear left at the giant pizza. When you see the two-for-one chili dog special, take the Pepto-Bismol turnpike east for five bathroom stops. . . . " You get the picture.

Can you imagine the chaos if a father indulged every whim of his child? Can you imagine the chaos if a mother never said "no" or uttered a certain "not yet!" Can you imagine the chaos if God indulged each desire of yours or of mine?

God's destiny for our lives is not momentary pleasure. He does not see His duty as that of making sure we never feel disappointed. Instead, God's overarching desire is that we reach the destiny of salvation and walk the road of an inheritance that can never perish, spoil, or fade.

When discouragement sets in, try to remember that God is more concerned with our heavenly destiny than with our earthly indulgences. God just wants to lead us home. And His itinerary includes stops that encourage and refresh His children, especially in our times of disappointment.

THOUGHT FOR THE HEART

I sense that I am feeling disappointed in these areas, yet I can see God at work to encourage and refresh.

— Max Lucado

● HIS APPOINTMENT

"Moses said to the Lord, 'O Lord, I have never been eloquent, neither in the past nor since You have spoken to Your servant. I am slow of speech and tongue.' The Lord said to him, 'Who gave man

his mouth? Who makes him deaf or mute? Who gives him sight or makes him blind? Is it not I, the Lord? Now go; I will help you speak and teach you what to say.' "Exodus 4:10-12

I heard a song entitled "Disappointment" once. It was a song about the struggles we all face in this world, but there was an interesting twist! Phil Keaggy, one of the pioneers in Christian contemporary music, wrote this line: "Disappointment, His appointment—change one letter and you'll see. . . . " A simple thought, but quite insightful.

Disappointments come when life brings something other than what we've planned or expected. The degree deepens when life brings something other than what we think we deserve. Disappointment comes when we want to say "no" to the circumstances before us.

Moses spent many years in a state of disappointment. You remember. He was a special child, protected by his mother and raised as the son of Pharaoh's daughter. Moses had everything a young man could want, but he was torn between two worlds.

Then came that day when he observed an Egyptian hurting a Jew, and he sided with his own heritage. Moses thought that the Israelites would appreciate his support, but they didn't know him. They didn't know why he had done what he'd done and they did not trust this young "Egyptian." Moses found his world in disarray, and he fled.

Years later, Moses was still running . . . not physically, you understand, but emotionally and spiritually. As he hid in the mountains, tending "the farm" and reflecting on where he went wrong, a voice interrupted his thoughts.

"Moses!" The voice was strong and powerful.

"Is that You, Lord?" he asked. "There, in the burning bush?"

"Here I am." And the great I Am spoke to His servant.

Moses didn't understand what was happenng, and the message did not become clearer. God wanted something from him, but for the life of him, Moses couldn't grasp just what God needed.

"I can't speak ... You should know that!" Moses argued with the Lord. "You don't want me to help You, that's for sure. Remember, I'm Your disappointment."

Needless to say, Moses learned to obey! He did not long remain "shy" and locked in the secrets of his past. Moses rose to the occasion and ended up a very different man than the one we find staring at the burning bush.

God had an appointment for Moses! Yes, the man had suffered a big disappointment. But at just the right time and in just the right way, Moses was used to lead God's people out of bondage and into their promised land.

I'm sure you have felt disappointment. In fact, you may be struggling with it right now. Please hold on. For every disappointment, God has His appointment. Be ready. You are His treasured child.

THOUGHT FOR THE HEART

It is not easy for me to see myself in light of God's pleasure. I tend to focus on what I am not rather than on who I am in Christ. Father, help me to await Your appointment.

—Shelley Chapin

●
DESERT DAYS

"Jesus, full of the Holy Spirit, returned from the Jordan and was led by the Spirit into the desert, where for forty days He was tempted by the devil. He ate nothing during those days, and at the end of them He was hungry." Luke 4:1-2

I was seated in a coffee shop in Philadelphia. Barbie and

DISAPPOINTMENT

Mary, my two youngest, were with me. I tried to take the girls along on one trip each year, and this was their trip. It was the first time the two youngest had been alone with Dad away from home. They were excited.

I was speaking at a Christmas conference for Campus Crusade and I took the girls out for dinner before my first session. They needed to eat early, but I would wait until after I spoke to enjoy a meal.

A young lady came into the restaurant and sat next to me at the counter. She ordered iced tea only and I remember thinking that strange, but I paid little attention at the time. The girls and I were in heavy conversation! The lady began to look at me, and I finally realized she wanted to talk.

"Do I know you?"

"Yes," she said.

"You're going to have to help me. I'm sorry, but I don't remember."

"I was at Cornell in 1971," she stated with nostalgia.

Cornell in 1970 and 1971 were two of the happiest months of my life. A month of Bible teaching with university-aged students, in a beautiful setting, with my family along, was great! God blessed and we all enjoyed our time there.

"How can I help you?" I asked, after a few moments' reflection. She told me a story of great expectations and great disappointment.

God had touched her life very specially during that summer at Cornell. She had given her life to ministry. As the month came to a close, she sent her application in to join the staff of Campus Crusade. Her roommate had done likewise, and they eagerly returned home to await a reply.

A couple of weeks later the roommate received her acceptance but this young woman did not. She called headquarters and was told "we'll look into it," and she tried to remain optimistic.

In the meantime, their church committed to support the roommate who was now eager about her new calling. The young woman again contacted headquarters and this time was told that they apparently had lost her application. The roommate went off to staff training, and this young woman went back to a bar that she had frequented in the days before Cornell.

As I listened to the sadness in her voice, she told me she believed there are two kinds of Christians in the world: those for whom God answers prayer and things work out, and those for whom nothing works out.

The young woman continued her story of resentment, anger, and departure from God. She ended up living on a university campus in Pennsylvania, and that brought us up to date.

"How did you get here?" I asked. And she looked at me with a smile.

"One day I saw a poster on campus with your name on it," she explained proudly. "I decided if anyone has an encouragement to offer me, it might be you."

By this time my daughters had finished their dinners and it was time for me to speak.

"Why don't you eat dinner with me after the session," I suggested. She consented.

I changed my message for that evening. I spoke from Luke 4 where Jesus, full of the Holy Spirit, returned from the Jordan and was led by the Spirit into the desert to be tempted by Satan.

I spoke on the desert days of life. They often come right after the minutes of greatest triumph. The Lord had just been filled with the Holy Spirit. This young lady had just learned the power of the Spirit in her own life. And both were led into the desert.

DISAPPOINTMENT

She had experienced the exhilaration, but she hadn't heard the rest of the story. The filling of the Holy Spirit doesn't mean that life is "happily ever after." It often means the deserts, disappointments, and lost perspectives of life.

We will all face disappointment. When the deserts come, do not turn away. Remember that we step through those deserts in the company of the One who gives us life and strength and hope.

THOUGHT FOR THE HEART

I have been struggling with disappointment lately, and I've been wanting to give up. Lord, grant me the courage to keep going with You.

—*Phil Hook*

RHYTHMS OF MY HEART

ENDURANCE

DON'T BE A CLOCK-WATCHER

"Those who trust in the Lord are like Mount Zion, which cannot be shaken but endures forever. As the mountains surround Jerusalem, so the Lord surrounds His people both now and forevermore."
Psalm 125:1-2

It is difficult to explain how I felt that first year with cancer. At first I was afraid and anxious about my nine-month prognosis. Being only twenty-eight at the time, I had never prepared for my own death. I had barely even thought of death in that first season of my life.

After several months passed, however, I began to prepare myself for leaving this world. Into a mind where heaven had been only a daydream came thoughts of a new reality. I was going home! I would soon be with Jesus. And all of the struggles of this world would pass into a never-ending light.

Each day that passed found me more and more comfortable with death. I will not boast of having no fear, but I will say that I became eager to be with the Lord. I felt ready to be with the Lord.

Nine months came and went. It was obvious the prognosis was not valid. And my friends gathered for a "staying here" party in my honor. We rejoiced, but I also grieved. Something inside me had prepared for death, and now that I would be living, my fears returned.

The next few months proved difficult for me. I was grateful for the chance to "stay here," yet sad over my delayed homegoing. There was so much for me to reconsider—such as living each day with physical pain. I didn't mind the pain so much when an end was in sight. But to live in pain for many years seemed an impossible task for someone like me.

God sent an angel to me in those months of inner turmoil. His name is Tom Quinn. He is a wise, older, gentle-man with years of experience as both pilgrim and servant of the Lord. We visited one day and I told him of my struggle.

"It sounds like you're a bit impatient," he said, smiling.

"I had counted on going home! I wanted to see Jesus. And I'm tired," I explained.

"I know. But remember, don't be a clock-watcher."

"A clock-watcher?" I must have looked a little puzzled.

"A clock-watcher!" he repeated. And the explanation that followed made everything quite clear.

You see, Mr. Quinn has been in business for himself for years. He has hired and fired, struggled and grown, lost and won. And he has learned much about people.

"There are few things worse than an employee who starts watching the clock at 4:30." His words hit home, and I readily understood their message.

It's fine to long for home, but God asks that we walk here attentively and actively as long as He allows. He asks that we honor Him with our hearts, with our minds, with our very lives.

I do hunger for home! But I have learned, in my years since 1982, that God always has a reason for His rhyme. I am here with a purpose and it is no mistake that my "nine months" has been extended again and again.

You too are here with a purpose. For some of you, that purpose may seem obscured by pain or loss or weariness, but make no mistake. Our God has a reason for "loaning" us to this world each day that we have breath.

Endure! Hold on to God's love for you! And try not to watch the clock!

■■■■■■■■■■ **T H O U G H T   F O R   T H E   H E A R T**

I feel tired, Lord. I feel tired of this world, tired of my pain, tired of the everyday commitments that I face. I am tired, and lately I've been staring at the clock! Help me to look to You and to endure for the sake of Your love and purpose.

— Shelley Chapin

●
STEP BY STEP, DAY BY DAY

"You say about this place, 'It is a desolate waste, without men or animals.' Yet in the towns of Judah and the streets of Jerusalem that are deserted, inhabited by neither men nor animals, there will be heard once more the sounds of joy and gladness, the voices of bride and bridegroom, and the voices of those who bring thank offerings to the house of the Lord, saying, 'Give thanks to the Lord Almighty, for the Lord is good; His love endures forever.' For I will restore the fortunes of the land as they were before, says the Lord."
Jeremiah 33:10-11

I'm hoping that it will help you as much to read these thoughts as it helps me to write them. Sometimes seeing my heart written down in words helps to solidify my own direction. Writing about endurance has helped me to do just that—decide where I am headed from here.

When I chose, in 1962, to travel to Africa as a "tentmaker" physician, I thought I would last only a few years. I thought I would get the wanderlust out of my system and then return to London for a respectable career.

Years later, I'm still tentmaking! And my travels have led me to many parts of Africa, Haiti, Belize, Venezuela, Romania, and the former Soviet Union. I've had a wonderful career! Yet lately I've been torturing myself, trying to decide where I "ought" to be.

"Am I in the right place?" "Could I do more somewhere else?" "Is God leading me to leave here; and, if so, where does He want me to go?" I have a lesson to learn from endurance.

ENDURANCE

The word *endurance* is an interesting one. Sometimes it means just gritting our teeth and carrying through on a task we dislike. Sometimes it means pushing on toward an incredible goal or prize. Sometimes it means placing one foot in front of the other, simply trying to live by faith. My guess is that most of us are attempting the latter.

I think of those who spend years training for the Olympics. They shine for a few moments during the years leading up to the competition, but mostly they work—day in and day out. For the hopeful Olympian, there might be a big reward, or there might not.

The swimmer might not swim fast enough that day. The runner might miss his push off the block. The skier might ski past the gate or lose control in the freshly fallen snow. The basketball team might be upstaged by a team that is faster and much more professional. The relay racer might miss the baton.

Why does someone train so many years for a fleeting possibility at reward? Why do so many enter the Games when so few leave with the medals?

For each of us, life is a game of endurance. It is measuring who we are against the task at hand and making a decision. It is trying not to lose sight of the task at hand so that tomorrow will have its opportunity. Life is much about endurance.

I could have run my race back in London. I could have changed careers. I could have chosen another country to give my life to or a different means of measuring my reward.

But to God, what seems to matter is the day-at-a-time "training." To God, what matters is the step-by-step journey of depending on Him.

I am no different than that hopeful Olympian. I work hard each day, but I can't help dreaming about that gold medal out there somewhere. Thus my current dilemma.

ENDURANCE

Sometimes we get bored with endurance and we want some exciting turn.

I simply need to remember that what sets the believer apart from anyone else is not the reward itself but the reason for that reward. We gain our strength from the daily privilege of knowing and serving Christ. Each day brings its reward for the Christian, even though the reward may seem simple or insignificant.

Endurance is all about a daily commitment. No one can win a marathon tomorrow without first having trained and prepared today. No one can win the prize tomorrow without today's endurance.

I do not know what decisions are before you, but I know that I have made my decision in the thoughts collected on this page. I will keep on serving God where I am, day by day. I will endure and grow and honor Him each day that I am alive.

Abraham walked with God day by day. Sarah believed one day at a time. Jeremiah did daily as he heard the Lord command. The disciples walked forward in faith. And I too will walk forward.

Endurance is a commitment to place one foot in front of the other and continue to walk with our Lord. It is a sweet "I trust You, Father" offered to a loving God. Endurance is a trust that says God knows just what He is doing and will bring His good to pass.

We can all endure! Just continue to walk with our Lord. We can all take one more step of faith today.

THOUGHT FOR THE HEART

I've been trying to make a big decision, Lord, as if my future depends on the "right choice." Help me to trust You instead of my decisions. Help me to simply walk in Your ways.

— *Pamela M. Reeves*

●

ENDURANCE IS A PROCESS

"But those who hope in the Lord will renew their strength. They will soar on wings like eagles; they will run and not grow weary, they will walk and not be faint." Isaiah 40:31

Do you ever get out your high school yearbook? I do . . . and wince. The young man in those pictures weighed 174 pounds, was broad-shouldered, and lettered in four sports during his senior year. When I graduated from high school, I was fairly obsessed with being in good shape. I did 100 push-ups every night in my college dorm room, and the first summer after graduation I swam across California's Lake Arrowhead, simply because it was there.

I married a perky little brunette, and we began our life of ministry together. Like every good servant, I was out most evenings, so my life consisted of eating, sitting, driving, watching TV, and sleeping. I gained forty-seven pounds in six months. It just snuck up on me — all over me, actually — until one morning I stood before the bathroom mirror and became depressed.

My stomach looked like something that should be named "Heartbreak Hill." It was a monument to spaghetti, stroganoff, hamburgers, fast food, slow food, and ice cream. "Is anybody home in there?" I asked. Something had to be done.

I'm an obsessive person so I don't do things halfway. If I needed exercise, I was going to hike a mountain to get it. So on a sunny January day, I began my return to good shape by hiking down a trail on a nearby, fairly deserted mountain.

Two hours and seven miles later, I felt great about my exercise and decided to return to the car. A fleeting thought that maybe the walk uphill would be harder than the walk down was pridefully dismissed, and I began the nightmare hike back home.

I knew I was in trouble when the minutes turned to hours. Before long, I was lying on a dusty trail, gasping for breath. I noticed a deer carcass close by which a bear had killed and eaten sometime that week and, believe me, I was not encouraged! A chill began to set in and I was shivering. I literally could not go one step farther.

"Lord Jesus, help me. This is my fault. I let myself go and I'm too weak to go on. Send help, Lord, or I'm going to die." And with those words, I curled up in a fetal position to wait.

The Lord graciously responded. Two young boys on a dirt bike appeared to ferry me back to my car. I lost fourteen pounds of liquid that day and could not walk normally for quite some time, but I had embraced some critical lessons.

I learned that we get weak slowly—so much so that we rarely even notice. And getting strength back is a process, not an event.

I learned that God not only helps those who help themselves, He helps the stupid, the weak, the obsessive, and the undeserving. He answers prayer, and He cares about even our follies.

And I learned that endurance is a process of waiting on the Lord and relying on Him for strength. It is not a result of "handling" life myself.

The strength is there—as we wait upon the Lord.

THOUGHT FOR THE HEART

I tend to run ahead of God in these areas.

—Gary Richmond

ENDURANCE

●
A PILGRIM'S PROGRESS

"Let us fix our eyes on Jesus, the author and perfecter of our faith, who for the joy set before Him endured the cross, scorning its shame, and sat down at the right hand of the throne of God."
Hebrews 12:2

I once read a story about a young man in East Africa who lived in the bush. He was given two books by some missionaries there: the Bible and John Bunyan's *Pilgrim's Progress*. As he read, he learned two things from the books. He learned that he is a child of God, and he learned that he can do what God wants him to do if he wants to badly enough.

This young man took his learnings to heart, and he soon pursued an education in the United States and has since returned to serve as a leader in his country. He "wanted to" serve God, and he was willing to travel 11,250 miles to prepare himself for a lifelong journey of service.

I have two lovely grandbabies who, at this writing, have recently learned to walk. They are twins, one boy and one girl. Little Morgan learned to walk first, and she learned to do it well! She walks very upright and flat-footed, sure and sensible and thoroughly prepared.

Her brother, Patrick, has a bit of a different approach. He stands up, gets his balance and determination in sync, and then turns loose to grab the world! With arms outstretched, he smiles with glee and takes the steps that will lead to his future.

Everyone's walk with God is different. We have a different beginning and a different path. We are simply asked to want the journey and to step one foot at a time.

I have a wonderful husband who has walked with me

through thick and thin for years now. We have parented two children and lived through sorrows and joys, side by side. The secret? We have wanted to support and love one another. And we have taken one step at a time.

Getting to know Pat has been a process of talking to him, observing him, and listening to him. It has taken each day that we've spent together to build the relationship. And we have not made it to the end of our journey.

Coming to the United States and getting an education is a process of endurance for the young man in East Africa. Learning to walk is a process of endurance for the twins. And building a healthy marriage is a process of endurance for both my husband and myself.

God leads us each step of the way as we make our own "pilgrim's progress." He provides the strength, He provides the grace and forgiveness. He provides the wisdom and the love — all that we need.

THOUGHT FOR THE HEART

I can see how endurance plays a role in our individual lives as well as our relationships. I want to grant patience to these people and these situations in my life today.

— Mary Dale Thomas

●
A WITNESS TO GOD'S HAND

"Some faced jeers and flogging, while still others were chained and put in prison. They were stoned, they were sawed in two; they were put to death by the sword. They went about in sheepskins and goat-skins, destitute, persecuted, and mistreated — the world was not worthy of them." Hebrews 11:36-38

My life has been changed by some of the most precious people on earth — the sick, the lonely, the hurting, and the dying. Earthly possessions of wealth, power, and prestige suddenly mean little when matched with human suffering and endurance.

I wrote the following poem for my friend, Evelyn. God has changed my heart and my direction in the years of her illness. He has given me blessings beyond measure which flow through me to others. I have touched lives, they have touched mine, and we will never be the same for the privilege.

"For Posterity"

One day the world stood still—
tragedy struck,
tentacles wrapped around life
breeding fear and uncertainty.
Unknown haunted the night,
weeping became a constant companion,
exhaustion consumed.

Struggle began its vigil
in torrents of pain and suffering.
Touch, comfort, listening and acceptance
became soothing oil,
dulling pain.

Death beckoned,
fighting futile,
but courage and perseverance
welled within
combating the shadow.

Monuments marked victory
over insurmountable odds;
proven character survived.

E N D U R A N C E

Temptation to exit prematurely,
alleviating pain, spread as a virus—
but character fought and won.

Conflicts dissolved into insignificance.
Resolution begat peace.
Forgiveness stood at the threshold and entered,
bringing comfort down deep.
Strength from within became a witness
to God's mighty hand.
Courage traveled the road of life
finding jewels of promise
glistening among the ashes.

Strength from God,
acceptance of reality,
adversity laced with fortitude,
forgiveness of self and others.
Knowledge, understanding, truth
and wisdom are the precious gifts
left for posterity.

THOUGHT FOR THE HEART

My life has been enriched by the pain and the endurance of these people.

—Marilyn Rhode

●
QUIET STRENGTH

"Blessed are the poor in spirit, for theirs is the kingdom of heaven."
Matthew 5:3

We've been exploring the Beatitudes in my share group lately—humility, perseverance, mercy, purity. . . .

ENDURANCE

When you look at the list, there is a thread of endurance that runs through them all. God's people must endure, it is a simple truth.

We find illustrations in our everyday lives of those who live the qualities Jesus described. God was gracious to me. My illustration walked in the door of my house.

He reminded me of the burly men I'd seen slamming each other on the Super Bowl turf. But this man was there to repair my sideboard, not to score a touchdown! He followed me quietly into the dining room and did not speak as I explained what I needed from him.

"Floyd, this is a piece I've hunted for a long, long time," I explained. "The cracked leg was not apparent when I found it; I only discovered the flaw after we moved it here. I was told you can fix it!"

"I believe I can, Mrs. Dobbs," he responded, his eyes only then leaving the sideboard to look directly at me.

"My tools are in the truck," he continued.

"It's heavy," I jumped in. "Can you lift it?"

Obviously Floyd was young and strong, but I had tried to lift the sideboard and had needed my gardener and two of his workers to succeed in the task!

"Don't you worry, Mrs. Dobbs," he assured me. "I'll fix this sideboard." And he did.

Floyd left the house, only to return quickly with a tool chest and a helper. They worked steadily for an hour and did not once disturb me at my computer.

"Mrs. Dobbs?" I heard Floyd's voice from the dining room. "We're done."

I entered the room and quickly observed the masterpiece of this man. He had repaired the sideboard with care and skill. It looked wonderful!

"What do you think?" I asked. "Will it see another hundred years?"

"Yes, Ma'am." He sounded proud. "It's a good piece."

In a few short sentences Floyd told me more about the styling of the piece, the nature of the burled wood, and the design of the hardware than the antique dealer had been able to offer. As he talked, Floyd touched the parts he was referringto. I could see that Floyd and the sideboard shared a rapport. I also noticed that Floyd spoke eloquently and easily when he talked about furniture.

"We adjusted this door too—just realigned the hinge." Floyd worked his way around the room. "We put some oil on this piece. These old pieces are often dry," he patiently explained.

Floyd pointed to a nearby credenza and moved to place his hands on it gently. "I noticed you lost the hardware on this door," he added. "I had a match so I put it on for you."

Basically, Floyd had repaired my sideboard, but that wasn't all he had done. He had taken care to fix other pieces as well. He knew about a job well done, and he knew about taking care of more than what was asked. I felt intrigued by Floyd's knowledge.

"You know antiques very well!" I wanted to admire this man a bit. "You must have some interesting pieces of your own."

Floyd hesitated for a moment and I could see him draw back into his shell. Floyd talked easily about furniture, but not so easily about himself.

"No, I don't," he spoke with hesitation. Then his face brightened softly as he added, "But I do like keeping these old pieces together." He continued surveying the room. "My work lets me do that."

"You do your job very well," I said. And I meant every word.

Floyd handed me a bill that was less than half of what I'd expected. He had not charged anything for his added work on the other pieces in the room.

E N D U R A N C E

"Thank you for your good work, Mr. Albright," I said as I shook Floyd's hand. And Floyd walked out the door.

Floyd ministered to me that day at my house. He knows his work, and he knows it well. He knows his limits, his abilities, his customers, and his pieces. He knows who he is and who he wants to be.

When I was with Floyd, I felt his peace. I felt his confidence, his quiet strength, his respect for his craft and for the world. When I was with Floyd, I sensed a wisdom beyond his years and a gift for humble endurance.

It is difficult for us to satisfy ourselves with endurance. We often push, pull, and prod ourselves to jump through one more hoop or experience one more activity. Men like Floyd are not typical of the rest of us.

To live the Beatitudes is to live with endurance. It is to run the race that is before us with humility and quiet determination. It is to not get sidetracked and lose life's real meaning. To live the Beatitudes is to live like Jesus.

■■■■■■■ T H O U G H T   F O R   T H E   H E A R T

I am tired! I feel like I endure, but I'm usually just "hanging on." Lord, help me to order my life around Your priorities. Help me to hunger for Your attitudes.

— *Sally Dobbs*

●

THE CHOICE OF ENDURANCE

"May the God who gives endurance and encouragement give you a spirit of unity among yourselves as you follow Christ Jesus, so that with one heart and mouth you may glorify the God and Father of our Lord Jesus Christ." Romans 15:5-6

Paul packed his few belongings and said his last good-byes. Then he sat for one more moment to pen the final words of his letter to the Roman church.

"I'm on my way to Spain, brothers," Paul wrote. "I have finished my work here. Though it may seem hard to believe, the Gospel has been fully proclaimed from Jerusalem all the way around to Illyricum. Just think of all the men and women who now know our Savior. God has been honored, and my heart is at peace.

"I'm going on to Spain because they too need the Good News of Jesus Christ. And you know me, I am best when laying a new foundation rather than building on someone else's work. The Gentiles in Spain need to hear about Jesus, and I know it is my purpose to share with them.

"I plan to stop and see you on my way there," Paul concluded. "Peace be with you. Pray for me. Your brother, Paul."

There was rarely a moment in Paul's life when he felt unsure. Ever since he was a young boy he had been taught to live with discipline. He had known what he wanted since before he could recall, and that assurance didn't change with his conversion. Paul's gifts lay in evangelism, and his audience awaited him.

Paul walked deliberately out of the familiar into the unknown. He felt a twinge of excitement and surprise, I'm sure, but he was ready for what lay ahead. Paul knew much about endurance.

We hear from Paul again, though the postmark does not say, "Spain." You see, he never quite made it to his desired destination. Instead, he was detained by the Roman police and placed under house arrest. Paul was forbidden to further his journey to those who needed the message. He had every reason to give up.

"You can't do this to me," I might have said. "I am a Roman citizen and I have rights."

By God's grace, Paul's response sounded nothing like mine. In fact, we see his endurance shine through even

ENDURANCE

though his dream was invaded by someone else's jealousy and fear.

"Dear Philippians," Paul wrote with care. "I want you to know that what has happened to me has really served to advance the Good News of Jesus Christ. Yes, the Gospel is being proclaimed, through the ranks of the guards and even into the household of Caesar."

Sound familiar? Didn't Paul realize he was in jail?

Paul had every reason to grow discouraged (and he did have his moments!) but he chose, instead, to believe in God and keep placing one foot in front of the other. Paul chose the way of endurance.

You and I each have our particular struggles and our deep disappointments. We have plans that are disrupted and dreams that go unnoticed. We have pain that courses through our hearts and leaves us uncertain and despairing. But we also have the choice of endurance—the choice to accept the realities that God allows and look for His opportunities in their midst.

Paul went to "Spain," though it was not called by that name. He lived his purpose and shared the grace of God with those who otherwise might never have heard. He proclaimed the Good News to every palace guard sent to watch "the prisoner," to every official who was curious enough to come see, to Caesar himself and those who were beloved by the ruler.

So many times we miss what God is doing in the throes of our own disappointment. Hold on to endurance! Know that God is using you, even when it seems like He has foiled the plan.

▬▬▬▬▬ THOUGHT FOR THE HEART

I have struggled with endurance in these areas or relationships lately, and I'd like a renewed sense of perspective.

—Shelley Chapin

RHYTHMS OF MY HEART

WEAVING A TAPESTRY

"Now when I went to Troas to preach the Gospel of Christ and found that the Lord had opened a door for me, I still had no peace of mind, because I did not find my brother Titus there. So I said good-bye to them and went on to Macedonia. But thanks be to God, who always leads us in triumphal procession in Christ and through us spreads everywhere the fragrance of the knowledge of Him."
2 Corinthians 2:12-14

I often think of Paul as a scholar, a teacher, and an academician. Sometimes it's hard for me to let him be a person.

Paul's conversion lost him his family, his inheritance, his heritage, his position, and probably all of his friends. He spent the first three years of his Christian experience in the deserts. And in his epistles we see the marvelous mind that God gave Paul, a mind able to weave theological truth with human need.

Occasionally, Paul gives us a glimpse into his own life, and his second letter to the Corinthians is full of such glimpses. We have much to gain from Paul.

The church at Corinth was full of rebellious teenagers in the faith. They seemed to have a love-hate relationship with Paul. They asked him questions and resented his answers. They opened up to him about their problems and then did not like his solutions.

Paul wrote the Corinthians at least three letters. He visited them several times. And on one visit he tried to fix the alienation, but that particular trip proved unsuccessful.

One day, Paul sent Titus to the Corinthians one more time to try to bring forgiveness and healing. Paul went to Troas to minister where God gave an open door. In short, the people of Troas were responsive, but Paul's mind was on other things.

FAILURE

Paul's concern for the church at Corinth was more than he could handle. He describes it this way: "This body of ours had no rest, but we were harassed at every turn— conflicts on the outside, fears within" (2 Corinthians 7:5).

Paul was hurting deeply, and his concern was such that he abandoned the ministry in Troas and went on. He simply could not continue there with so much unresolved in his relationship with the Corinthians.

The end of this particular story is great. Titus came to Paul with the good news that reconciliation had been reached in the relationship with the church at Corinth. Paul could rest now about that particular problem, and so he rejoiced by penning "thanks be to God."

In the midst of both failure and success, bad news and good news, losses and gains, Paul could see the hand of God moving and working His good. God's hand was weaving a tapestry which Paul did not understand at the moment but which you and I can reflect on and see as beautiful.

We tend to see failure as an "end" and as a "bad thing." When we abandon a work we feel called to, the burden seems unbearable. When we cannot bring forgiveness even though we believe it is best, we feel helpless. It is in those moments we do best to remember that God is still at work.

Paul abandoned the ministry at Troas, but God did not abandon that work. Paul could do nothing more about the Corinthians' anger, but God was free to work.

Try not to label yourself as "failure." Certainly we fail, but God is always at work to bring about His good. He does lead us in triumphal array, even when we're unaware of the parade.

THOUGHT FOR THE HEART

I have been counting myself a failure in these areas. I would like to

195

begin to expect God to work even in those areas or relationships where I have "failed."

— Phil Hook

●
THE RIGHT TO FAIL

"Some time later Paul said to Barnabas, 'Let us go back and visit the brothers in all the towns where we preached the Word of the Lord and see how they are doing.' Barnabas wanted to take John, also called Mark, with them, but Paul did not think it wise to take him, because he had deserted them in Pamphylia and had not continued with them in the work. They had such a sharp disagreement that they parted company." Acts 15:36-39

The 1992 election year found many candidates running from their pasts or from the unfounded accusations of those who objected to their campaigns. One woman in Texas recalled her Phi Beta Kappa graduation, though she never completed her B.A. degree.

Why would this successful woman falsify her academic record? Why do we strive toward a state of perfection when such a goal is impossible to achieve?

I don't know why, but when I think of "failure" I think of the "right to fail." Though the world around us does not seem to agree, I think that people need the right to fail in order to be authentic. We cannot be perfect, so why place that kind of pressure on ourselves or our children?

Think of it this way: if one is, what I call, a "hundred percenter," the risks of life are so great. For those who have that over-perfectionist need, it seems inevitable that feelings will have to be denied, masked, or covered up in some way. The amount of energy it takes to be "perfect" is immense.

Those of us who fear failure must either redefine what

FAILURE

we mean by success or, as in the case of the Texas politician, resort to living a life of duplicity and subterfuge. Unfortunately, when we lie about our own accomplishments no one is served or satisfied.

It is so much better to grant one another the right to fail. It is an inherent part of being human. And it's a critical ingredient to healthy families and relationships.

You've heard the illustration about the glass that's either half empty or half full. My feeling is if there's anything in the glass at all, it's a positive! After all, we cannot get away from the reality of sin in our lives. I don't look at the glass that is 98 percent empty and say, "I've missed the mark almost 100 percent." I look at what's there and say, "Wow! I'm doing 2 percent well!"

I'm not trying to start a new brand of optimism; I simply want to encourage you to build relationships which allow people to be who they really are. For me, it is very liberating to know that I don't need to pretend—not with God, and not with those I love.

If perfection were the goal, God could accomplish that purpose much easier without us. God *is* perfection and we *do* fail.

Perfection isn't God's purpose for you and me. God allows us to participate in life much like a father allows his son to help with some project around the house. It's almost a given that the father could do the job better and faster than the son, but the goal of the father-son relationship isn't "better" and "faster." The goal has much to do with the building of relationship and the realization of worth.

Grant those around you the right to fail. We all need that privilege.

THOUGHT FOR THE HEART

I tend to place pressure on these people to accomplish what I want accomplished in a way that seems "best" to me. I will work at granting those I love the right to fail.

—Jay Kesler

DOWN BUT NOT OUT

"Simon, Simon, Satan has asked to sift you as wheat." Luke 22:31

The night had been a strange one, indeed. Usually the Passover meal was eaten with joy, but not this time. Jesus seemed unusually close, as if He were trying to touch the disciples in some special way. And yet He seemed distracted. He spoke of suffering and betrayal, servanthood and the New Covenant. And then he dropped the bomb.

"Simon, Simon, Satan has asked to sift you as wheat."

Wait a minute here! Can Satan do that? He did it to Job. And he did it to Peter. Maybe he can do it to you and to me. Yes, he can. And if you feel you are flopping into the sifter, you're in good company.

Peter could hardly have known that just a few hours later he would face—and fail—the greatest test of his life. Peter would be faced with the opportunity to defend or deny his Lord. Satan was sifting him, and he failed. But was he out of the game? Was he benched for all eternity? No way!

Jesus finished His statement with a wealth of encouragement for His servant, Peter. "I have prayed for you, Simon, that your faith may not fail. And when you have turned back, strengthen your brothers" (Luke 22:32). Though Peter would suffer a failure, he would then be used to strengthen others—a legacy with which we are well acquainted. The man of great failures became the leader of the first church! Oh, the great gift of grace!

Whether you know it or not, Satan would desire to sift

you as well. He loves to entangle our faith until we are a drain rather than a strength to one another. However, as Jesus prayed for Peter, so also He prays for you and for me. He uses our failures and He strengthens others through our pain. Such is His commitment.

Jesus helps us to weather Satan's storms, and then He strengthens us so that we can strengthen others. Our failures will come, but they are not greater than His grace.

▬▬▬▬ THOUGHT FOR THE HEART

I am aware of feeling like a failure in these areas of my life. In these areas, I am willing to let Jesus strengthen me and others through me.

— Tim Hawks

●
MRS. BOAZ

"Therefore, I will boast all the more gladly about my weaknesses, so that Christ's power may rest on me. That is why, for Christ's sake, I delight in weaknesses, in insults, in hardships, in persecutions, in difficulties. For when I am weak, then I am strong." 2 Corinthians 12:9-10

I had always been afraid of failure. It's almost as if I believed that to fail is to be flawed. For years I felt the responsibility of the world on my shoulders, so it seemed that failing was tantamount to letting others down. I remember struggling with this imbalance from the time I was very young.

My fourth-grade teacher was one of the best teachers I've ever known. Her name was Mrs. Boaz, and she had taught generations of students by the time I reached her classroom.

Mrs. Boaz stretched her students. She wanted us to

learn. And I wanted to please her almost as much as I wanted to please my parents. To fail Mrs. Boaz would have been one of my deepest disappointments.

One fateful day in October, we were scheduled to read our book reports before the class. Mrs. Boaz had given us plenty of time to prepare, but as children sometimes do, I forgot completely about the assignment. I was all settled in my seat when I heard her call my name.

"Shelley," her voice pierced my daydream. "Why don't you begin by reading your report."

"Report?" My mind raced wildly. *Had I forgotten something? Oh, no! I did forget!* And the more I panicked, the more I felt flawed. I was sure that "failure" was written all over my face.

What did I do? The brave thing, of course! I took a blank sheet of paper out of my notebook, stood up at my seat, and proceeded to read my "written" report! Needless to say, no one was fooled, least of all Mrs. Boaz.

I will never forget what my teacher did for me that day. She allowed me to read a report that didn't even exist! Yes, she pretended to be interested, thanked me when I was done, and waited until class was over to approach my deceit. And even then, Mrs. Boaz was gracious and kind to me. She acted as if she understood — as if she might even have done something like this sometime in her fifty-plus years.

Mrs. Boaz did not shame me that day or any other day of my fourth-grade education. She did not make a classroom spectacle out of me or any other children. Mrs. Boaz taught me lessons in math, science, geography, and English, and she taught me lessons of life. She allowed me to fail without being a failure.

God knows that we fail. Failure is no surprise to Him. Yet much like an adolescent fights to cover the blemishes, we fight to hide the unsightly flaws of our character.

FAILURE

It's not that I feel we should be satisfied with less than that of which we are capable; it's that I do believe we place tremendous pressure on ourselves and on our children when we pretend to be always more than we are. When we pretend to be "above" failure, we do ourselves and those we love a great injustice.

Living as a human being in this world includes failure. It includes forgetting homework from time to time. It includes blemishes on our faces, varicose veins in our legs, a "shifting" of our physical assets as we age, and wrinkles in our skin. Living also includes wrinkles in our behavior, our attitudes, and our relationships.

If we never admit our failures, we never deal honestly with one another. And what do we have if we must conceal the very heart of who we are and how we relate?

Jesus accepted the woman at the well. Jesus loved the tax collectors and "sinners." Jesus took pleasure in restoring the naked man in the graveyard. And Jesus was happy to accept the disciples—fears, jealousies, misunderstandings, limitations, and all!

Look around you today. There is probably someone in your life who is standing before you, blank piece of notebook paper in hand. Give that friend, that child, that husband or wife, that employer or employee, that pastor or counselor the gift of your love and acceptance. Let that person know that to fail is very different than being flawed.

THOUGHT FOR THE HEART

I am aware that sometimes people feel afraid to fail around me. I would like to help those I love feel "at home" with me. I would like to set them free to fail, free to succeed, free to be who they truly are.

— *Shelley Chapin*

●
GRACE-CONTROL

"For the wages of sin is death, but the gift of God is eternal life in Christ Jesus our Lord." Romans 6:23

Some years ago, I encountered the book, *Failure: The Back Door to Success.* As I perused the material, I had two very different reactions. My brain thought, "This is so true!" But my emotions sent out a distress signal that read, "Nothing could be further from the truth! People who succeed don't fail."

I found my dilemma interesting, and I attempted to solve my struggle at the rational level. Thoughts like, "Nobody succeeds all of the time!" "Even hall-of-fame athletes lose their share of games," "Tom Landry didn't even win a game in his first season with the Cowboys" crossed my mind, but the thoughts didn't resolve my conflict.

No matter how many examples I offered of those who had failed before succeeding, my emotions simply wouldn't budge! They "dug in" around the fear of failure at the deeper, irrational level, and they just weren't buying what my mind was trying to sell. In the weeks to come, I discovered an intense fear of failure in my life that I'd never even realized before.

My terror of failing was more invasive than I knew. It even affected me when I won or succeeded. In order to even try, I had to call upon my entire reserve of risk-taking courage. Thus, by the time the challenge was over, I was too emotionally depleted to even savor the victory! After all, the next possibility for failure was gaining on me and I had to be ready. No time to celebrate!

As the age-old (and still wise) saying goes, "To err is human, to forgive, divine." But I had never learned to allow myself the privilege. I couldn't fully accept the failure-prone nature of my humanity. And I wasn't at all sure God would accept or look favorably upon "losers" like me.

I'm grateful that God introduced me to that simple book with its life-changing principles. My emotions were literally turned inside-out in a matter of weeks. I began to see verses like, "for all have sinned," not just as a verse about salvation, but as a truth about Christian living as well.

We all fail. And we all fall short. And we all "die" just a little with the sins and failures of our lives. But the good news is that we are forgiven. And there is grace when we fall. There is no failure that remains so, only failures that God then uses to create His good in our lives.

The knot in my stomach is still there at times, but it no longer keeps me from giving life and relationships my "best shot." I've put my heart on grace-control. And I'll continue down the rocky road to the successes and failures God has charted.

■■■■■■ THOUGHT FOR THE HEART

I tend to "beat myself up" after these failures, and I am willing to apply the healing balm of grace to my wounds.

— *Boyd Luter*

●
FAILURE IS NORMAL

"And we know that in all things God works for the good of those who love Him, who have been called according to His purpose." Romans 8:28

I once sent for a book that was entitled, *The Seven Deadly Virtues.* Probably never sold to many more people than myself, I couldn't pass it by when I saw the advertisement in the magazine. Here's what it said.

FAILURE

"Beware of the man who has never been caught."

Isn't that great? Beware of the man, woman, child, organization, family, university that has never been caught! Caught? Caught doing what? Let me see if I can explain.

If you take a sweeping look around Christendom, you will notice that we rarely discuss our failures until we are "caught" in the midst of a lie or a relational sin or some other wrongdoing worthy of notice. For as long as we can escape the curious eye of parishioners, friends, family members, coworkers, we will.

We avoid the word *failure* as if it is the worst possible thing that could happen to a person. We avoid it as if a simple mention of the word might bring its plague upon us. But in my humble view, failure is a normal occurrence that happens to all of us regularly! It is part of being, how should I say this . . . human!

Failure isn't the "bad news," it is a reality. Failure is to be expected. It even teaches us great lessons upon which to stand in years to come. Let me offer some basic reasons why both the admission of and open discussions about failure can mean so much to the Christian community and the communities we belong to at large.

First, if we remember our own humanity, we stand on equal ground with those around us. When we hear one person's story of sin or struggle we won't immediately separate ourselves from that person.

I am a university president, but that does not set me apart from the students in the area of humanity. Being the president means I'm a bit older and, hopefully, wiser. It means my job is to see that the students get educated in ways they may not even realize, much less appreciate at this point. But it also means I share a common heritage and reality with each of them. I do my best to walk with them, human to human and child of God to child of God.

Secondly, it helps to remember that God allows failure

to come into each of our lives. If we are aware of our own humanity, it makes all the difference in the world as to how we respond when the failures come.

When Adam and Eve "failed," God was not resting or surprised. He allowed them to eat of the fruit. He allows all of us choice in our relationship to Him. He is not surprised nor is His plan thwarted when we fail.

If we never take on any challenges in which we can fail, then we tend to live "in a bubble," afraid of the environment and our response to all it holds. If we step out in areas even though we expect our share of failures, then we grow in experience and wisdom.

Thirdly, God uses our failures. Remember the familiar verse we quote so often? "In all things God works for good" (Romans 8:28). This verse does not apply only to "all successes." This means that the believer has an immeasurable privilege of having a Father who helps us learn and grow from any and every situation.

You may be thinking, "I know I'm not perfect, Jay!" And I agree that we know this intellectually. But I watch as we attempt to display our brand of perfection—what we wear, what we own, what we demand of one another, what we try to do ourselves, what we believe, what we think "critical" in the world. We display these preferences as if they are marks of our success or indicators of someone else's failure. Such behavior limits the world around us and limits our view of God.

I remember when I first started writing. I had lots of ideas to share, but I worried that the article or book wouldn't turn out "just right." I wasn't sure if I would choose the "best word." I felt immobilized by the limitations and failures I feared might lie ahead.

Then I read the biography of William Barclay who said that God had given him a second-rate mind. (I couldn't help but chuckle at that point! If *he's* got a second-rate mind, I'm in real trouble!) He never felt obligated to write the great English novel, and he was not too proud to write on demand! He said every book he wrote began with a phone conversation from someone who said, "Bill, would you write a book on. . . . "

This simple explanation saved my writing career! If you have to write the great American novel, then you never write anything. You focus on doing something "perfect" rather than responding to a need. You focus on "what if I fail" rather than allowing failure to be part of the process of maturity.

We are all going to experience failure. Allow God the privilege of growing you and loving you through those failures. And allow others the opportunity to fail.

■■■■■■■■ THOUGHT FOR THE HEART

I am afraid that I tend to chastise or judge myself or others in these relationships. I would like to begin to accept, allow, and even expect failure so that I can watch God work His good.

— *Jay Kesler*

RHYTHMS OF MY HEART

FAITHFULNESS

FAITHFUL IN THE DARK

"Even though I walk through the valley of the shadow of death, I will fear no evil, for You are with me; Your rod and Your staff, they comfort me." Psalm 23:4

Much of our travels down roads of recovery seem filled with treks through dark valleys. Valleys the psalmist spoke of that reflect the shadows of death. It is in these times that the darkness is so deep that we don't see God.

For most of us, darkness doesn't bring comfort. For many of us, darkness reminds us of bad things that have happened or fears that have long lurked within. Darkness has a habit of obscuring our way. The path is not clear and we cannot see the patches of cluttered confusion or unforeseen potholes.

En route, the psalmist spoke only one claim: the knowledge of the presence of God. As he sensed the road under his feet, his only choice was to walk forward. Nothing in his circumstance gave light, so he chose to focus on the Lord of Light.

We have the same choice as the psalmist. We often cry out, thinking we need to see and understand, but the darkness still encompasses us. We are asked simply to walk forward, trusting that God is there.

This Scripture brings to mind certain memories of nighttime camping and hiking adventures. Embarking up trails, my friends and I relied only on our guides. How could we trust them? How could we not! We were out alone in a place where we had to depend on the ability of our guides, and they came through. We were able to do this difficult activity because we could trust the ones who were leading us.

The psalmist seems to have accepted this very important part of his relationship with God. God designed roads for David—roads to walk with growth in mind. And sometimes God took His servant on "night hikes," where David's only option was to depend. The result? David was never let down by God. Instead, he was faithfully cared for in God's purposed design.

David had confidence that God would be with him on his journey. Faithfully, in the dark, David expected God's comfort and that is what he received.

Our relationship with God hinges on faithfulness—God's faithfulness to you and to me. Without any assurance that things will turn out the way we might desire, we are simply asked to depend on Him and to take comfort in His faithfulness. There is ample evidence that He will be there for us, just as He was for David.

Our Heavenly Father will surely invite us on spiritual night hikes. And we can count on the fact that, at times, those hikes will be difficult indeed. But we can also trust the Shepherd who will be our guide for the journey. He is faithful to guide, even in the darkest hour.

THOUGHT FOR THE HEART

I am having a difficult time trusting God's faithfulness in these areas of my life.

—Ellen Quarry

●
SIMPLE TRUST

"How long, O Lord? Will You forget me forever? How long will You hide Your face from me? How long must I wrestle with my thoughts and every day have sorrow in my heart? How long will my enemy triumph over me? Look on me and answer, O Lord my God. Give light to my eyes or I will sleep in death; my enemy will say, 'I have overcome him,' and my foes will rejoice when I fall. But I trust in Your unfailing love; my heart rejoices in Your salvation.

F A I T H F U L N E S S

I will sing to the Lord, for He has been good to me." Psalm 13

I have been "reinventing the wheel," so to speak, in the last few years. I have been working on "me" — trying to grow old gracefully and with wisdom.

I have realized, through the years, that elderly people can be divided into two groups: one is a group that many love, search out, and enjoy being around. The other is a group of people we try to avoid. I have committed myself to seek membership in the first group of individuals!

As part of this commitment, I joined an "ACOA" (Adult Children of Alcoholics) 12-step group several years ago. This has been one of the best things I have ever done, though it has not been easy.

The first step — admitting my life had become unmanageable — was fairly easy. Life has always been chaotic, so it was not hard to see how the chaos had left me out of control in recent years.

The second step — believing in a Power bigger than myself — was something that I have taught many people through the years. I fully believe that there is one God, the only true God; God, who brings order out of chaos.

Step three — turning my life and will over to God — proved to be a little more difficult to grasp. Twice I worked my way through this step, and each time I came to the conclusion that trusting God has been a habit of my life. Yet the book I am using clearly states, "If you've concluded that you are already trusting God, you aren't telling yourself the truth!"

One day I invited an Old Testament professor out to lunch and asked him what it means to trust God. My friend said that the root of the word *trust* means "to lean on something." Trust is a very "simple" word!

The professor then went on to say that in the Hebrew Scriptures, the longer we walk with God the greater the trust that God demands. Suddenly he got my attention.

It seems, as I take a look back, that the longer I have walked with God, the less I have needed to trust Him. I have hundreds of messages I can give to a group. I know which ones work and when. I have friends I know I can trust to help me in emergencies.

I have worked hard to build up a retirement account. And I am fairly comfortable that I can sustain my lifestyle in the coming years. As I go down the list, I realize that I have built a life that requires very little trust of God.

After my lunch with the professor, I began a process of once again learning to trust God. As a habit of each day, I want to learn to lean on Him.

The spring of 1992 found me teaching a class in cross-cultural studies. One of the themes I chose for the class was trusting God. We committed to one another that we, as a group, would "work" at trusting God. We had a great opportunity to practice that commitment!

Our major project for the semester was to spend ten days in Poland. With a language we did not know and a culture foreign to our own, we committed to place ourselves in God's hand—to serve, to learn, and to trust.

The trip went well. And the last weekend was spent in the mountains of southern Poland. Two of the young people with us had never experienced snow and were disappointed to find no snow on our excursion. We decided to "trust God" for snow, and it snowed all weekend! It snowed so hard that we became snowed in to our mountain retreat.

On our last day, I began to worry. A neighbor brought his horse and wagon to pull us out, so we stacked our luggage on the wagon and walked out of the mountains behind him. We arrived at the train station on time. One by one the bags came off the wagon and then . . .

"The train does not operate today," we heard in shaky

translation. It seemed that the tracks were in repair and we had twenty minutes to reach another station. I became angry and very frustrated with God.

Tired and ready to get home, I did not want to miss our train and our plane. I wanted to go home! And I guess my frustration showed on my cold, bearded face.

One of the students came up and put his arm in my arm and asked the question of our trip. "Phil, are we trusting God?" "Not right now," I replied, "but let's start again!" The nearest station was several kilometers away.

We put our luggage back on the wagon and trotted behind an old horse. After three kilometers we came to a highway. The man with the horse went up to a farmhouse and asked if we could get a ride to the station. That farmer took three students and the luggage.

Next, our friend stopped cars on the road. They too agreed to help these funny Americans until we all ended up at the right place at the right time.

Somehow the Lord made the clock stand still. We covered that distance with time to spare! And one more time, trusting God in the simple parts of life was honored.

I have missed trains and planes through the years. Many times trusting God requires waiting and patience and answers we might not understand at the time.

But if we will simplify our wants and be grateful for His offerings, if we will keep Him in mind as we rush through the tasks of the day, if we will trust Him with our well-being, if we will pause long enough to "check in" with our Father, He clearly comes through.

What a great lesson to grasp in my aging years, yes? And what a great lesson to pass on to those who will enjoy being around.

■■■■■■■■■■■■■ THOUGHT FOR THE HEART

I have a difficult time trusting You, Lord. And trusting You for the "little things" rarely even crosses my mind. I would like to commit my heart to leaning on those everlasting arms.

— Phil Hook

●

GOD'S SHOES

"How beautiful on the mountains are the feet of those who bring good news, who proclaim peace, who bring good tidings, who proclaim salvation, who say to Zion, 'Your God reigns!' " Isaiah 52:7

I am an observer of feet, in general, and shoes, in particular! I have found a man's shoes speak volumes about his personality, character, and the like. I can't help but cast a glance at the feet of people I meet — especially the feet of those I know well and love dearly.

The foot is a most humble part of the body! It is the epitome of lowliness (you can't get too much lower!). As looks go, it's in a kind of perpetual adolescent state: not exactly attractive, kind of awkward, and oddly proportioned. But functionally, nothing is more perfectly suited to its purpose than the foot!

The foot is highly sensitive and extremely agile. The foot is dirt-proof, waterproof, and almost fireproof. The foot rarely complains, although it's doing most of the heavy labor, and it almost never fears!

It is nothing short of miraculous that feet support and set into motion a body over thirty times their height and forty times their weight! When all is said and done, the feet are critical to our day-to-day living.

I am also intrigued with the way that we clothe these quiet servants of ours. Some shoes are sleek and well-polished fare. Some barely protect the foot from the dust of the earth. Still more are heavily constructed, thick and strong to protect the foot from heavy responsibilities.

Some shoes carry feet in colored array. Some provide their masters with an experience in style! While still others prepare the foot for just the right job. Yes, shoes play a very important role!

Our Lord has personally delivered "good news" to you and to me. With His life, death, and resurrection, He has taught us that we can accept His salvation. But there are still those who haven't heard.

God needs you and me to be His shoes! And the shoe that bespeaks the owner's greatest delight is the well-worn, comfortable, steady shoe. These shoes reveal something of the owner's interests, his habitual ways, his personal style, and above all, his humility. There is nothing that the worn, comfortable shoe declares more eloquently than the humility of its owner.

In the fulfillment of its loving duty, the comfortable shoe speaks in a language all its own. It says, "I am His and He is at home with me. I've been many places already with Him, and I'll walk with Him anywhere He wishes."

Be shoes on the feet of our Lord today. Be faithful to His teachings and purposes. Be comfortable in your gifts and ready to go with a simple, "Not my way, but Yours."

The feet of our Lord are beautiful . . . share the journey.

THOUGHT FOR THE HEART

For Your incredible orchestration of love, Lord, I thank You. I would like to be shoes on Your feet today—to serve You and share Your light to all around. Help me to remember the humility and strength of the feet. And help me to find great joy in serving You.

—Chris McCray

●
LET GOD BE GOD

"I will listen to what God the Lord will say; He promises peace to

F A I T H F U L N E S S

His people, His saints — but let them not return to folly. Surely His salvation is near to those who fear Him, that His glory may dwell in our land. Love and faithfulness meet together; righteousness and peace kiss each other. Faithfulness springs forth from the earth, and righteousness looks down from heaven. The Lord will indeed give what is good, and our land will yield its harvest. Righteousness goes before Him and prepares the way for His steps." Psalm 85:8-13

I've been working on understanding faith lately, and it isn't easy to grasp the concept! I have noticed, in recent years, that I want God's kingdom to be designed to suit me and my desires. I want God to fix things. And if He will not fix them, I want Him to tell me what He is doing and why. I want Him to let me in on His plan *now!*

I imagine that I am not alone in this struggle with faith. Probably some of you also wrestle with its everyday implications. We know that God is faithful, yet sometimes the knowledge just doesn't seem sufficient to suit our need for assurance. It is difficult, at times, to live by faith.

Job had to learn a lot about faith. What was Job's relationship to God? How did Job hang on during the horrible time in his life? After all, he lost his children, his possessions and, ultimately, his health.

Job did love the Lord, and He was called according to God's purposes. But that did not protect Job from pain. Even in his pain, he persistently called to God. Sometimes he cried out in rage at the pain, regretting that he had ever been born. Sometimes he recited his own deeds of righteousness. Sometimes he questioned why God was allowing this to occur.

When Job's friends insisted he was steeped in sin, Job was adamant about his own goodness. When Job's wife suggested that he curse God and die, Job refused.

Job acknowledged the justice of God, but he could not

accept that God would allow a righteous man to suffer such extreme loss and pain. Job's faith was in crisis. His life was in shambles. He needed God to respond to his cries for understanding. At last, God answered.

The reply Job received was nothing like what he expected. Instead of answering Job's questions directly, God asked Job some questions of His own.

"Where were you when I created the earth and its amazing creatures?" "Can you set the universe in motion and give the sea its boundaries?" "Are you able to give wisdom to the birds of the air, the beasts of the field, the fish of the sea?"

As Job listened to God, he realized how small his own understanding of life had been. He realized how little he had really understood about God. Job realized his place in the scheme of God's creation. He was a precious and unique child of the Creator.

Job at last understood what I am just coming to realize. God is sovereign! He is wise. And I am never going to be able to understand all that He does. Furthermore, God is not going to consult me about what He does at the moment I seek the consultation. He does not owe me bits of insight or explanation.

Implicit in the word *Lord* is sovereignty, and that is where faith begins. God is faithful to Himself, He is faithful to His creation, He is faithful to His children. He is Lord.

Faith is all about giving up what I think I need and welcoming what God knows I need. Faith is all about letting God be God.

■■■■■■■■■■ THOUGHT FOR THE HEART

Job learned a secret about faith that I too long to learn. I want to trust God's faithfulness. I want to live, "He is Lord."

—Carolyn Means

F A I T H F U L N E S S

•
YOU HAVE WHAT YOU NEED

"And my God will meet all your needs according to His glorious riches in Christ Jesus." Philippians 4:19

I was standing on the steps of the main building at Wheaton College, looking at a 1967 red and white Cougar with California license plates. I didn't know the boy who was driving, but I knew the girl who climbed in beside him.

Wendy was brilliant. An "A" student among "A" students. And she was deeply troubled. She had gotten into many difficulties and her behavior became such that it was time for her to leave school.

I had spent many hours with her throughout the semester. She even baby-sat our children. But there seemed no way to help as I watched her drive away. A deep sense of failure filled my heart and mind.

My wife and I prayed for Wendy often, but there was no news from her for a long period of time. I'm still not certain all that she experienced during the silence, but God graced us with her presence once again.

Several years later, a letter arrived in the mail. She was a student at one of the University of California branches and she had met a couple there who opened their home and their hearts to students. Wendy had found a place to belong. And in spending time with them, Wendy got her life with the Lord straightened out.

Our whole family was ecstatic, and we reestablished our communication with her right away. She began to write me a letter every three or four weeks, keeping me up to date on what was happening in her life. The letters would always finish with a sermon "Wendy style." She said I'd preached to her so many times she owed me some!

One day Wendy's letter concluded this way.

"My sermon for you this time is nine words long, so get ready! If you ain't got it, you don't need it." (It was her paraphrase of Philippians 4.)

Wendy's little sermon has become the basis for many of my more elaborate sermons. And it has stayed in the forefront of my mind ever since it was delivered.

I have a great tendency to start my thoughts with the words, "if only" or "when." Those two phrases explain that I can't do what I should do today because I don't have what I need and I'll be able to do what I should do just as soon as I get what I need! Confused?

In other words, I am great at making excuses for my behavior or lack thereof, but the truth is simple. God has promised that I already have everything that I need in order to do what He wants me to do.

I know that life doesn't seem to be summarized in those nine words very often, but I encourage you not to forget Wendy's sermon. If we wait for the circumstances and ingredients to be "just right," we'll never act on what God is doing right now.

God gives us what we need. That's a promise.

THOUGHT FOR THE HEART

This is what I have right now . . . and I'll do my best to accept that this is also what I need.

— Phil Hook

●
"I LOVE YOU"

"Shadrach, Meshach, and Abednego replied to the king, 'O Nebuchadnezzar, we do not need to defend ourselves before you in this matter. If we are thrown into the blazing furnace, the God we serve is able to save us from it, and He will rescue us from your hand, O king. But even if He does not, we want you to know, O king, that

we will not serve your gods or worship the image of gold you have set up." Daniel 3:16-18.

I overheard a conversation one day that inspired me to do some thinking. I was cooling down after a brisk walk when I heard a young man speaking to a gentleman his senior.

"We're much more sophisticated these days," he said. "We can travel anywhere; we make more money. We are much better educated and we have so many opportunities. Life is much better now than when you grew up, Pop." And with that the grandfather smiled.

"Tell me, son," the grandfather spoke ever so respectfully to this young man he loved. "Do you think people love each other more today than we did yesterday? Do you think people love God more now than when I was young? Do you think people are more true to their convictions these days?"

Interesting questions, yes? I certainly found the conversation thought-provoking.

At first glance, life does seem better than it used to be. We certainly do have more amenities and choices. And I must admit that I enjoy many of the pleasures which have come with time and technology. But what makes life better? What makes life worthwhile? What is truly important for you and me?

The Israelites were defeated. Sadly, the battle didn't take much effort on the part of Nebuchadnezzar. This ruler of Babylon had many advantages, so Israel's Southern Kingdom fell in stages—the land, the temple, the people were all affected by Babylon's rule.

In the midst of captivity stood four young Hebrew boys: Daniel, Hananiah, Mishael, and Azariah. They were considered the "cream of the crop" and Nebuchadnezzar wanted only the best. He summoned these four young men wth a plan to train and "perfect" them for his services. He gave them new names: Belteshazzar, Shadrach, Meshach, and Abednego.

As I learn about these young men, I am amazed by their commitment and dedication. I can only surmise what I would have done in their place, but I am not at all certain that my maturity would have prepared me for such a task. In their late teens, these young men exhibited a faithfulness to God that is almost unprecedented. They stepped into their new role with grace and quiet determination.

You've heard the story before, I am sure, so I'll spare you the specific details. Just step back with me, for a moment, to a time and place when three of the four boys were threatened with extinction.

"As soon as you hear the sound of the horn, flute, zither, lyre, harp, and all kinds of music, you must fall down and worship the image of gold that King Nebuchadnezzar has set up. Whoever does not fall down and worship will immediately be thrown into a blazing furnace" (Daniel 3:5-6).

The ultimate test of allegiance was placed before these young men. For Shadrach, Meshach, and Abednego the choice was cut and dried. Either bow down to an idol created by the king—or die.

Perhaps the three remembered all they had been taught by their fathers and mothers. Perhaps the young men recalled the stories of Israel, persecuted and held in captivity. Perhaps they simply loved God and wanted to please Him.

For whatever reason, these young men made a choice that day that has long since affected the lives of people like you and me. In the face of persecution, they chose not to bow down. They chose not to excuse. They chose not to falter in the faith of their fathers.

Faithfulness grows out of simple commitment. Faithfulness grows out of love. Faithfulness is a condition of the heart, not a decision of logic. Faithfulness is a promise God makes to His people, and a privilege He enjoys in return.

We do know more these days. We've all been exposed to far more information than those who lived before us. We are more sophisticated, more traveled, more rewarded, and more educated. We are more exposed to life's offerings.

But I'm not so sure we are "better." It's hard to get any better than three young men who risked their earthly lives to stay faithful to their God.

Faithfulness grows out of relationship. It's a wonderful gift to present to God. And it's a gift that need not be measured, classified, or compared.

Faithfulness is a gift that says, simply and clearly, "I love You."

━━━━━━━━ **THOUGHT FOR THE HEART**

It is difficult for me to feel like I'm being faithful to God right now. I am struggling with some of the circumstances God is allowing in my life. I will think about these young Israelites and ask God for a touch of their courage and perspective.

— Shelley Chapin

●
THE IMPORTANCE OF DISCIPLINE

"I have fought the good fight. I have finished the race. I have kept the faith." 2 Timothy 4:7

While walking along the beach in southern Florida, one sees some unusual sights! As I took my morning walk, I observed people of all sizes, shapes, and age-groups and I was impressed! Most of the people much older than me were taking walking *seriously!* They were not out for a leisurely stroll along the water; they were working with great dedication!

I was walking at a good pace myself (or so I thought!) until a couple of seventy-five-year-old ladies passed me by! Then I began to take notice! I even watched as some men went the length of the beach several times. They did so with the commitment of one who is training for a marathon race!

Have you ever considered how important discipline is to the Christian life? We often talk about God's faithfulness, but we rarely talk about our own! Yet if we expect to grow in faith and become strong, it takes some responsibility and faithfulness on our part!

God doesn't wake us up and knock us out of bed in the morning and say, "Get up and pray!" Nor does He tie us into a chair and say, "You're not getting up until you read the Bible!" He doesn't even give us a wake-up call so that we won't miss church or Bible study or time alone. God respects our decisions.

I wish good marriages automatically happened, but they don't. I wish God would leave a sermon on my desk each Thursday, but He doesn't. I wish we could be good parents simply by wanting to be, but that's not the way this system works!

The Apostle Paul knew this secret about faithfulness. He understood that just because of his calling or the great things God had done through his ministry, there was no coasting! He had to work at keeping his relationship with the Lord fresh. He had to keep running the race (1 Corinthians 9:24-27). He had to remain faithful to that which he had begun.

To be faithful to God is to offer Him a great gift. This doesn't mean that we have to pretend to like everything that happens. It doesn't mean that we shouldn't cry or struggle or question. Faithfulness to God is a commitment to trust His leading and to act on that which we know to be true about Him.

Don't wait for some "zap" from heaven to make life perfect. Don't look for an emotional experience to bring you to spiritual maturity.

God has given us a Book and a living example of life-changing principles. Let's commit to faithfully following that which He has provided.

If you need some inspiration, go to a beach or a mall and watch some senior citizens walk! Or focus on men and women like Paul, Daniel, Joseph, Hannah, Esther, and Ruth. It is a privilege to offer God the blessed gift of faithfulness.

THOUGHT FOR THE HEART

I have been thinking about my responsibilities in my relationship with God. I'd like to begin to focus on these aspects of running a good race faithfully.

— *David Lynch*

THE OBJECT OF OUR COMMITMENT

"Go, gather together all the Jews who are in Susa, and fast for me. Do not eat or drink for three days, night or day. I and my maids will fast as you do. When this is done, I will go to the king, even though it is against the law. And if I perish, I perish." Esther 4:16

I am haunted by the memory of Cynthia's pain. She was a beautiful and talented young Christian girl whom I'd known and loved for several years. I knew Cynthia was valuable, but Cynthia didn't believe in her worth. She thought she did not belong anywhere.

Cynthia had grown up early. She didn't have a mom

and a dad who spent time with her, listened to her, and cared about her world. Instead, she had to take care of herself. She had to be the adult. There was only one problem: Cynthia wasn't an adult. She needed someone to love and guide her.

By the time Cynthia was in high school, she had long since ceased to make wise decisions. She had much knowledge and experience, but no love and direction. Such was the setting that led up to one of the most painful situations in Cynthia's life.

There was a knock on my door one night. I opened it to see Cynthia standing there. She was literally shaking and in tears as she pushed past the door and into my home. She locked herself in the bathroom and, in a story that took several hours to unfold, told me of the day's events.

Cynthia had been pregnant. She had not known what to do. She had chosen to have an abortion that day. She had suffered all alone. My heart literally sank with grief for the pain I saw etched on her face.

We talk about how much "older" our children are today than when we were young. They look more mature, they want to be treated as adults at a far younger age. They are educated in issues we didn't even *want* to know about. And they speak a language which far surpasses the extent of our former experience.

When I take a look at all that our adolescent culture knows and is exposed to on a daily basis, it is easy to agree that, "Yes, our young people are growing up faster than we did." But when the definition of "growing up" changes from faithfulness, commitment, and love to exposure, independence, and opportunity, I'm not so certain our societies have made great strides.

Children sell and deliver drugs for adults since children can only be charged as minors. Children have abortions. Children give birth to children. Children fend for themselves on the streets. And children of all ages, cultures, and financial status put their lives and their hearts at risk to simply belong somewhere.

Young Esther had only one person in her life she could trust. We don't know the details of her family history, we simply know that she was raised by her cousin, Mordecai. And we know that he was faithful to Esther and that he loved her. We also know that Mordecai loved God and was highly concerned about the mistreatment of God's people.

King Xerxes was what we might call a typical king in his day—more concerned with himself and his own happiness than most anything else. When his wife refused to honor him in the way the law required, he had her put away and the search was on for someone beautiful to replace the queen. To make a long story short, Mordecai volunteered Esther for the pageant.

For months, Esther was primped, preened, and otherwise prepared for her suitor. And she won the gaze of the king. He liked Esther more than any other woman, and she became queen.

God has a great sense of irony, doesn't He? The king, whose servants were persecuting the Jews, married a young Jewess—a fact he did not even realize nor think about. Mordecai was not so unaware. He knew that a Jew in the house of the king might very well provide the Jewish population with a voice. Mordecai could see no other way to rescue his people and so he begged Esther's help.

This request might seem small to us unless we recall that the queen was not allowed to speak to the king unless she was invited. Esther had no such invitation, so to talk with Xerxes might mean death. Mordecai knew the risks. He laid out the facts and left Esther alone to pray.

Despite the risk, this young woman put her own well-being aside for the greatest cause one could serve. She chose to be faithful to God, no matter what the cost.

How sad I feel when I compare Esther's cause to that of so many young people today. We have children starving their bodies to look lean and in fashion. We have children who are too afraid to "just say no" to boyfriends, girlfriends, drugs, or peer pressure. We have children who are too afraid to live out their own true convictions. We have children carrying guns and killing other children. And we have the Cynthias, who are all grown up yet not grown up at all.

Take a look at that to which you are committed these days. I don't mean to paint a bleak portrait, merely one of observation. We are all faithful; it is simply a matter of what or who we choose as the object of our faithfulness.

Ask your heart if your faithfulness is spent on the only Person that matters. Ask your heart if it's ready to spend your faithfulness on God. And if you have been blessed with children or grandchildren, ask God to help you write love on their hearts. There is no greater purpose than His.

THOUGHT FOR THE HEART

Lord, I know You must compete, from time to time, with my friends, fortune, dreams, or pride. I would like to honor You as Esther did. I would like to offer You my true devotion. And, Lord, thank You for being faithful to me.

— Shelley Chapin

RHYTHMS OF MY HEART

● CALM IN THE STORM

"A furious squall came up, and the waves broke over the boat, so that it was nearly swamped. Jesus was in the stern, sleeping on a cushion. The disciples woke Him and said to Him, 'Teacher, don't You care if we drown?' " Mark 4:37-38

I have no idea what kinds of things move you to fear, but I can tell you that there are several situations which are sure to inspire fear in me. One of those fear-inspirers for me is found high in the sky, up above all other movement. I am not a great fan of flying.

Though not exactly enamored with the idea, I said yes one day when a church member offered to fly me and a friend to a nearby town for lunch. The appointed day came and the sky was blue, so I felt relieved. After all, blue skies and bright sun make for a perfect flying day, right? Not exactly!

I soon learned that a low cloud cover causes turbulence and that even though the sky is blue, the air can be quite bumpy. As we took off for our getaway, the pilot advised that the ride would be rough, and rough it was. As the small plane bounced and swayed, I held on tightly to the arm rest. *I* felt fear, but as I gazed at the face of my pilot friend, I knew he was assured. The one in charge was not at all disturbed by the turbulence.

Our bumpy ride that day reminded me of one boat ride taken by the disciples and our Lord. Everything was fine until the storm hit, then all of the disciples grew fearful and distraught. I can understand their anxiety, but Jesus didn't seem disturbed by the storm.

Jesus was asleep in the back of the boat, a fact I'm grateful was not duplicated in my airplane story! And the more the disciples feared, the more frustrated they became with Jesus' seeming lack of sensitivity to the situation. How could He be so calm when they were experiencing such fear?

Our Lord was calm because He was in control. The storm didn't bother Him any more than a little turbulence worried my pilot-friend. It was me and the disciples who let our fear get the best of us!

I relaxed a few times on the return trip, and I am trying to learn to relax on life's journey as well. There are many situations I can fear, but my fear belies a very important truth.

God is in control of our lives. The turbulent situations of life do not catch Him off guard. He is in control—always. And He never tires of graciously reminding us that He will not leave us or forsake us.

There is no storm we face that Jesus hasn't already weathered. And He promises to accompany us through everything we experience. Perhaps this assurance can soothe our fears and provide us with calm in the midst of the storm.

THOUGHT FOR THE HEART

These are the storms of life in which I feel most afraid. I would like to invite Jesus to accompany me in these fears.

—David Lynch

●
IN THE LAND OF FEAR

"A word was secretly brought to me, my ears caught a whisper of it. Amid disquieting dreams in the night, when deep sleep falls on men, fear and trembling seized me and made all my bones shake."
Job 4:12-14

Dictionary definitions of "garden variety" fear do not do justice to the emotion that can paralyze even the strongest of individuals. Can even the unabridged version adequately describe the knot in the stomach or "weak in the knees" feeling that appears when fear steps in? Can any written words portray that sense of "bounce off the walls" panic or futile paralysis that so often handcuffs you and me to even the most basic bouts with fear? No way!

We express these clarifying questions as ones who have had virtual "careers in fear." Admittedly, we haven't always been cooperative slaves of fear. Quite often we have looked fear full in the face and done something very courageous or bold—occasionally even risky! But, just at the point of congratulating ourselves for overcoming our burden, that old familiar fear tracks us down and "blindsides" us again. And we find ourselves doubly ashamed at descending into the snakepit of fear once more.

Somewhere along the ongoing treadmill of fear, a radical thought occurred to us: *Maybe the forces of fear aren't an elite unit! Maybe most people experience fear. Maybe we are not so alone after all!* We liked this newfound theory and decided to test its validity.

One hesitant interview after another revealed a fellow pilgrim in the land of fear, and this helped us deal with our sense of aloneness and shame. Our discovery also convinced us of the reality that fear is a chronic condition that will never completely go away or leave any of us at peace. The chronic condition of fear is one that we must recognize and evaluate—not one that we can expel at will.

Perhaps you too see yourself as a "fearful" person. Perhaps you too have tried and subsequently failed to conquer your fear through all of the prescribed means. Perhaps you too have doubted your own spirituality and value due to that feeling we call fear.

Paul understood the anxiety as well as the longing to overcome. Yes, Paul, who penned those familiar words,

F E A R

"Do not be anxious about anything" (Philippians 4:6), found himself to be anxious when in Troas without a friend (see "Failure" reading by Phil Hook). The "door" for Paul's evangelism was open. People were willing to hear. And Paul walked away! He felt anxious being there without Titus.

Paul also understood fear through the eyes of his young friend, Timothy. Paul believed in Timothy, taught him well, and even wrote regularly to encourage his disciple. Still, Timothy struggled with fear from time to time and Paul did not chide or chastise the nervous pastor. Paul advised Timothy to "take a little wine" for his stomach (1 Timothy 5:23), then keep on keeping on.

Some of us struggle with feelings of fear more than others. Perhaps we have been physically or emotionally harmed by someone. Perhaps we have been misunderstood or punished or mocked for our needs. Perhaps we just feel inadequate in the midst of a very big world.

Take heart. God understands our fear. Job, David, Jeremiah, Isaiah, Hosea, Abraham, Sarah, Hannah, Peter, Timothy, Mary Magdalene, and Mary, mother of our Lord, all had their bouts with fear. And all were sustained by the understanding, the mercy, and the kindness of our Lord.

Talk to God about your fears. Give them a name. Allow Him to help you explore the source and allow His love to be your guide. God is kind to those He loves, so please be kind to you as well. He will lead you in triumphal procession!

■■■■■■■■■ THOUGHT FOR THE HEART

I am aware of feeling fear in these specific areas of my life. I would like to invite God to walk with me in these fears.

—*Boyd Luter & Shelley Chapin*

F E A R

●
"FEAR MONSTERS"

"Moses answered the people, 'Do not be afraid. Stand firm and you will see the deliverance the Lord will bring you today. The Egyptians you see today you will never see again. The Lord will fight for you; you need only to be still." Exodus 14:13-14

I once overheard a teacher talking to the children in her class about "fear monsters." They knew right away what she was talking about. Fear monsters are those creatures that hide under your bed and in your closet. They usually creep out when it's dark and when you're all alone, and they're very hairy and scary!

The unfortunate thing is that fear monsters do not stay behind with our childhood! We bring them with us into adulthood. Fear monsters seem to enjoy hanging around in the misty dark of the unknown—an uncertain economy, potential environmental disasters, global political instability, and other social, political, or personal struggles. These monsters may not be hairy and scary, but they are just as intimidating.

We may fear failing in our marriage or on the job. There is the fear of blowing it once again in a promise we have made to ourselves or to someone we love. Fear monsters come in all shapes and sizes, and they do not stay in the closet or under the bed! They are parasites which draw their nourishment at our expense.

Moses was a man who was acquainted with fear monsters. Could this be the same man who made the bold statement recorded in Exodus 14:13-14?

In Exodus 3, God instructed Moses to bring the Israelites out of Egypt, but the fear within Moses was greater than his confidence in God. The fear monsters each spoke in turn to the prophet.

FEAR

"Who am I to do this?" "How do I know God won't let me down?" "What if they don't believe me or listen to me?" "And what if they kill me?" "Lord, You know how weak I am in this area." "Maybe You ought to send someone else!"

In response to each of the fears, God spoke with strength, confidence, and faithfulness. "I will be with you," He assured His servant. "I am who I am! The God of Abraham, Isaac, and Jacob has appeared to you. I will help you speak and will teach you what to say."

Fear monsters are not easily pried off our bodies, but God is a God of patience and understanding. God walked alongside Moses in the middle of his fears, and Moses began to see and experience a God of strength. Yes, God worked His oil of peace into Moses' fearful skin until one day the prophet himself was able to say to a people paralyzed by fear:

"Do not be afraid . . . the Lord will fight for you."

■■■■■■■■■■■■■ THOUGHT FOR THE HEART

I have several fear monsters hiding in my closet. Lord, fight for me!

— Shelly Cunningham

•

JUST STAND UP

"I can do everything through Him who gives me strength." Philippians 4:13

It was a normal day in chapel. I walked into the side entrance where the president, the speaker, and the musician wait for chapel to begin. Dr. Edman was in his last years as president of Wheaton College and his eyesight was already poor.

"Is that you, Phil?" Dr. Edman asked.

FEAR

"Yes, sir," I replied, a little unnerved by the tone in his voice.

"Would you sit on the platform with me this morning?"

"Uh, certainly, sir," I answered. How could I say no?

There were five chairs on that platform. I knew them well from months of sitting through the services. The middle chair was always occupied by the president. To his right, the speaker would be seated and to *his* right, the song leader. The other two chairs needed to be filled, and I was a designated "filler" for the morning.

It was my first year on the Wheaton faculty, and I definitely felt out of place in that seat. I have often said jokingly that I could not have met the entrance requirements of the students, so I had to come to Wheaton as a faculty member! I spent most of my time that first year feeling very afraid.

I was the last person to walk out on the platform and I took the end seat. It was time for chapel to begin.

As usual, the chapel was full of students and the balcony full of guests. There were probably well over 2,000 people there that day, and I knew each person was aware of my discomfort. I had never sat on a platform with that many people in my life!

The organist began to play, and the time-honored tradition said that we were all to stand and sing the first stanza of an old, familiar hymn. I heard the introduction, knew the hymn, but when it was time to stand I had a problem. My legs literally would not work. My body was frozen!

My father had always pastored small churches. I had never seen a crowd like this. And all I could think about was the panic in the pit of my stomach. What was I going to do if my legs wouldn't cooperate?

A quick check of all systems told me my arms were willing even though my legs were not, so I used my arms to push myself out of the chair. I was able to stand for the

FEAR

song, and when it was done I sat down in my refuge again, thankful that the only thing I had to do in chapel that day was accomplished.

One of the frequent phrases in the Scriptures is "Don't be afraid." The angel spoke those words to Zechariah and Mary, John and the shepherds. Jesus spoke the words to His disciples. The refrain is repeated frequently.

When I read the words, however, my reaction is, "Who wouldn't be afraid?" If an angel were speaking to you or a storm were about to overtake your boat, fear would be a fairly natural response! And particularly it has been a natural response for me.

Fear was one of the governing emotions of my life: fear of not being accepted, fear of failure, fear of not performing well before a crowd. Fear had frequently paralyzed my mind and body, and on this day in chapel I began to come face-to-face with that paralyzing fear.

I imagine you too might wrestle with fear from time to time. I don't think God is trying to be insensitive when He says, "Don't be afraid." I think He simply knows that He is in control and that He will provide the strength to enable us to face whatever it is that we fear.

I have found Him adequate to give me the courage I need, and I encourage you to give Him a chance to support you as well.

Though it isn't easy to do, perhaps all God asks is that we just "stand up."

■■■■■■■■■■■■■■■ THOUGHT FOR THE HEART

I am aware of feeling afraid in these areas of my life. I will try to "just stand up" and let God do the rest.

—*Phil Hook*

239

FEAR

●
WHAT GOD PROVIDES

"For God did not give us a spirit of timidity, but a spirit of power, of love, and of self-discipline." 2 Timothy 1:7

My thoughts turned to the audience as chapel ended that day. I had been asked to sit with the college president on the platform and as I looked out at the students, a thought crossed my mind that left me paralyzed with fear.

Someday, I'm going to have to speak in chapel, I thought. *Faculty members are expected to speak in chapel, and I'm a faculty member!* It was a brilliant deduction—and one that left me cold.

I left the stage and quickly dismissed the fear. After all, surely it would be a long time before I was asked to speak.

This is my first year, I thought, *so I should be safe. There are plenty of experienced faculty members who are sure to be invited before me.*

I was sitting in my office near the end of second semester when the phone rang. It was Dr. Earl Cairns, then chairman of the Chapel Committee. He wanted me to speak in chapel during the last week of the semester. It is not a request that one turns down!

As I hung up the receiver, the paralyzing fear gripped my body. I immediately began to prepare the message, and within a few hours it was ready. I preached the words to myself hourly, daily, constantly. In the tradition of fearful people, I overprepared and then overprepared some more!

The best way to describe my fear is to say that it was dangerous to be away from the bathroom long enough to drive to school, and I was only fifteen minutes away! My stomach was literally tied in knots.

The day came for my chapel engagement. Many people

240

were praying for me and I was certainly praying for God's very gracious blessing. I walked out onto the stage, sat in my chair, and waited.

The Lord blessed the time. Funny, isn't it, how we're always surprised when God fulfills His commitments to us? I was relieved to be "done" but, horror of horrors, they invited me to speak again. Fortunately, summer vacation intervened.

When I next spoke in chapel the following fall, the process was a carbon copy of the first time. I was fearful, God blessed me, and I was invited again! Somehow I had to deal with my fear.

One day as I was standing behind the platform, waiting to speak, I struggled with an important decision. Should I go to the bathroom one more time before I reached the platform? After all, if I waited it might be too late!

The platform won. It was time. And as I began to walk up the four steps, it was as if the Lord spoke to my heart.

"Phil, whose message are you giving?"

Yours, Lord, my heart replied.

"Whose people are you talking to?" He seemed to ask again.

Yours, Lord, I thought.

"Then why are you so afraid?"

The Lord brought the verse in 2 Timothy to mind. God gives a spirit of power (the ability to do what we need to do), a spirit of love (the reason to do what we need to do), and a spirit of disciplined thinking (the mind to do what we need to do).

There's no way to explain it, but my fear disappeared on the way to the platform that day. When I finally gained perspective, I was able to see myself not in the fears of my childhood, but in the ability of God's Spirit.

I have since lived many years and I still wrestle with fear. But I have not forgotten the power, love, and discipline that are provided for me by my God.

These are some of the areas in which I struggle with fear. I would like to learn more about the power, love, and discipline that God offers.

— *Phil Hook*

●

FEAR OF THE UNKNOWN

"Immediately Jesus reached out His hand and caught [Peter]. 'You of little faith,' He said, 'why did you doubt?' And when they climbed into the boat, the wind died down. Then those who were in the boat worshiped Him, saying, 'Truly You are the Son of God.' "
Matthew 14:31-33

One of my best emotions is fear. It's true! For as long as I can remember, I have been very good at feeling fear!

I was almost always afraid in my room at night. I thought "something" lived under the bed, in the closet, down the hall, and in our yard. I knew that "something" only came out at night, and I was certain that "something" knew whether or not my parents were sleeping!

I can't help but smile each time I read of Peter's first steps on water. I guess I relate to Peter because of my own propensity to speak first and think later. Peter was energetic and enthusiastic, and he often volunteered his opinion way before it was prudent to even have one!

It had been a long day. John the Baptist literally lost his life to a promise that should not have been made, and Jesus was grieving the loss of his lifetime friend. Our Lord withdrew to a solitary place to pray, but He did not find solitude. He found, instead, the crowds who needed Him. He set *His* needs aside and began to care for *their* needs.

FEAR

As evening approached, the disciples wanted Jesus to send the crowds away.

"This is a remote place," they argued, "and it is already late. Let them go to a nearby village and buy food." Jesus heard their request and responded with an idea they had not entertained.

"You feed them," He suggested. "They do not need to go anywhere else for food." The disciples stared at their teacher, frustrated and probably a bit angry. I imagine more than one was thinking, "Why doesn't He ever take care of *our* needs?"

The feeding that followed has served to touch hearts and minds for two millennia. Well over 5,000 men, women, and children were fed that night—with just five loaves of bread and two fish. The disciples had much yet to learn.

When everyone was satisfied, Jesus sent the disciples ahead in the boat. After everyone else was satisfied, He took time for Himself—time to grieve John's death and to prepare His own heart. He took time alone with the Father for restoration. And when this time was over, He took the shortest path to His friends.

Enter: worry and the unknown. The disciples were out on the water alone at night without their Teacher, so I imagine they were just a bit concerned. They probably wondered where He had gone, how they would find Him, what He was doing. And then, as if someone were playing a trick on them, their eyes beheld a figure, walking on water.

"It's a ghost," they cried in fear (sounds a bit like my childhood speculations about "something"). They literally cried out in their terror and they had no place to run.

"Don't be afraid," Jesus quickly assured. "It is I!" I would give anything to see their faces as He walked closer and closer to the boat.

Did they try to pretend they weren't really afraid? Did

they release each other and straighten their clothing in embarrassment? Did they wonder if they were losing their minds?

"Lord, if it is You, tell me to come to You on the water." Leave it to Peter to break the silence and think of such a request!

"Come," Jesus replied. And Peter jumped right out there in the middle of the lake.

Enter once again: worry and the unknown. Peter immediately began to walk, and he was thrilled! But he also had a problem. Men cannot walk on water! Men sink if they try! Men who try to walk on water are not very bright! At that precise moment, the beloved disciple began to sink in his fear.

Fear is a powerful emotion. It grows out of our own system of worry, anxiety, concern, and beliefs. And when that worry is mixed with some unknown, the reaction can be overwhelming.

I don't know about you, but my fears have matured right along with my body and mind. No longer do I fear "something" and his under-my-bed or in-my-closet domain. Now I fear people and situations and those things which fall totally out of the realm of my control.

My fears have changed, but God's response has not. "Do not be afraid, it is I" still applies today just as much as it did 2,000 years ago on that midnight boat ride.

God can be trusted. There is no unknown to Him. And He is always in control.

I won't suggest that you never be afraid, because I know that both you and I will have our moments. I simply want to suggest that you store His words in the memory banks of your heart. He is there, and He will never let you out of His sight.

F E A R

*I do feel afraid at times. I find I am particularly fearful of these pos-
sibilities or these people. Lord, help me to come to You before sinking in my own anxieties.*

— *Shelley Chapin*

•
WORKING THROUGH OUR FEARS

*"Why is life given to a man whose way is hidden, whom God has
hedged in? For sighing comes to me instead of food; my groans
pour out like water. What I feared has come upon me; what I dread-
ed has happened to me. I have no peace, no quietness; I have no rest
but only turmoil." Job 3:23-26*

Fear is a powerful emotion. Fear can cause even the most
rational of individuals to act in ways that are not explained by the reasonable mind. But when fear is married
to lack of intelligence or lack of exposure, the result can be
ridiculous — or devastating.

I've encountered fear many times through my years of
treating medical conditions in Third World countries. People there do not have the information of a more developed world nor the capabilities. In general, their wisdom
is passed down from generation to generation.

Sometimes the shared wisdom is life-transforming and
can teach us all a valuable lesson. Sometimes the information is based on speculation or fear alone. It is the latter
beliefs that are so hard to crack and which often do so
much damage.

I recall my first exposure to motherhood in Haiti. The
weather there is hot and humid, yet the babies were
always wrapped in clothing suitable for a harsh winter. I
would undress the baby for examination and the mother

would immediately return the child to its "tomb." Try as I might, I could not break that tradition. Mothers insisted that the clothing was necessary to protect the baby from harm.

I also recall going to a home late at night to answer a cry for help. A young child in the home was ill with malaria. His fever was high and the night was blistering.

I noticed as I approached the home that all of the shutters were closed tight and that a light was on in the window. The home was tiny in size and very hot when I entered, so I suggested they open the shutters. A look of fear crossed the mother's face. She would not even consider such a thing! By opening the shutters she would be inviting demons to enter her home. How could I possibly fight that belief?

Fear comes in all shapes and sizes. I can mock another man's fear, but when it comes to my own, there is nothing funny about the feeling.

Possibly you have some fears of your own. Perhaps you're afraid to let your child grow up and face the world. Perhaps you're afraid to fly. Perhaps you fear the night hours or driving in heavy traffic on the freeway. Perhaps you fear growing old.

My encouragement is simply this. Examine your fears. I don't believe that we must strive to eradicate all fears from our experience, but I do believe that an unexamined fear is hazardous to our emotional and, often, physical well-being.

Examine your fears. Allow God to work with you to grow through those which seem manageable right now. A resolved fear can make the difference between a cool, refreshing breeze or a hothouse of unbridled terror.

THOUGHT FOR THE HEART

I would like to work through my fears, and there are a few, in par-

ticular, that I feel ready to examine. Lord, help me to enter my fears with Your truth and perspective as my guide.

—Pamela M. Reeves

●

SHRINKING FEARS DOWN TO SIZE

"The fear of the Lord is the beginning of wisdom, and knowledge of the Holy One is understanding." Proverbs 9:10

Unlike my father, who retired from the U.S. Army after twenty-five years of service, it is not so easy to resign from the ranks of fear. Even if I seek an honorable discharge, fear never lets me go without a fight.

Make no mistake, though . . . while fear may grow to seem "friendly" in its familiar companionship, it is no more a friend than any other taskmaster who demands servitude. Though a certain element of fear is healthy, fear that is "out of control" can devastate and manipulate us into actions and reactions which threaten to destroy.

So how can we deal with our fear? Where can we send those feelings which threaten to take over our very lives and relationships?

While fear can hurt us greatly, it can also be used for good purpose! Over and over again in Scripture, the anecdote to fear is faith and the interchangeable idea for faith is "the fear of the Lord!" In other words, the *object* of our fear makes all the difference as to the *outcome* of that fear and the feelings which accompany its presence!

The kind of fear that haunts our lives, sapping us of peace and joy, is fear of our circumstances or of people who have either hurt us or threaten to harm. The more we fear, the more those circumstances or people grow into giants, capable of all kinds of assaults on our strength. Our fears may even be well-supported, but the logic doesn't take away the overwhelming sense of discouragement.

On the other hand, "the fear of the Lord" whittles such situations back down to real-life size and disables their power to destroy our well-being. Our God is the biggest, strongest, most powerful Being in the universe. He is God. And no person on earth nor unresolved conflict can destroy or overpower the One who made us all.

I am not suggesting that you and I can walk away from all of our fears, simply by focusing on God. We still live here amid the circumstances and people who threaten harm and can often carry out the threat.

What I am suggesting is that focusing our attention on God Himself can help us to prioritize, to accept, to better comprehend and plan. And focusing our attention on our Heavenly Father can give us support through even the toughest of times.

My attention immediately turns to Job for an example of "the fear of the Lord." Though lost in the storm of his pain, Job finally turned toward God. And as Job began to listen to God's voice, he found purpose again—purpose for his pain and purpose for his life.

We are the children of God. And part of our inheritance includes the open invitation to wrap our emotional arms around our strong and caring Father. We have an ever-increasing trust fund of love and assurance available to us all, and such love and assurance help turn our focus off of this world's fears to our Father's provision.

The fear of the Lord is the beginning of wisdom for all who desire the gift. The fear of the Lord is the powerful reminder that God will take care of His own.

█████████████ THOUGHT FOR THE HEART

I would like these fears in my life to shrink to "real-life" size once again.

—Boyd Luter

FEAR

●
UNEXPECTED TURNS

"Now all has been heard; here is the conclusion of the matter: Fear God and keep His commandments, for this is the whole duty of man." Ecclesiastes 12:13

As Jesus rode into Jerusalem on a donkey that day, the people proclaimed Him a king. They welcomed Him as Messiah—Savior of the people! Yet as He went about the city over the next few days, the accolades faded away.

Jesus challenged the religious authorities. He threw money changers out of the temple. He made choices of His own, even when those choices conflicted with the law that the people had been taught. Finally, as He hung on a cross between two thieves, those who had proclaimed Him King mocked Him. Those closest to Him fled.

Had Jesus misrepresented Himself and His kingdom? No. Jesus had told people the truth, but few really listened. Had Jesus failed to prepare His disciples? No. Jesus had prepared His followers, but they grew frightened as He was arrested and taken away. His friends could not stay faithful when life took an unexpected turn.

I have never really put myself in the disciples' place. I know how the events of that week turned out, so I've never imagined I could truly understand those who ran in fear. Much like the men on the road to Emmaus on that Sunday long ago, I have seen myself as having the advantage of Scripture. After all, I have God's Word and 2,000 years of church history to confirm what Jesus said about Himself.

In recent years I have come to take a personal look at the events of Jesus' last week on earth. Through the struggle of some close friends, I have come to admit that I too am fearful. I don't really want to accept the kingdom on the terms Jesus offers. When I have prayed, "Thy kingdom come," I have really meant "*my* kingdom come."

Sometimes we get fearful about what God seems to be doing in our lives. Yet, Jesus was never fearful of circumstances. The only thing He seemed to struggle deeply with was separation from the Father.

Just as Jesus did not fear His Father's leading, He does not intend for us to feel afraid of His rule over us. When we can accept who we are and who God is, we will have peace and rejoice in His kingdom.

The disciples ran because they had expected the kingdom to be designed on their terms. They had expected God to fit their political and religious systems. They had expected God to fix their diseases. They had not expected God to turn their lives upside down.

Just like the disciples, we tend to turn away when the kingdom isn't like we want it to be. When the King keeps His plans hidden from us, we want to know what is going on. We fear the unknown.

Jesus answered the disciples' fears. He said, "Look at Me and be saved." "Give Me your life and you will gain new life, abundant and free." "Trust Me with your family, your health, your job." He answers our fears today, but it still isn't easy to let go.

Fear grows out of our own uncertainty that God will take care of our needs. The disciples felt comfortable with Him until storms arose or people walked on water or soldiers came to arrest. Fear says, "I'm not so sure of this person I am trusting."

You and I do have the advantage of Scripture. If we look back, we see that Jesus *did* take care of His followers. We see that He *did* prepare them, He *did* supply their need, He was fully trustworthy. Hindsight teaches us to release our fears; it is trusting God with the unknown that we find so difficult.

FEAR

It is normal to fear, but God does give the answer. He has given us Jesus as a perfect example of the relationship He desires for us to have with Him. As His children, we will have life. Our job is to love Him, to obey Him, and to trust Him.

It wasn't easy to be a disciple then! And it isn't easy to be you or me. God understands! He understands our fear, and He supplies our need.

THOUGHT FOR THE HEART

I do find that I fear the unknown — the way that God leads from time to time. Help me to trust You, Lord. Help me to trust Your love and provision.

—*Carolyn Means*

RHYTHMS OF MY HEART

FORGIVENESS

● SET THEM FREE

"Don't be afraid. Am I in the place of God? You intended to harm me, but God intended it for good to accomplish what is now being done, the saving of many lives." Genesis 50:19-20

One of my heroes of the faith has always been a young man named Joseph. He inspires me.

Born into a family wrought with strife and jealousy, Joseph was the "shining star" of a mother who longed to give birth to a child and a father who longed for a happy wife. For years the beloved wife, Rachel, had been barren while her sister, Leah, bore children to Jacob. And for years the jealousy had increased, threatening to rock the very foundations of the family.

Enter Joseph. At last God opened Rachel's womb and a baby boy was born. His mother smiled, his father felt relieved, and ten older brothers looked on as a new child was celebrated.

Through the years, Joseph was honored with special treatment. I doubt either mother realized the resentment that was brewing in the hearts of the brothers, but the fire grew hotter and hotter until one day those same brothers sold Joseph into slavery and told their father he had been killed. Ten men plotted a course that would influence the future of every family member, and the effect was sobering.

The specifics of Joseph's captivity are recorded in the Book of Genesis. In summary, Joseph was a man who tried to honor God and who suffered for his attempts. He was also rewarded in time, and given great responsibility because of his character and wisdom.

The years were good to Joseph's heart. I've never understood how he responded with forgiveness and grace, but that is exactly what he did. God fathered Joseph personally and the end result was a man who resembled our Lord, both in action and attitude. Joseph did not let the sin of his brothers destroy his life; instead, he took responsibility for his own pain and chose to set them free from their debt.

Any time we are freed from a debt that we owe, there are no words to describe the relief. And when we are freed from this debt without even asking, the gift is almost beyond comprehension.

Many years later, Joseph looked into the eyes of his brothers and extended forgiveness. He set them free. He demanded no payment in return, and he wasn't asking for gratitude. He forgave to honor the God he knew and loved.

I'm not sure if you are struggling with forgiveness right now, but I know I have times when I long to forgive but can't seem to escape the anger or the pain. Forgiveness itself often hurts, but the end result is an unburdened soul and a heart that is free to receive the grace that is daily ours through Christ.

Look around. Examine your heart and your hurts. Take note of those who might even deserve the "cold shoulder" or the careful avoidance.

Look around, and when the hurts pile up, offer forgiveness. Set people free.

THOUGHT FOR THE HEART

I have difficulty forgiving these people for these hurts, but I am willing to work on setting them (and myself) free.

— Shelley Chapin

●
ANYTHING BUT CHEAP

"Then He called the crowd to Him, along with His disciples and said, 'If anyone would come after Me, he must deny himself and

take up his cross and follow Me. For whoever wants to save his life will lose it, but whoever loses his life for Me and for the Gospel will save it.' "Mark 8:34-35

American military presence in the Philippine Islands was being phased out. We had been there for years, yet now it was time for our power to fade. A chaplain and his family who had served there for some time began to prepare for departure.

"There is much we haven't yet seen," they decided. "Let's spend our final days visiting the sights we've put off until now." The plan seemed like a good one.

It was Easter Sunday, not long after the family had made their resolution. The chaplain conducted four services and then threw the children into the car to head for downtown Manila. They wanted to see the Easter celebration at the great cathedral, and they were just in time for the final portion.

They parked as close as possible and began to make their way toward the square. As they walked along, they passed vendors who were selling all kinds of religious merchandise: candles, incense, veils, rosaries, prayer books and, of course, jewelry. They could hardly believe all the trinkets that were available for purchase in the middle of such a great event.

As the family rounded the final corner toward their goal, a surprise awaited them. There stood a man adorned in crucifixes! Yes, draped on every available appendage and piece of clothing were crosses of all shapes and sizes.

"CHEAP CROSSES FOR SALE," read the hand-lettered sign, hung crudely around the man's neck. "Cheap crosses sold here."

Can you imagine such a message, and on Easter! As if a cross could somehow be construed as "a bargain."

There was nothing cheap about the cross borne by our

Lord. It was an instrument of death, stained with blood and marked by the nails in His hands and feet. There was no bargain there.

In order to offer forgiveness, the price Jesus paid was immense. There is no human way to imagine, much less describe, the burden carried by our Lord. And yet He chose to carry the load in order to offer forgiveness.

Jesus had already prepared His disciples for the meaning of the cross. And He had extended the meaning to include those who would long to follow in His steps.

"If anyone would come after Me, he must deny himself, take up his cross and follow Me."

Is Jesus literally asking us to die on a cross? No. Nor is He suggesting that we strap ourselves to a piece of wood or carry a cross up a hill. Such an act would accomplish nothing—forgiveness is already ours!

Jesus is asking us to commit our lives to Him and to all that the cross meant and means. He is asking us to commit to forgiveness, reconciliation, and eternal perspectives. He is asking us to give up ownership to the only worthy Lord. He is asking us to align ourselves with His love and purposes.

Forgiveness is anything but cheap. It is the root of reconciliation and restoration. It is the foundation for Christianity. It is the great gift from our Lord that keeps on giving its gracious rewards.

We do not have "cheap crosses" or "cut-rate forgiveness" for sale. We have a Savior to share with the world whose love, death, resurrection, and life have set us free!

THOUGHT FOR THE HEART

I long to grasp the real meaning of forgiveness in my own life. And I long to pass this gift along to everyone I know.

—David Lynch

FORGIVENESS

•
WITH MATURITY'S VIEWPOINT

"If you love those who love you, what reward will you get? Are not even the tax collectors doing that? And if you greet only your brothers, what are you doing more than others? Do not even pagans do that? Be perfect, therefore, as your Heavenly Father is perfect." Matthew 5:46-48

God is perfect and we are not. It is that simple! God is perfect, but He is not a perfectionist. That is not so simple for us to remember! God is without sin by definition, but we struggle with sin from the moment we are born. Though it is difficult for us to comprehend, God, in His perfection, loves you and me! And though we could offer nothing in return, He chose, in His love, to offer forgiveness. Though we are weak, God is strong. He reaches out with love.

How can God be perfect and yet willingly offer forgiveness to you and to me? What can we learn from Matthew's description of God's love?

Matthew refers to a perfect God, but I really don't think that the point of Matthew's words is God's righteousness. I think that the heart of Matthew's description lies in this: God is complete. God is mature. God is not lacking.

Maturity or completeness is the ability to accept the normal. Maturity or completeness is the ability to see the end from the beginning. With maturity's viewpoint, forgiveness is assured. Forgiveness grows out of the love of God.

In the fall of 1992 a mother of three came to my office to talk. She was a partner in an unhappy marriage in which her husband left her with total responsibility for the children and household. He wasn't available nor was he particularly interested, and he made no attempt to hide his apathy.

FORGIVENESS

The children regularly competed for their father's attention and, thus, for hers. When they didn't receive that attention, they fought and created a scene. All in all, the family was in disarray, and this unhappy woman came to me for some kind of relief from her grueling world. She felt the weight of disappointment and anger on her shoulders.

"How do you behave when the children get angry?" I asked. She seemed surprised by the question.

"I get angry too," she replied with a note of defense. "I scream at them just like they scream at each other." She looked away and I think I detected embarrassment. I decided to press on.

"How would someone tell who the mother is at your house?" I asked. I smiled slightly, hoping to lighten the tension, but my guest looked uncomfortable all the same. She made no attempt to respond.

During the hour that followed I attempted to offer encouragement. She was certainly struggling, and I knew that if she continued on the same path her pain would increase. Somehow I needed to help her discover the freedom of maturity.

What would it mean to be a mature mother? Slowly but surely she began to realize that a mature mother has the ability to see the beginning and the end. A mature mother has the ability to see that children are children. A mature mother has the ability to maintain her own love, even when it seems that the ones she loves are the enemy. A mature mother can forgive because her eyes are on the bigger picture.

I imagine that you, like this mother, have difficulty loving and forgiving at times. Even when we know we should rise above the occasion, it is difficult to do so. Yet we are not without help or guidance.

It is fortunate that God can see both beginning and end.

FORGIVENESS

It is fortunate that He does not act like we act. He understands our weaknesses and He understands our limitations. And He accepts us, limitations and all!

There is forgiveness with God. His eyes are on the bigger picture. He can forgive because He paid the price that we might be free.

I struggle to forgive at times. And I find it difficult to act maturely with certain people or in certain situations. Lord, I am so grateful for Your love and forgiveness. Help me to see others through Your eyes of love.

—Phil Hook

●

EASIER SAID THAN DONE

"Then Peter came to Jesus and asked, 'Lord, how many times shall I forgive my brother when he sins against me? Up to seven times?' Jesus answered, ' . . . not seven times, but seventy-seven times.' "
Matthew 18:21-22

As a young believer, forgiveness seemed to me to be both a basic and an easy concept in Christianity. At that early stage of spiritual growth, I basked in the warm glow of the Lord's incredible mercy in pardoning my sins. I was like a small child on Christmas morning—completely delighted in the wonderful gifts received with little or no thought about giving to anyone else.

For well over a decade, my "easy as falling off of a log" approach to forgiveness continued, at least on the surface. Then, while teaching at a college in Texas, I was asked to preach a series on forgiveness in a local church which was fragmented due to bitterness and a very angry spirit.

Initially, it seemed like a rather boring and disagreeable

assignment. After all, who would want to confront such angry factions? Besides, I wondered how committed to the Lord such people could be, considering they were "blowing it" in what I considered the easiest part of Christian living.

As distasteful and forbidding as the prospect seemed, however, I decided to go ahead and plow through that month of messages on forgiveness. The money was good and, I must confess, my pride enjoyed believing that they needed someone as well versed in forgiveness as myself.

God was gracious to me—even in the pride of the moment. Through the process of teaching the messages, two astounding things happened. First, a significant number of people in the shattered congregation reached out to each other with forgiveness. Equally amazing and even more personally surprising, however, was the change that occurred in me.

Over a year before presenting that sermon series on forgiveness, I had been angrily assaulted—frontally and through widespread gossip—by a church board member. He was "out to get me" because I had called his hand at a crucial juncture, preventing a limited "power play" he had orchestrated.

I was taken back by this man's anger, as I had once been close to him. He was unwilling to even admit his bitterness. So, being the wise, mature person in this spiritual "cold war," what did I do in response? I followed suit, reasoning that I was the innocent party in the situation and that I had every right to be angry and hold a grudge. After all, I had been wronged in the line of duty!

Why hadn't I faced this issue earlier? I'd certainly had my chances to do so. Every few weeks my wife had been asking if I were ready to forgive that man, and I, of course, had replied, "I forgave him long ago!" But there is a considerable difference between mouthing pious words and opening up your heart to release such a painful memory. It required a major "spiritual housecleaning" for me to fully forgive that man, and I was greatly humbled in the process.

What was it that got to me and melted my unforgiveness? Primarily, it was the fascinating story taught by Jesus in Matthew 18. The Lord has forgiven each Christian more than you and I will ever have to forgive one another. It made me realize from the top of my head to the bottom of my feet, just how hypocritical it is to seek and accept God's forgiveness yet then refuse the same forgiveness to others.

Because of the heat of emotions and wounded pride, those of us who refuse to forgive are attempting to "play God" in other's lives. At the same time, we end up locking God out of working in our own lives by holding on to that self-righteous pride.

While I still believe that forgiveness is very basic and quite simple to understand, I no longer hold the illusion that forgiveness is easy to practice and live. I have come to realize that forgiving painful wrongs is one of the hardest things in life—very much "easier said than done."

THOUGHT FOR THE HEART

I am aware of holding a grudge in relation to this person. I would like to seek God's help in loosening the grip on my bitterness and anger.

—*Boyd Luter*

●

FORGIVENESS OPENS UP THE SOUL

"If you, O Lord, kept a record of sins, O Lord, who could stand? But with You there is forgiveness; therefore You are feared."
Psalm 130:3-4

FORGIVENESS

I went years telling myself that I held no grudges against my father. I told everyone I met that I had a fine family — a bit quiet, but fine. I insisted that my father was behind me 100 percent and that he didn't visit because the conditions in Africa are not conducive to the elderly. I was a very good con artist when it came to hiding my feelings.

My family was indeed quiet and I have since come to understand that my parents struggled deeply with their own identities. They were not raised to feel good about themselves or their accomplishments. They did not raise me to feel good about myself or my accomplishments.

My mother died suddenly when I was sixteen and away at school, and that was the end of "family" for me. My father rarely communicated by letter or phone. When I came home for the holidays, we had few conversations. He was not cruel; he was simply unavailable to his only daughter. I had no idea what to do with the emotions I felt, the needs I experienced, the pain deep inside.

I became a physician! If I couldn't feel good about me with me, then I would spend my life helping everyone else. And my strategy worked quite well! I've poured hours and years into service and I love my work.

Little did I know that a small child would be my emotional connection. I had no idea my defenses were down, and no thought that this child could invade my space with healing. The story still amazes me.

A small boy was brought to me one day, and he looked just like other small children I had treated through the years. He was gaunt, he was lifeless, he couldn't even cry while I examined him. He was just existing.

Like most children in his situation, I admitted him to our clinic and prescribed a diet of nutritional supplements and food that would actually help. And I told his family that he would need to remain with us for at least one month. They agreed and left, and I immediately saw a look of relief cross his face. I made a mental note, but was too busy to pursue my observation.

Several weeks came and went, and he began to grow strong. I think he actually grew a few inches, though I know that isn't possible. What I attributed to increased height was actually increased confidence. My young friend was growing up and feeling just a little bit better about himself.

One night, I was at the clinic late. There were papers to complete and charts to study and I was feeling a need to clean off my desk. I thought I felt someone looking at me and when I turned to the door, there was this young man.

"Doctor?" he said. This was the first time I remember hearing him speak.

"Doctor, are you happy?" he asked gently.

What a strange question, I thought to myself. *Why would he ask such a thing?*

"Why, I think so," I answered. I felt myself smile a bit. "Why do you ask?"

"You never really look at me," he said. "At home, that means that my mother is not happy."

I took my young friend back to his bed and assured him I was quite pleased with his progress. I even tucked him in, but I was aware of something for the first time that night. The boy was right. I had a hard time looking into the eyes of suffering children. Something inside of me felt it would break if I stared into those fearful, lonely eyes.

I decided to "go to work" on the inside of me. I solicited the help of a trusted physician who worked with me in the clinic, and we worked hard.

I had to release my pain—the anger, the fear of abandonment, the isolation, the sense that I was not loved or lovable. I had to release the pain of my mother's death and bearing it all alone. And I had to release honest anger against my father for years of silence.

FORGIVENESS

I have a simple message about forgiveness. When we withhold forgiveness, we become enslaved to avoidance, to anger, to deceit. I was always kind and cheerful, but I was also unavailable emotionally. I had to hide the hurt inside or express it, and I didn't think I could do the latter.

When we withhold forgiveness, our relationships suffer. I didn't realize it at the time, but the quality of my relationships has changed drastically since my "growing up." I have a whole range of emotions now that I never knew before.

Forgiveness opens up the soul and releases angers, fears, and insecurities. It gives us opportunity to love and be loved, often for the first time ever.

I have since repaired my end of the relationship with my father. We are more free with one another because I am more free, more honest, more open with him.

My earthly father will never play the role I would like him to play, but my Heavenly Father has stepped in and more than made up the difference.

If you're avoiding someone or some relationship, I simply encourage you to learn from my young friend. Your eyes tell the story, whether you want them to or not.

THOUGHT FOR THE HEART

I am withholding forgiveness. I have been hurt and I want that other person to help carry the burden or at least feel my pain. Lord, I know I need to forgive. Help me to allow Your forgiveness to run through me.

—Pamela M. Reeves

●

BEWARE OF ARROGANCE AND PRIDE

"Do you see this woman? I came into your house. You did not give Me any water for My feet, but she wet My feet with her tears and

*wiped them with her hair. You did not give Me a kiss, but this
woman, from the time I entered, has not stopped kissing My feet.
You did not put oil on My head, but she has poured perfume on My
feet. Therefore, I tell you, her many sins have been forgiven — for
she loved much. But he who has been forgiven little loves little."*
Luke 7:44-47

At eighteen, I was fairly certain about my theological
views. I knew all about salvation, forgiveness, sin and, of
course, righteousness. After all, I had been a believer since
age nine. Certainly that was long enough to be an expert,
right?

How little I understood about our humanity back then. I
thought I was completely in control of my own destiny! I
thought that God and I had crossed those critical bridges
of life. And I thought I had won all the battles! I was
certain that there would be no surprises.

Have you ever noticed how easy it is to be sure when
we're young and how hard it is to be sure as we age?
Have you ever noticed how arrogant we can be, even
when we're trying to be holy? Have you ever noticed how
easy it is to get sidetracked from that which really
matters?

Simon and the other Pharisees were certain of their theology too! They wanted only one thing from Jesus the
night they invited Him to dinner. They wanted to trick
Him into saying something that would jeopardize His
ministry. They wanted to find a hole in His teaching. They
wanted to find a way to disable His incredible relationship
with people. After all, they knew the teachings backward
and forward, and they knew that Jesus' brand of theology
didn't match their own. They thought it their duty to
reveal His flaws.

As Jesus approached Simon's home that night, I can
almost hear Him sigh. He knew what awaited Him. He

knew the night would be a theological tug-of-war, and I imagine He was weary from the battle before it had even begun.

Jesus entered the home of His "hosts" that night. As usual, the streets were dusty, the weather warm—and He waited for their hospitality. The hospitality did not come. They were so enamored by their own agenda that they failed to offer the basic kindnesses afforded all guests. They did not wash His feet, they did not anoint Him with oil, they did not greet Him with the customary kisses. In short, they ushered our Lord into their world and into their traps without even a hint of concern for His honor.

The evening progressed uneventfully for the most part, until a woman entered the home. Almost undetected by the preoccupied men, she knelt down behind our Lord and wept. She couldn't believe that Jesus—the honored guest—was being so mistreated. She saw the dust on His feet and the tears started to flow.

This woman was a sinner. Like you and me, she had failed in her life. She had committed acts for which she was not proud and she had lost her way from time to time. When she gazed upon our Lord, she saw her own sin and His glory, and she couldn't hold back the love. Washing His feet with her tears and her hair, she anointed Him with oil and smothered His feet with kisses. This woman loved Jesus, and her love rang out like a cathedral bell on a crisp winter morning.

The Pharisees still didn't get the picture. Simon thought to himself that Jesus should know better than to let this "woman" touch Him. *If He were really a prophet,* Simon thought, *He'd know that this woman is a sinner.*

Jesus knew she was a sinner! And that made the woman all the more dear to Him. Few things give Jesus more pleasure than the love of one of His children. She was His child. She knew she was a sinner. She knew she needed

Jesus. She longed to honor Him.

Jesus' statement to Simon rings through *my* mind like a bell on a crisp winter's day. I just wish I had understood the simplicity of His love in my younger, more vulnerable days.

"Her many sins have been forgiven—for she loved much." Jesus' words cut right to Simon's bone. "But he who has been forgiven little loves little."

Sometimes we forget how much we need His forgiveness. We get caught up in our own greatness—the accomplishments, the knowledge, the issues which seem so clear to us. And before we know it, we forget how much we need Him. Without realizing the change, we begin to debate and argue rather than weep and wash.

The very essence of our relationship with Jesus grows out of the reality of His love and our humanity. We cannot reach God on our own. We cannot pay for our own sins. And so our Lord stepped into this world to offer unfailing love and immeasurable forgiveness.

Each day we are bathed in God's forgiveness, and each day we need His love and understanding just as much as we did yesterday. It is through recognizing our need for Him that we have love to offer. It is through remembering our need for Him that we have love to give.

Hold on tight to the reality of God's love. Let Him remind you daily of the relationship that literally sets you free. Lay aside the false securities and lay hold of the gift that brings security. Lay hold of forgiveness.

■■■■■■ THOUGHT FOR THE HEART

I tend to forget my own need for God. In fact, my pride has been leading me astray in these areas. Lord, help me to receive Your forgiveness so that I too can truly love.

— Shelley Chapin

RHYTHMS OF MY HEART

GRACE

●

THE UNEXPECTED GIFT

"But God demonstrates His own love for us in this: while we were still sinners, Christ died for us." Romans 5:8

Grace comes in all shapes and sizes and from all sorts of sources. The "trick" is to be ready! Watch and see! Grace will come.

There was a war in the house of Saul, and everyone knew about the battle. Saul was a king at war with himself, and thus with everyone else.

Though not to oversimplify, Saul's problem was at least in part due to the way he viewed himself. In God's eyes, Saul was fit to be king. In his own eyes, Saul was not. Tragically, Saul's view of himself spoke loud to his soul until he had destroyed just about everything that he held dear.

David was a gentle man. He loved Saul and wanted to protect him from the war. And he loved Saul's son, Jonathan. David and Jonathan were kindred spirits, and David did all in his power to defer Saul's anger and restore peace between the households. David tried to stay the most tragic of endings, but his goal was thwarted. For by the end of the accounts in 1 Samuel, Saul and Jonathan were dead.

There were more than a few casualties in this battle born of jealousy and fear. Not only were Saul and Jonathan dead, but so were the futures their families would know. And so was peace in the kingdom. For years, David fought to restore what was tragically broken down. And for years he mourned the death of his dear friend.

Enter grace. One day, in an unexpected conversation, David asked a question.

"Is there anyone still left of the house of Saul to whom I can show kindness for Jonathan's sake?" The answer returned to the king through a servant of Saul named Ziba, "There is still a son of Jonathan; he is crippled in both feet."

Mephibosheth, so the story goes, had fallen in the middle of one of the angry battles. Just a child at the time, he injured his feet, but there was no medical help to offer him. As a result, he had lived his life as a crippled man.

"Bring him to me," David requested.

Put yourself in the world of Mephibosheth for a moment. He had only heard stories of David, he had not known the king. And it's probable that the stories he heard from his jealous grandfather were not flattering.

Mephibosheth had lost his father. He had lost the use of his feet. And he had lost many of the dreams a young boy dreams, all in the wake of a battle no one really understood.

And then there is a message: "King David wants to see you." *Who, me?* he might have thought. *But why?* I doubt it ever crossed his mind that David wanted to show kindness to him and restore him to his land and treat him as a son. It took time for all this grace to set in.

Grace is surprise! It comes like a thief in the night with no expectation. It comes without deserving. And it comes without our ability to earn its gifts.

God reached out to us as David reached out to Mephibosheth. We were crippled in sin and unaware of His world. And we never expected a gift that would yield forgiveness and eternal life. We didn't even know we needed such a gift!

Let God surprise you with grace today. Let Him remind you of your worth. And let Him give to you freely, openly, lovingly, and eternally.

THOUGHT FOR THE HEART

I have been feeling like Mephibosheth these days. God, grant me grace in the depths of my crippled soul. Grant me Your kindness.

— Shelley Chapin

●
THE PARENT WHO NEVER STOPS CARING

"Which of you, if his son asks for bread, will give him a stone? Or if he asks for a fish, will give him a snake? If you, then, though you are evil, know how to give good gifts to your children, how much more will your Father in heaven give good gifts to those who ask Him?"
Matthew 7:9-11

Remember that first time when you heard or said, "I didn't ask to be born!" Well, that statement is true (though it usually doesn't help the situation at hand!). Think about it for a moment! We don't ask to be born. We can't! A parent has certain responsibilities to the child growing out of this simple reality.

We didn't ask to be born — not to our parents and not to our God! We didn't ask God to create the world or to create us as part of His plan. We didn't ask Him to allow us choice in the midst of our wonderful Eden. I'm not complaining, but the reality is a powerful one.

Why does God extend grace to you and to me? Why did He send His Son to make the utmost sacrifice for our sin? Why does He continue to lead us, to reach out to us, to forgive and comfort? Because He chose to create us and He takes responsibility for that choice.

Grace has a lot to do with parenting. There are countless moments when Janie and I had to go the extra mile, give up what we desired, or forgive when the child wasn't even aware of his wrongdoing. Grace goes along with parenting, and it goes along with being children of God.

God has extended (and will continue to extend) grace to you and to me. He knows what we're capable of and He knows what choices we'll make. And He knows that He has allowed us to live in this situation.

God knows that we cannot live life on our own but that we'll try to time and time again. He knows that we need Him, even though we're always trying to say, "Let me do it!" God knows that we cannot atone for our own sins and that we don't even fully understand what that means. Grace is God's gift to these humans that He has created.

What parent will give a stone when a child asks for bread? What loving parent will give a snake when a child needs fish? If we humans give good gifts to our children and care for them, how much more is our Heavenly Father in the business of caring for you and me?

God has given us grace because, as our Parent, He is committed to our well-being. He is committed to doing all that He can to guide and save and prepare us for life. God extends grace because we literally couldn't make it without Him.

Do you need a little more grace? He's already getting it ready to send your way. And He doesn't give begrudgingly. He'll give you grace because He loves you and He has created you.

After all, you didn't ask to be born, did you?

THOUGHT FOR THE HEART

It is often difficult for me to allow God to give me grace. I'm generally trying to take care of "me" my own way. I would like to be more willing to allow God the joy of parenting me.

—Jay Kesler

●

EXQUISITE COMPANIONSHIP

"But He has said to me, 'My grace is sufficient for you, for My power is made perfect in weakness.' " 2 Corinthians 12:9

GRACE

Remember the popular movie *Love Story?* I'll never forget how it swept the country with its sentimental view of relationship. And one of the most poignant statements in the movie was, "Love means never having to say you're sorry." I can still see the look in their eyes as the young couple pledged these words to one another.

Even as a non-Christian, I could see the transparent lunacy in such a statement. Though the message sounds romantic, to love someone without ever saying "I'm sorry" just does not work! Still, long after becoming a believer in Christ, I continued to make a parallel mistake in my outlook toward God's grace.

Though I might have mentally known better, my preferred perspective toward God's grace could have been expressed as "grace means never having to suffer." And this cockeyed viewpoint was the product of an illogical leap, anchored securely in midair! Let me outline my midair leap.

First, I was delighted to discover that grace is God's undeserved favor, extended to you and to me.

Next, I was humbled to learn that grace is most bountifully expressed through Christ's death on the cross in my (and your) place.

Therefore (my own midair leap), I concluded that since grace led Christ to suffer in my place, surely grace would also mean I would not have to suffer! And I really liked this conclusion!

In case you didn't notice, reasoning like that puts "2 + 2" in serious jeopardy! Also, such a conclusion virtually ignores the many biblical passages which teach the positive role of suffering in the Christian life. Mostly, this reasoning simply reflects my personal unwillingness to include suffering in the repertoire of my life of faith.

My simple equation for grace proved helpful only a short time. You see, I encountered suffering. And instead of reevaluating my own faulty deduction, I kept thinking that the Lord had placed me on a grace-free diet. I waited and waited for God to remove the obstacles, but the practical and emotional sides of life began looking more and more like grace-less wastelands.

Fortunately, as I grew in the Lord and His Word, a midcourse correction began taking place. I started to see God's amazing grace in every aspect of my life, even the dark corners. Still, it was not until I was asked to write on the Apostle Paul's understanding of grace that I really saw how the Lord works His grace in and through our painful trials.

Nothing makes me feel weaker and more helpless than ongoing suffering. But, I now realize joyfully that God and His grace do not desert me in the bomb crater of my pain. If anything, I am permitted to watch the Lord take a spiritual "ninety-eight-pound" weakling like me and put me through His classic strength clinic.

God's grace is not the absense of pain, though all of us would prefer to live without the sufferings. God's grace isn't even threatened or slowed down by the painful trials of this world.

Instead, God grants us the exquisite companionship of His grace as we live through each moment of life on this earth. His grace provides the strength and comfort to help in our times of need. Grace means never having to live alone in this world, and never having to face our sufferings without the sufficiency of God's strength, wisdom, love, comfort, and understanding.

THOUGHT FOR THE HEART

I am aware of God's grace in these areas of my life, even though I may be experiencing pain.

—Boyd Luter

GRACE

●
ANOTHER CHANCE

"The grace of our Lord was poured out on me abundantly, along with the faith and love that are in Christ Jesus." 1 Timothy 1:14

"Go and make disciples of all nations!" (Matthew 28:19) Such is the well-known command given by our Lord to those who knew and served Him during His ministry on this earth. Some eighteen years later, Paul, Barnabas, John Mark, and others set out to do just that — proclaim the Gospel to those in need of the Good News.

Though we do not know exactly what happened, somewhere during that missionary trip John Mark decided to go back home. Such a decision did not please Paul, who was not one to desert a cause.

The trip nonetheless was a success and they were pleased with all that God accomplished during their journey. No one seemed to remember John Mark's leaving until it was time to begin the next missionary journey.

"I'd like to go along," John Mark announced to Paul. And whether the young man expected this response or not, Paul said no. Thus began a real struggle between the members of the missionary team.

Barnabas wanted John Mark to be included. Paul (the perfectionist) could not accept bringing a "quitter" back on to the team. For Paul, efficiency, effectiveness and, above all else, commitment to the cause, were of utmost importance. John Mark had proved unreliable.

Barnabas viewed John Mark through a different set of glasses. John Mark was his nephew and a long-time "child" of the older disciple. Barnabas was a "son of encouragement," so in keeping with his name he wanted to give John Mark another opportunity.

Where Paul saw failure, Barnabas saw possibilities. And

the dispute became so intense that they literally parted company, separating a team and a friendship that had been important for years. Paul took one missionary journey, and Barnabas took another— both effective, and both in keeping with their gifts and vision.

From Paul's perspective, John Mark did not deserve a chance. But Barnabas saw through eyes of grace. He saw someone to be loved, understood, forgiven, and graced with another opportunity to serve.

The rift between the friends did not last long. Years later in another epistle, Paul acknowledged the work John Mark had accomplished. And the grace continues! John Mark also authored one of the greatest letters we have— the Gospel according to Mark.

There are times when our vision is not as clear as God's. When in doubt about another person's worth, allow God's grace to shine through.

▮▮▮▮▮▮▮ THOUGHT FOR THE HEART

I am aware that this person needs the gift of my grace right now. I will pray for the courage and softness of heart to give that grace.

—Phil Hook

●

EQUAL FOOTING, EQUAL NEED

"But because of His great love for us, God, who is rich in mercy, made us alive with Christ even when we were dead in transgressions— it is by grace you have been saved. And God raised us up with Christ and seated us with Him in the heavenly realms in Christ Jesus, in order that in the coming ages He might show the incomparable riches of His grace, expressed in His kindness to us in Christ Jesus. For it is by grace you have been saved, through faith— and this is not from yourselves, it is the gift of God— not by works, so that no one can boast." Ephesians 2:4-9

GRACE

One of the most unattractive things about Christians is our desire to dispense grace rather than accept grace. In essense, we often send the message, "I am perfect so I can allow you to be imperfect. I'll grant grace to you." Another way of stating this might be, "I am superior and you are fortunate that I'm willing to extend grace your way."

In truth, grace is equally distributed to all of us. We are all in need of grace. And not one of us is "superior" or "above" the need for such a gift. Grace is all about a favor that is granted to us through the sacrifice and servant-hood of Jesus Christ. It was never meant to be a measuring rod for our own ideals of perfection.

A great place for a Christian to stand on grace might sound something like this: "I accept my own humanity and I can live with a bit of a sense of humor about my foibles. I can accept this reality in me and in others. We are all recipients of God's gift of grace."

Since what I have suggested may not sound too different to you from the first position, let me clarify one simple point. The reality is that we all need grace, even if we sense that we have "very little sin." From God's point of view, we have a lot of sin! And a "little sin" was worth dying for. In short, there is no "minimal" need for grace. We all need this all-significant gift from God.

I don't know if you've ever stopped to think about this or not, but Eve's wrongdoing took the form of a nibble and an offering. She tasted a piece of fruit that had been forbidden and she offered that same fruit to her husband. Adam accepted. Those small acts of will alone altered history for each and every one of us.

Would we have behaved differently from Eve or Adam? No. We might not have succumbed at just that moment, but somewhere in the experience of the garden we too would have begun to doubt. We too would have allowed the tempter his moment on the witness stand. We too would have begun to question God's wisdom or motive. And the story would have unfolded in much the same way.

We Christians have a tendency to remove ourselves from the list of those who really need grace and pride ourselves on the fact that we are willing to extend such grace to others. Simply beware. We are all recipients of God's gentle mercy. And we are all in need of that open door to salvation and life: God's grace.

THOUGHT FOR THE HEART

I find myself thinking "I'm a little bit better" or "a cut above" this person or that situation. Help me, Lord, to stand humbly before You, a child in need of and surrounded by Your grace.

—*Jay Kesler*

●
BE A GIVER OF GRACE

"Remember, O Lord, Your great mercy and love, for they are from of old. Remember not the sins of my youth and my rebellious ways; according to Your love remember me, for You are good, O Lord. Good and upright is the Lord; therefore He instructs sinners in His ways. He guides the humble in what is right and teaches them His way." Psalm 25:6-9

David and his ragtag band of soldiers returned to Ziklag. They were weary from the battle and ready for refreshment, but to their horror all of their wives and possessions were gone. They had been stolen. In the bitterness of their loss, the men wanted to stone their king.

"This isn't fair. We've worked hard for him," they said among themselves. "He deserves to die." Yet before they carried out their angry threat, another plan emerged.

In their midst was an Egyptian—a swarthy man who

promised to lead them back to their families. And so the men were persuaded. They set out for battle to reclaim that which was rightfully theirs.

A full third of the men were too weary for battle. After all, they'd already defeated one army. And so they stayed behind. They simply could not press on. Though their pride said, "Go," their bodies would not cooperate.

Soon the remaining men caught up with the band of marauders. They fought, we are told, from evening of one day to evening of the next. And they recovered everything that had been taken, including the possessions of the Amalekites.

When the successful ones returned to the group which had been too weary to fight, those who had gone to battle made their position clear.

"Since they did not go with us, they cannot share in the plunder," the men declared. "They have no right to the reward."

David remained quiet for a moment, perhaps surprised by their attitude or perhaps not.

"No, my brothers," David said firmly. "We must not deal this way with the grace that God has given to us. We will share the reward equally among all." The pronouncement was clearly not available for discussion.

Grace is a difficult gift to offer at times. The undeserving are always willing to welcome the reprieve, while those who consider themselves "better" are rarely willing to share. Such is the way with children and adults. We want grace when we need its healing power, but we are slow, at times, to extend its balm to others.

What made David such a good king was his understanding of grace. He knew he was undeserving of God's mercy, yet he also knew God insisted on granting such a gift. How could David give anything less to those he ruled?

GRACE

Be a giver of grace. When we try to measure by what we deserve, each one of us falls short. But when we're willing to give that which is freely given us, there is plenty for everyone.

████████████████ THOUGHT FOR THE HEART

It is difficult for me to extend grace to these people. I will ask God to help me better understand His mercy.

— Phil Hook

●

WHEN GRACE BEGAN

"Your attitude should be the same as that of Christ Jesus: who, being in very nature God, did not consider equality with God something to be grasped, but made Himself nothing, taking the very nature of a servant, being made in human likeness."
Philippians 2:5-7

We often speak of grace as the gift which brings us salvation, and it is! But grace is much more than that moment on the cross when Jesus gave His life in our place. It is more than the resurrection morning when we knew that hope had come to pass. Grace began long before the Ascension. Grace became flesh.

We have all struggled with sin and rebellion, some of us to a lesser degree than others, but the heart holds the same potential in us all. It is such reality that brought Christ into this world.

We could never hope to bridge the yawning gap that separates us from the awesome holiness of the living God of all creation. Only God could accomplish such a task, and His limitless love made Him willing to do so in spite of the price such love required.

The King of the universe, the Lord of glory, the God of

creation voluntarily stepped into this world as a baby . . . a pauper . . . the child of an unwed mother. He borrowed a place to be born, a place to sleep, a donkey to ride on, a boat to preach from, an upper room to use for His last supper, and a tomb in which to be buried.

This God-man did not enter the planet in power and glory. He entered in the weakness and vulnerability of an infant who would grow to become the lover and servant of the poor, the sick, and the sorrowful.

During the years of His ministry He would continually minister to the needs of the multitudes and the disciples. And He would willingly endure the rejection and the ridicule of His own people.

As if this were not enough, this God-man would suffer His face being slapped and covered with spittle. He would allow His beard to be ripped out and His clothing to be torn away. He would allow His back to be lacerated, His head to be wreathed with thorns, and His hands and feet to be pierced.

His eyes would be filled with tears, His ears would be filled with mockery, and His heart would be filled with grief as He bore the incalculable weight of human sins. The world had never seen anything like it before, nor will it ever again.

Jesus the Messiah — the incarnate Word, the embodiment of truth and life, the Creator and Lord over the heavens and the earth, the visible and the invisible came to this world to shed His grace on you and me.

It is not enough to begin our discussion of grace with the Cross or with the Resurrection. To gain the true picture we must begin with that act of God choosing to become man . . . choosing to become infant child in need of our care.

Let grace speak to you through the love of our Lord. Let grace give purpose to your life and to your worship. The grace of our Lord was a lifestyle He chose, an attitude that He lived with each moment of the day.

███████████ THOUGHT FOR THE HEART

It sobers me to think of the love that caused our Lord to leave His throne and step into humanity. I am so grateful for Your grace, Lord; so grateful that You chose to give Your grace to me.

—Ken Boa

●
SAYING NO, SAYING YES

"For the grace of God that brings salvation has appeared to all men. It teaches us to say 'No' to ungodliness and worldly passions, and to live self-controlled, upright, and godly lives in this present age, while we wait for the blessed hope—the glorious appearing of our great God and Savior, Jesus Christ, who gave Himself for us to redeem us from all wickedness and to purify for Himself a people that are His very own, eager to do what is good." Titus 2:11-14

Pitching was a real gift to me, the love of my life, my dream. It was also a real gift for me financially. I got jobs when there were none available to most anyone else. During the summer months pitching dominated my life. I was paid to pitch!

Every team has people who "hang around"—people who used to play ball or wish they could play ball or who just want to be around ball players. They were fun to have around and they were useful to the team. They ran errands, picked up bats, and often paid the bill for dinner.

One of these men was small and old. I imagine he played ball once upon a time, but he was retired. He hung around the dugout during the game to see if there was anything he could do to help.

One evening I was pitching and pitching well. Between

innings as I relaxed on the bench, the old gentleman sat down beside me and asked a question that changed my life.

"Phil, how long are you going to be a softball bum?" he asked.

A softball bum? Had I heard him correctly? What was he talking about and why would he say such a thing? I pretended not to be bothered by the question, but the words would not stop ringing through my mind.

I thought I was a softball star, not a bum . . . but as I thought about it, I realized he was right. I had lost perspective on who I was and what I believed in order to play more games and make more money.

How long was I going to be a softball bum? That would be my last season to play ball that way.

I relate this story to you because I imagine you too occasionally succumb to the temptation to be someone you are not. We do this all the time. Whether for convenience, personal gain, fear, acceptance, or other reasons, we accept invitations to be something other than what we are.

One of the greatest gifts of God's grace lies in His ability to help us be who He has designed us to be. Paul's letter to Titus reminds us of this privilege. The same grace that brings salvation (the eternal transformation of the soul!) also brings transformation of our lives. He helps us say no to those things that threaten our well-being and yes to those choices that guard our well-being.

When God comes into our lives He brings order — creation and salvation show the wonder of His love. And that love doesn't stop there. He also brings order to our daily lives. Sin brings disorder, but God brings order. Sin brings distress, but God brings joy.

It is difficult at times to say yes to self-controlled living. It is a decision built upon trust and honesty. And it is a decision that requires patience. I didn't have much patience or trust in those early days.

I think I knew that God cares but I lived as if He doesn't get directly involved in our daily choices. I lived as if I were in charge of my destiny rather than God.

In my later years, I'm relearning old lessons. I'm realizing more and more how much God cares and how active He is in our everyday needs and decisions.

God's grace enables us to receive His order. His grace enables us to exercise our gifts and become all that He has specially designed us to be. His grace helps us say yes to that which is good and pure and eternal.

▬▬▬▬▬ T H O U G H T   F O R   T H E   H E A R T

Lord, grant me the grace to be who You have designed me to be. Grant me the grace to say yes to living for You.

— Phil Hook

●

GOD'S PROMISES

"Your house and your kingdom will endure forever before Me; your throne will be established forever." 2 Samuel 7:16

Most of us know the story of David's adultery, but there is a story which precedes that one that many do not know. It is a story of God's grace. It is a story of redemption. It is a story that reminds us that God's love is unfailing.

David grew up as a shepherd boy in a house of older brothers and sisters. He loved his job. It was his duty to take care of the sheep, and a good shepherd he was.

Then one day, when he least expected the visit, Samuel came calling and chose David as the next king over Israel. I don't know what was in the young man's mind at the time, but I do know this: he had no idea how to be a king, and he had no idea how much shepherding had prepared him for the duty!

Many years passed and much had occurred in the life of this young king. He had served his people well and, above all, he had loved his Heavenly Father. David had a heart for God, there was no mistaking that fact.

Then one day David realized that an injustice was being done. He as king of the Israelites was living in a magnificent palace while the ark of the covenant continued to dwell in a tent. David wanted to honor God by building a beautiful temple for Him.

"O Lord, here I am, living in a palace of cedar while the ark of God remains in a tent. I'd like to build a house for You, Lord. I'd like to put the ark in a sacred place where You belong," he prayed.

God graciously sent a message to David through Nathan the prophet. God reminded David that He'd been living in a tent for quite some time and that He was fine! He encouraged David in all that the king had done. And He promised David that He would make his name known, "like the names of the greatest men on earth."

Once again, God shed His grace on His servant. David had gone to God desiring to honor Him, and God had turned the blessing back on His child instead. How God loves to bless and encourage those He loves! God's response continued:

> The Lord Himself will establish a house for you: When your days are over and you rest with your fathers, I will raise up your offspring to succeed you, who will come from your own body, and I will establish his kingdom. He is the one who will build a house for My name, and I will establish the throne of his kingdom forever. I will be his Father, and he will be My son (2 Samuel 7:11-14).

GRACE

I imagine David could hardly believe his ears; after all, what does every father long to hear before he dies? God told David that his own offspring would be king, that he would be cared for by God as His son. God even promised that David's son would build the temple. David's dreams had come true, even though that son had not yet been born.

Only a few sands of time passed through the hour glass before David was on the roof watching Bathsheba as she bathed. For a few moments he forgot his commitment to keeping God's commands and lost sight of all God had promised for the future. For those moments, David was a man attracted to a woman who wasn't his. And instead of controlling the temptation, he succumbed.

David and Bathsheba conceived a child together that night, and David's whole world turned upside down. Instead of honoring God the way he had done for a lifetime, David spun a web of lies, deceit, and premeditated murder. The king was in trouble.

Did God know about this coming sin when He extended the promises to David? Did God grant those promises anyway, in light of the new information?

The answer to both questions is a resounding yes. Solomon, the son of David and Bathsheba, became the fulfillment of that promise. And Solomon's wisdom touched the kingdom (and our lives!) for many a year.

God knows what stands in our futures. He knows the steps we will take, the temptations we will succumb to, the sins we will commit, the triumphs we will share. Such knowledge does not change His gift of grace. Instead, it makes His grace all the more precious to David, to you, and to me.

David sinned, yes. And there were severe consequences for the sin. But the consequences of our lives do not cancel grace. Grace is the free gift of God.

GRACE

Even in our sin we are the beloved children of a faithful Heavenly Father. Hold on to this gift! It's enough to last a lifetime.

THOUGHT FOR THE HEART

It amazes me to realize that God knows my needs, my fears, my sins, my doubts, my secrets — and grants me grace anyway! Grace is mine because He loves me. And it is mine yesterday, today, and forever.

— Shelley Chapin

RHYTHMS OF MY HEART

G R I E F

●

GOOD GRIEF

"We do not want you to . . . grieve like the rest of men, who have no hope." 1 Thessalonians 4:13

I will always be impacted by the funeral of a twenty-eight-year-old woman. She was the daughter of a special friend and colleague, and her death was totally unexpected—a shock to family and friends.

In the course of the funeral service, many wonderful memories were expressed, painting a clear picture of a godly and vibrant young woman. Yet, the happy anecdotes never proceeded very far without the interruption of a tear, a quivering voice, or an awkward silence. This kind of heartfelt expression of joy and pain upon the loss of a Christian loved one represents what can be called, for lack of a better term, "good grief."

Unfortunately, there are many people, including quite a few believers in Christ, who view "good" and "grief" as mutually exclusive categories. Like oil and water, they think that the two ideas don't mix: that grief cannot be good and that good has no place for grief.

Some proponents of this position say that God has removed all suffering, so we need not experience grief. Some Christians take the approach that there need be little or no grief associated with the death of a believer. After all, a believer's death means "promotion" into the Lord's presence, so why should we grieve?

The phrase, "that you may not grieve" is often ripped violently out of its context in Paul's letter to the Thessalonian church, suggesting that there is a way to stop the emotional pain of our losses in this world. Yet in the high-noon light of God's truth and the reality of living, this astoundingly prevalent outlook is a house of cards, providing temporary shelter for stoics and others who flee real-life pain and emotions via denial.

I make these firm statements, not as one who is some-how better or more aware, but as one who squatted in that same lean-to for many years, attempting to avoid the frightening storm of grief. But I had the protective bubble of grief-less living cave in on my head. I experienced a grief I could not deny or misplace. I experienced a grief which stayed with me and threatened my perfect way of escaping pain.

Back in 1988, my father died unexpectedly. I did not, at the time, break down in grief over losing him or even over the lost opportunity for a better relationship. But, gradual-ly, the stress of carrying around that unresolved grief caught up with me. There was an infected hole in my heart that refused to be filled or healed, except through honestly facing the pain of my loss.

Lest we lose sight of God's whole message, we must embrace the entire sentiment of Paul's encouragement, "That you may not grieve, as do the rest who have no hope." We are not asked to avoid grief, nor are we urged to quickly remedy our grieving. We are encouraged to grieve through the perspective of hope.

And what does hope have to offer the one who is griev-ing? The reminder that God is in control, even though we are not. Hope is the commitment that what we know to be true about God and His promises remain, even in the midst of our loss. Hope is our future and our entire reason for being.

We all will experience grief in this world — in all kinds of ways and through all kinds of trials. But our grief is sand-wiched between hope that is sure and true and eternal.

It is entirely possible to open-heartedly grieve in the good company of hope! It is possible to experience "good grief."

GRIEF

I am aware of feeling grief over these situations in my life. My hope can provide strength in these ways.

—Boyd Luter

●

"BOTTLED UP" NO LONGER

"When they came together in Galilee, He said to them, 'The Son of Man is going to be betrayed into the hands of men. They will kill Him, and on the third day He will be raised to life.' And the disciples were filled with grief." Matthew 17:22-23

I have told this part of my life to few. I don't know why I am telling it now, except that I've come to believe that our pain can help turn another person's pain into joy. Our past can be the path for another man's future. I am hoping my theory plays out in this way for you.

I grew up in England—the proper England, back when tea time, school uniforms, and morality were all upheld . . . at least we thought they were! I grew up in a world that appreciated Jane Eyre and Charles Dickens, crumpets and good conversation, walks in the late afternoon and etiquette. My family practiced all of the graces and I learned them well.

As the only child in our home, I learned early on that I would be the avenue for the family pride. How I looked, how I studied, and what I became would be our ticket into tomorrow. I felt the pressure from the preschool years on.

No one fought in our home, at least not that I heard. We had a big table at which we took our meals and that was the only place I remember even the slightest volume in my parents' voices. They had to speak loudly there due to the amount of space between the seats. Other than that, we all spoke politely, evenly, and respectfully.

I don't recall spankings because I don't recall much about childhood. I was a child, but a child in our home was merely a younger, smaller version of the adult. A child was never actually a child. I didn't question the family rules.

As I grew, I obeyed. Whatever my father thought best, I accomplished. I joined certain clubs in school, I acted certain parts in the plays, I read certain books in the summer, and I always, always excelled. That was a requirement for living in our home; it never seemed an option.

I continued my perfect behavior for most of my life. In fact, I think that the perfect behavior almost kept me away from the Lord. I never sensed a need for God, until my mother died.

I was away at school and barely sixteen when a telegram arrived. The headmistress beckoned me out of Latin, and I entered her office somewhat puzzled. She too was proper so I knew right away that something was odd. She seemed to fidget in her chair, and she must have brushed back her hair and straightened her glasses a dozen times. Finally, she settled on simply reading the telegram. I will never forget its contents.

"Mistress Pamela M. Reeves. Please inform Mistress Reeves that her mother has died of natural causes. Services will be held in two days." And that was the end of the message.

Grief is such a powerful emotion. I have felt its power in my later years. Grief is born from a small seed way down inside that grows and grows until finally it bursts. Like a weary dam once destined to stay strong, grief releases the pressure.

I had seen people grieve, but I didn't know the proper form. I felt as if I would burst in her office that day, but I'd never seen feelings expressed. So I locked the grief away, deep in the dungeon of my own pain.

Two days later we buried my mother and two days after that I was back at school. For the remaining years of my education, vacations were just the same as they had been before. Only this time, my father and I shared the long table together at meals. No one spoke loudly anymore; we simply didn't speak at all.

I did not feel my grief until well into my thirties. A physician myself at that time, I had charge of an elderly African woman. When she died, I watched how her children cried and I learned, for the first time, to grieve.

Your story might not be as stoic or dry as mine, but the message should translate. Allow yourself the ability to grieve. I never knew all that was bottled up inside until I cried with that African family. I had no idea the freedom of grief until I opened that door which had been closed for so long and allowed the grief to flow.

I have still never seen my father grieve, though I've grieved for him more times than I can count. Try to learn from one who held it in for so long; let grief show! It is a natural response to our losses.

Let it go! Let it show to all the world. Expressing grief is one of the great perks of being human.

■■■■■■■■■ THOUGHT FOR THE HEART

I just might be holding in grief of my own. It is easier, somehow, to pretend that I am not bothered by the losses. Help me, Lord, to learn to express my grief. And thank You for expressing Yours.

—Pamela M. Reeves

●

THE DAY AT AUSCHWITZ

"If a man dies, will he live again? All the days of my hard service I will wait for my renewal to come. You will call and I will answer

GRIEF

You, You will long for the creature You have made." Job 14:14-15

It was a rainy morning when our taxi cabs arrived at Auschwitz. We didn't need the dreary weather to go with the dreary atmosphere, but we got it all the same. The buildings, the guides, and the bad weather only combined to sink our spirits before we even started the tour.

Ahead of us was a group of Jewish young people from Israel. For me, watching them was more interesting than the displays. Their hurt and anguish were obvious.

They carried several Jewish flags which they frequently waved as a gesture of solidarity and patriotism. Sometimes they wrapped themselves in the flags and wept. All in all, it was a moving sight. At times it even seemed that they recognized fellow Jews in the pictures, though this would have been impossible. After all, the horrors of Auschwitz occurred some fifty years earlier.

I remained somewhat of an observer until we entered a room which boasted a mound of shoes. Shoes. All shapes and sizes of shoes were piled before our eyes. I stood and stared and allowed the sight to penetrate my emotions. Then I saw them—a pair of shoes that live on in my memory.

In the midst of the pile, a little to the side, was a pair of high-topped, leather boots that must have belonged to a boy of nine or ten. Somehow a chord struck deep within me. They reminded me of shoes I would have worn. They brought back memories of being a child with dreams— dreams that would never be fulfilled.

I grew up in the years of the Depression and World War II. I thought about a little boy whose last memories were those of being separated from family and friends, gassed by the enemy, and left virtually alone to die. I thought about how horrible it is that such a thing can happen to a young, undeserving child.

GRIEF

I also realized, watching that pair of shoes, that many of my own dreams never came true—simple dreams like a bicycle or freedom or normalcy. Dreams like a father playing catch or store-bought toys under the tree at Christmas were gone with yesterday's excuses.

I know how much I had growing up compared to that little Jewish boy, but I also know how much I lost within the dreams of my own world. He and I shared something in common—we shared broken dreams.

We all have dreams. We all have hopes and longings, expectations and possibilities. It is not wrong to dream, nor are those dreams always out of our reach.

Many of my dreams have come true. And opportunities that I never even dared to dream have occurred for me in my lifetime. I reflect and I am thankful.

But I also learned, that day in Auschwitz, that it is important to grieve the loss of dreams gone by. Those young Jewish observers were not personally harmed by Hitler's insanity, but they needed to grieve for the dreams of family members and friends gone by. I needed to grieve for the longings of my youth that still remain only a dream.

Thousands visit Auschwitz every year. They go there to visit their own losses. They go there to explore, if only for a moment, their pain. Yes, there is a cleansing in the emotion of grief that is powerful and healing.

Perhaps you too can find time to grieve over a pair of high-topped, leather shoes in your life. Perhaps you can find time to grieve for that which mattered.

███████████ THOUGHT FOR THE HEART

I've been avoiding grief. It is uncomfortable to feel the emotions of loss. Lord, help me to allow Your healing to visit even those painful areas of my heart and mind.

—Phil Hook

G R I E F

●
NECESSARY SORROW

"For with much wisdom comes much sorrow; the more knowledge, the more grief." Ecclesiastes 1:18

It is a seeming paradox that wisdom brings grief. How much more we would enjoy wisdom if grieving were not involved in the process of maturity. The more we know about our world, the more we grieve over what life *ought* to be, but is not. Wars and refugees . . . homeless and poor . . . criminals and victims . . . divorce and abuse all remind us of the unfairness of the world around us. All of life includes its pains, and pain produces grief.

The process of grieving is part of living life and accepting what it brings. The more we choose life and thus grow in wisdom, the more we feel pain. The more wisdom we gain, the more sadness we see. Not one of us escapes the reality of our bittersweet journey in this world.

Those who marry experience joy but must also face the struggles of deep relationship. Those who have great talents must also face defeat. Those who are gifted with beauty or athletic ability must age. Those who have children must suffer the empty nest. And those who have jobs must give them to the next generation. All of life includes loss, and grieving about our losses is where a foundation of wisdom begins to take root.

As the writer of Ecclesiastes tried to convey, wisdom and grief are companions. Though we do suffer the griefs of letting go, the sorrow we feel is necessary for the soul. With the sadness comes a sense of understanding and compassion that lead to wisdom. With loss, we simply understand much more about life.

Though it is difficult to remember, meaning in life does not come when we are assured that we will never suffer loss. Rather, the opposite seems true. Meaning in life comes through the One who gave life to us. Grief and wisdom go hand in hand; meaning comes from God granting His grace and perspective to each and every situation.

Grief is not an enemy, though at times the pain seems much too difficult to bear. Grief is a sign that we are growing, and that wisdom is there for the taking.

▬▬▬▬▬▬ THOUGHT FOR THE HEART

I am experiencing these losses right now in my life, and I am beginning to be aware of these gifts of wisdom in the midst of my grief.

—*Mark Cosgrove*

●
PERMITTING YOURSELF TO GRIEVE

"Why are you downcast, O my soul? Why so disturbed within me? Put your hope in God, for I will yet praise Him, my Savior and my God." Psalm 42:11

One of the most difficult periods of my life was the decade of the '80s. I had plans and dreams and places to go, but I was stopped in my tracks before I even got started. I am a cancer patient, and I was first introduced to its grief in October of 1982.

I remember well the variety of emotions I experienced during those first few weeks with cancer. I was not expected to live long, and I simply did not know how to respond. I felt a deep sense of sorrow and pain as I wondered what God could possibly be doing in my life. And I grieved for the loss of all those dreams that I feared I would never fulfill.

It is easiest to think of grief as an emotional response to a painful event. When a relative dies, when a child leaves home, when we lose a job or change our employment, when a marriage dissolves, when we feel betrayed, when we've tried but seem to get nowhere . . . we experience grief.

We are promised in Scripture that this world will be a difficult place. Jesus Himself outlined some of the pain the disciples would suffer, yet they were not able to grasp the realities about which Jesus spoke so candidly. Much like you and me, the disciples tried to look on the "bright side," avoiding the pain and choosing to opt for the easier possibilities.

When we deal with suffering, whether physical, mental, or emotional, grief is part of the process. Unfortunately, grief is often characterized as a negative emotion and carries with it a sense of embarrassment or frustration.

"I should be able to handle this pain." "If I really had faith I wouldn't feel this badly." "I can't let people know how I'm feeling." "Everyone else seems to be able to handle their lives." "If I were really trusting God, I wouldn't feel so discouraged."

These thoughts are mere representations of the frustrations we feel as we come face-to-face with grief. Somehow when we're wrestling with grief we see only the smiles and abilities and confidences of others. We feel certain that everyone else is much more equipped to handle life and that we are somehow letting God and family down.

What I wish we could all understand and accept is that grief is a natural and healthy response to our losses. It is not a feeling that suggests we are unspiritual; it is a feeling that expresses our sadness over saying good-bye to a friend, a child, a job, a future, health, or a dream. Grief is an emotion of disappointment, hurt, *and* growth.

Be patient with your grief! Feel the pain and grasp the learning.

GRIEF

I am feeling the loss of these people, dreams, or expectations in my life.

— Shelley Chapin

●

RESPONDING TO LOSS

"In this you greatly rejoice, though now for a little while you may have had to suffer grief in all kinds of trials. These have come so that your faith — of greater worth than gold, which perishes even though refined by fire — may be proved genuine and may result in praise, glory, and honor when Jesus Christ is revealed."
1 Peter 1:6-7

I have been a cancer patient since 1982, and I've lived with a great deal of physical pain in the aftermath of surgery. I say this simply to reveal that grief and I are not strangers. We've shared many moments in communion with one another.

In the wake of dealing with my own pain, I have discovered something very significant about grief. It is felt by everyone, yet admitted and discussed by only a few. Simple observation, I know, but seemingly accurate.

While I don't know where our fear of grief began, I do know that it is an unnecessary fear. Grief is not an enemy; it is a very important friend. Without the healing balm of grief, we would grow little and understand even less about the experiences God allows in this world.

Where would we be if God had not grieved over the brokenness of sin? In Genesis 6, we see His heart break as He observes the world and feels the weight of sin's devastation.

Where would we be if Jesus had not grieved over His

304

people? "O Jerusalem, Jerusalem, you who kill the prophets and those sent to you, how often I have longed to gather your children together as a mother hen gathers her chicks under her wings, but you were not willing" (Matthew 23:37).

And where would we be if Peter and the other disciples had not grieved the suffering and subsequent death of our Lord? Can you see how natural it is to grieve if we simply take a look at its cause?

Which one of us is surprised when a widow grieves the loss of a husband she's known and loved for years? Which one of us is surprised when a father grieves during the marriage celebration of his only daughter?

Which one of us is surprised when a couple grieves the death of a child or the loss of a pension or the change of a job? Which one of us is surprised when a child, far away from family for the first time, grieves for the safety and love of home?

We have only brushed the parameters of grief's causes, yet it is easy for us to understand the sorrow that accompanies life in this world. We grieve, and the grief brings growth.

Peter knew that his friends would soon be hurting deeply. The Roman leaders who had once been sympathetic to the Christian cause had been replaced. And those new in power had no warmth for believers. The persecutions had already begun and Peter knew they would intensify.

How does a leader in the faith encourage his followers? For beginners, Peter spoke truth. Instead of pretending things were fine, he let them know that their griefs were real and should be expected.

Peter then reminded his followers that the pain would not be in vain. In fact, he likened their trials to the refining of gold. Just as gold must be heated to remove the impurities, so must we travel through various sufferings. And just as gold becomes refined in the heat, so do we become more like Jesus in the midst of our griefs.

Finally, Peter encouraged the believers by reminding them of the reward for our faith. Though we grieve for awhile, we have hope. And hope will unite us all with our God for eternity. The privilege is beyond our ability to yet grasp.

Don't hide the grieving. It is a healthy response to the struggles we face in this world—a response that was modeled for us time and again by our God and Father and by our Lord Jesus Christ.

It is normal and healthy to grieve over our losses. It is a privilege to grieve as those who have hope.

███████████ THOUGHT FOR THE HEART

I am aware of feeling grief in these areas or relationships of my life. I would like to begin to express that grief openly and healthily.

—*Shelley Chapin*

RHYTHMS OF MY HEART

GUILT

TRUE GUILT, FALSE GUILT

"Ah, sinful nation, a people loaded with guilt, a brood of evildoers, children given to corruption! They have forsaken the Lord; they have spurned the Holy One of Israel and turned their backs on Him." Isaiah 1:4

Being an emperor or a president must be a horrible job. Terribly alone and so vulnerable, the person in that position has much to gain but even more to lose. To have absolute control over the lives of people and to be hated at the same moment you are loved is a difficult position to be in.

According to tradition, Herod visited Rome and stayed in the home of his brother. This was probably not the first time he'd made the trip, but there was definitely something different about this journey. When Herod returned to Jerusalem he took his brother's wife along *and* her young daughter. One more time he was trying to meet the need inside while on the outside breaking all the rules.

John the Baptist was a preacher of righteousness. He seemed to fear no one, including Herod, and so he preached openly to the ruler about the immoral relationship. John did not mince words.

Herodias, Herod's new "wife," reacted with understandable anger.

Who is this man to judge my position? she thought. *I have left husband and home, and if I lose this relationship, I'll have nothing.* She grew angry at the thought of John's intervention.

Herodias badgered Herod until he arrested John, but still the messenger continued. Herod and John spoke together by day and then Herod slept with his brother's wife by night. Torn between the truth of John's preaching and the pleasure of his new wife's bed, Herod listened but refused to heed John's teaching.

Finally the opportunity arose for Herodias to silence her accuser. Herod gave a party for himself and invited all his people. Those who worked for him could not refuse, and so the festivities began.

Herod grew drunk with the attention and the alcohol made the party bearable, but still there was something missing. Finally Herod invited his new stepdaughter, Salome, to entertain the crowd.

"My daughter will dance for you," he announced. And everyone watched with the kind of attention one must pay to the king's command. Then, in an act of magnanimity, Herod promised his daughter anything she wanted, up to half the kingdom.

Enter the plan of Herodias.

"I want the head of John the Baptist on a platter," the young girl said emphatically. A hush filled the room.

"You want what?" Herod asked, hardly able to believe what he had heard.

Herod was forced to choose between the truth of John and the folly of his own promise. Pride won. John the Baptist's head was delivered on a platter that night, but Herod could not rejoice.

I have often wondered if Salome's nightmares filled the silent halls of the palace. She could not have slept well after carrying the head of a man. One thing I do know, however: the head of John must have slept between Herod and his brother's wife for the rest of their lives.

Jesus or any other good man reminded Herod of John. He was haunted . . . guilty . . . without peace.

Guilt has its place. It is our response to the pain of sin. But when guilt festers inside and takes root, there is no feeling more devastating or helpless.

Don't let guilt be the foundation for your actions and thoughts. Guilt deceives and discolors. Where you have wronged, deal with the pain.

████████████ THOUGHT FOR THE HEART

I continue to wrestle with this root of guilt. Lord, help me to deal with pain I feel I have caused and release the guilt that is unfounded.

— Phil Hook

●

FREED FROM YOUR BURDEN

"My guilt has overwhelmed me like a burden too heavy to bear. My wounds fester and are loathsome because of my sinful folly. I am bowed down and brought very low; all day long I go about mourning. . . . O Lord, do not forsake me; be not far from me, O my God. Come quickly to help me, O Lord my Savior." Psalm 38:4-6, 21-22

I could not have been more than six years old when it happened: I got caught in a major mistake in our household! I got caught lying!

For as long as I can remember, my dad has said, "Just don't lie to me. It will be much worse if you lie." (Those words are etched in my brain!) And if telling me weren't enough, there was always the story of what happened to my sister the time *she* lied.

It seems that she had been climbing on the fence in our backyard, which was something she was forbidden to do. When my parents asked her about her climbing experience, she denied it vehemently. The only problem was her legs were covered with splinters! Pretty hard to get splinters from the fence if you're not climbing!

The story always had the same impact on me. I was determined not to lie. And all went fairly well until "the incident." Then I discovered that things look different when you're guilty. And this time I was guilty!

I set a wet washcloth down on a very nice wooden table in my parents' sitting room. We all passed the table dozens of times daily, so it didn't take long for someone to notice the washcloth setting there, taking off the lovely finish with each passing moment!

Well, my dad got everyone together and asked us very nicely who had left the washcloth there. He sounded nice, but I quickly calculated that this might be one of those offenses for which one gets a spanking. Therefore, I determined that I was not about to say, "Me!" I would sit quietly and wait for him to stop asking!

Time passed and no one admitted to the deed, so we were all allowed to leave the room AFTER the reminder: "Everything will be much better if you just tell the truth."

I made it about twenty feet down the hall before I burst into tears, and the rest is old news! But I learned a big lesson that day: guilt feels worse than the punishment.

Have you ever noticed that guilt feels terrible? There are few human emotions more difficult to bear than guilt. And it seems to increase, not lessen, with the passing of time.

I have great news for you. The believer in Christ is not asked to carry guilt. It's that simple, though the feeling's a bit harder to shake.

We all err. We always have and we always will. We have some control over the sins we will succumb to, but there is not one of us who is without sin. Paul reminds us of that truth over and over again. We are forgiven in Christ and we are freed from the burden of guilt, but we will all experience remorse.

Allow me to draw a distinction for a moment: guilt is a spiritual condition, remorse is an emotional response to sin. We all have both ingredients in our lives, and making the distinction helps a lot.

When I'm aware of feeling guilt, I get away for a while

and spend some time searching my heart for its source. Then, when I discover the reason for the guilt, I ask the Lord for support and for help as I seek to make amends, to forgive, or to love again.

The next step is the all-important one: I try to let the guilt go! Let it go. Our sin and guilt have already been atoned for. We do not need to carry that burden.

Remorse is a response to sin that we feel from time to time, even from events long since past. There are a number of situations that still cause me to feel remorse.

But remorse is an emotional response to the sin and pain of this world. Guilt is a theological condition.

Good news! The condition has been atoned for! Guilt is not ours to carry. Jesus paid it all.

THOUGHT FOR THE HEART

I seem to carry guilt from these events or relationships in my life. I would like to give that guilt to my Lord and let Him carry it for me.

— *Shelley Chapin*

●
FACING YOUR "PURSUERS"

"The wicked man flees though no one pursues, but the righteous are as bold as a lion." Proverbs 28:1

The father of three daughters always has one special responsibility. It is his job to take care of the cars. When home from school or from college, there is always that familiar statement, "Daddy, there's something wrong with the car."

One day, Mary came home and in checking her car I realized that the inspection sticker was out of date. With great generosity I said, "Mary, drive my car tomorrow and I will take care of your inspection." I had forgotten that I had an appointment downtown early the next morning.

As I drove Mary's car the next day, it seemed that the inspection sticker was about one foot square and that everyone was noticing its delay. I found a parking place near my appointment, but unfortunately the side of the car toward the street was the side of the car with the outdated sticker! I knew that to park there meant a ticket, so I began the search for that "right" parking place where I wouldn't get caught!

Minutes later I found a place and arrived at my appointment ten minutes late. Haunted by the specter of the ticket, I quickly went through the ritual of the meeting and left. I returned to the car as swiftly as possible, fully expecting both a ticket and a public lashing. There was no ticket when I returned.

I often think about that inspection sticker. As I struggle with the guilts of my life—whether a small thing like being late or a large thing like disappointing or hurting my family, I am aware that guilt causes even the innocent to cringe. When we feel guilty, we lose perspective and begin to run even when no one pursues.

We have two choices of what to do when guilt emerges. First, we can stay with the guilt and run from our imaginary pursuers. We can excuse in our minds and justify our actions and remain alone in the powerful world of guilt.

Or we can work through the cause of the guilt itself and gain freedom from that which haunts us. This is my recommendation!

Sometimes the solution is simple to enact. Immediately after my meeting I drove to a service station and had the car inspected. Sometimes, however, the solution takes a bit more time and a lot more courage.

Work on the source of the guilt. Lay aside the imaginary pursuers and face the life that is yours for the taking.

GUILT

My imaginary pursuers look like this right now. I'd like to learn to face them.

— Phil Hook

●

THE GUILT MACHINE

"This then is how we know that we belong to the truth, and how we set our hearts at rest in His presence whenever our hearts condemn us. For God is greater than our hearts, and He knows everything."
1 John 3:19-20

Many of us suffer from deep guilt. And because of what our past has taught us, we often accept guilt as being from God. We walk around in inner conflict and confusion with merely an intellectual knowledge of a whole bunch of Scriptures that tell us, "We are free in Christ," "We are no longer condemned," and "We are accepted as the beloved."

On an emotional level, there is still something that blocks us from accepting these truths as reality. The fact is that most of us still feel guilty. And I call the struggle which blocks us from freedom, "the guilt machine."

The guilt machine exists within us, even though Christ died on the cross to free us from its grasp. We are spiritually free indeed, but our emotions still spew forth messages of rejection, self-hatred, and unrealistic demands. We are burdened and bound by the cruel chains of "shoulds" and "shouldn'ts."

As if they are bullies, we allow our feelings of guilt to push us back into a corner. Then, like fearful children forced to obey, we try to please the demands. Tragically, we think that satisying our own messages of guilt also satisfies God. Yet we couldn't be further from the truth.

The only way to truly fix the brokenness of our guilt machine is to turn to the Lord. He invites us to rest in the sweet assurances that our load of sin and failure is no longer an issue with Him. After all, it was Jesus, and not ourselves, who did something about the guilt. It was Jesus who carried the load of the sin. And it is Jesus who removes us from the burden, each and every day.

God is greater than the fallenness that resides in our hearts and threatens to condemn. He has and will continue to release us from the sentences of guilt that still spring forth. And His love will continue to extinguish all of the flames of anguish we feel.

Try to give the guilt to the only One who can take that pain. We are all good at denial, blame, and shame, but we need those tools no longer. The guilt machines can be retired.

THOUGHT FOR THE HEART

I am aware that my "guilt machine" works overtime in these areas.

— *Ellen Quarry*

●

NO REST FOR YOUR SPIRIT

" 'Although you wash yourself with soda and use an abundance of soap, the stain of your guilt is still before Me,' declares the Sovereign Lord." Jeremiah 2:22

At least there was something to enjoy. As he walked to the open window, the moon peered down, casting its silver glow on all that the eye could behold. When the night offered no rest, at least the moon and the stars brought relief. A deep sigh escaped from his dry lips.

"How can I rid myself of this man?" "When will the dreams end?" "What else could I have done?" Questions raced through his mind. He couldn't remember the last time his spirit rested. Guilt hung heavily on his heart.

He knew that Jesus had been innocent. He had known it all along. If he had ever met a man of God, it was the King of the Jews. This Jesus was a real prophet and He spoke the truth with so much conviction! Yet they wanted Him dead. A long and steady sigh passed his lips. "I thought the Jews were supposed to listen to their prophets."

"I gave them every opportunity to change their minds," his defense continued. "Their anger was so deep and consuming. They never even heard my verdict." Pilate turned to go back to his bed.

Every night since the Crucifixion, Pontius Pilate found himself awakened by a disturbing sense of guilt deep within. Pilate was the ruling authority, the Roman governor in power at the time of the crucifixion of Jesus Christ.

When he first heard about Jesus, Pilate had worried that this new prophet might incite the Jews to riot. He'd never considered that the riot might be turned against the prophet himself. Yet that is exactly what happened.

He pulled the covers up tight against his chin. "I literally begged the Jews to release Jesus," he spoke to an unseen accuser. "Why won't you leave me alone . . . leave me alone?" His eyes became heavy.

"Crucify Him, crucify Him!"

"You don't want to be an enemy of Caesar, do you?"

"It is our law . . . we want Him dead!"

"Crucify Him!"

Suddenly Pilate was in the middle of a crowd of angry Jews. As in all of his dreams of late, the crowd became bigger and bigger and the faces grew distorted. He was trying to defend himself, but they wouldn't hear.

In the dream he would try to calm the crowd with logic, but they would not listen nor would they be stilled. Then,

G U I L T

as quickly as they had come, the crowds would disappear and Pilate would be left alone, trying to wash blood from his hands.

We don't really know the depth of Pilate's struggle, but we do know that he was deeply disturbed by the response of the Jews. We know that he seemed to listen to Jesus and that he had a sign, "King of the Jews," fastened to our Savior's cross. We also know that he washed his hands to cleanse himself symbolically from this unnecessary death. Unfortunately for Pilate, a symbolic cleansing does little to assuage guilt.

I have chosen this example in Scripture because it is extreme. Few of us will ever feel the sting of guilt quite like Pilate. But we do wrestle with guilt's hold on our hearts. From time to time, it is difficult for us to "wash our hands" of that which plagues the soul.

Guilt is a powerful emotion. It can move us to terrible sin. Guilt can move us to covering our inadequacies. Guilt can move us to denial and to anger. Guilt can keep us up late at night.

Guilt can guide our dreams, our thoughts, and our actions. Guilt can guide our fears. Guilt can also move us toward Jesus.

There will be those times when we, like Pilate, wrestle with the choices we've made and their ensuing results. We will hurt some that we love. We will wrong some that we care deeply about. We will disobey the Lord and choose our own way. And we will experience guilt.

The good news for the believer is that we are forgiven! Washed and cleansed in the blood of the Lamb, we no longer carry the weight of sin. We no longer have to rid ourselves of guilt's hold.

Pilate carried the weight, as far as we know, for the rest of his years. I'm sure the dreams lessened in time, but I am equally certain that he never escaped the uneasy feeling of justice gone awry.

GUILT

Release your guilt. Learn from it quickly. Take your pain to the Lord and receive His forgiveness.

We need not live between midnight and dawn. We can truly and eternally experience the daylight of God's love.

████████████ THOUGHT FOR THE HEART

Like Pilate, I have a hard time shedding the clothing of guilt. Intellectually I know I am forgiven, but I struggle to receive the release that Jesus brings. Help me, Lord, to lay the burden down.

— *Shelley Chapin*

●

"NOT GUILTY"

"If a person sins and does what is forbidden in any of the Lord's commands, even though he does not know it, he is guilty and will be held responsible. He is to bring to the priest as a guilt offering a ram from the flock, one without defect and of the proper value. In this way the priest will make atonement for him for the wrong he has committed unintentionally, and he will be forgiven. It is a guilt offering; he has been guilty of wrongdoing against the Lord."
Leviticus 5:17-19

Guilt is fairly cut-and-dried in an African tribe, at least in the tribes I've known and observed. The rules are fairly simple and accepted by all, and the price for breaking those rules is always the same.

I knew this young man was struggling the first time I visited his village. He was about thirteen then, and he was fighting the rituals which had long been accepted by his father, his grandfather, his great-grandfather before him. It was his time to become a man, but he was not at all comfortable with what that meant to his family and his peers.

I observed him and judged him to be hurt and troubled.

320

G U I L T

He acted angry, but I did not see anger there. I saw a young boy who needed attention badly. I wanted to help.

I never knew exactly what he did wrong; I only know that I heard one day that the young man had been exiled from his people. He could not have been more than sixteen at the time, and he had failed to comply with tribal law. He was no longer welcome.

The next time I visited the village I casually inquired about him. I was not given any information. In fact, my inquiry was ignored. It was as if the young man no longer existed in their minds or hearts.

The point of this story is not about the young man as much as it is about me. I felt afraid to see him abandoned. I feared for his future and I felt for his pain, though he probably reacted very differently than I imagined.

The tribe had a system. Everyone knew the system. Everyone accepted the system and the rules for punishment. And everyone complied. It was really rather marvelous to watch people work in such a united way.

But guilt is so final. Guilt condemns, separates, breaks apart, and leaves its victims in disrepair. With guilt, there is no way out.

Thanks be to God, I've thought to myself many times since then. *Thanks be to God that we are not consumed. Thanks be to God that we are forgiven, loved, transformed, and renewed. Thanks be to God that there are now no "rules" which threaten to disqualify me from my family.*

I am grateful, Father, for Your Son, our Lord. I am grateful for the price You paid in my place. And I am grateful that I am no more known as "guilty."

I have never seen that young man again. As far as I know, his name is never spoken among the people of that tribe. As far as I know he is still lost to love.

We, on the other hand, are far from lost. We have been found.

GUILT

It is overwhelming to think of the love God has shown us in sending His Son. Lord, help me to release the load of guilt and accept Your yoke of love.

— Pamela M. Reeves

RHYTHMS OF MY HEART

HOPE

HOPE NEVER DISAPPOINTS

"We also rejoice in our sufferings, because we know that suffering produces perseverance; perseverance, character; and character, hope. And hope does not disappoint us." Romans 5:3-5

I remember the day well. It was not yet dawn when I heard the frantic pounding at the door. I stiffened and cast an anxious look at John.

"Could it be soldiers?" I asked in a whisper. "No one move." We stood frozen as John cracked the door, just enough to see.

"Mary," John gasped. "What's the matter?"

"Come. Come quickly," she panted. "The body of Jesus is not in the tomb."

"What?" We all gasped at the news. "What do you mean?" John demanded.

"A young man in shining robes told me that He has risen," she relayed. We heard the words, but none of us was sure what to do.

It seemed like hours before we moved, but then our feet caught up with our hearts. John glanced at me and I at him and we dashed out the door.

As fast as we could, we ran straight to the tomb. Moments before Mary's arrival, we were too afraid to leave that room. Now we were running through the streets at full speed, unaware and unconcerned about the consequences.

Mary had spoken truth. We looked into the tomb and saw that only the linen cloths remained. This was too hard to believe. What was going on? My mind recalled His words, "On the third day . . . " but could this possibly be true?

John and I churned with hope, but we kept it hidden inside. We had been through so much in the last three days. I had denied Him not far from this very tomb. "I do not know Him," I had insisted. And then I watched in the shadows as they made Him carry His wooden accuser toward Golgotha.

We ran back to tell the others about the empty tomb, and then waited, once again, in our room of fear. The high priest's men would surely come, and they would blame us for stealing the body. The hope that had sparked inside now seemed too risky to enjoy.

As quietly as she had come the first time, Mary arrived again. I saw her face and I knew. Mary's eyes shone as never before. "He is risen," she claimed. "He is risen, just as He said." She believed, and I wanted to desperately.

Before we had time to reply, there was someone else in the room. Was it a ghost? No. It was our Lord. And He urged us to touch Him. He showed us His hands and His feet, and then He ate as if He'd never been gone. Yes, He was alive, and my fear grew pale in His assurance.

Hope burst from within me, splitting the darkness that had been my companion since I had heard the rooster crow. The hope came from within and radiated out—beyond the room, beyond time, and beyond this world.

Never again will I fear the risk of believing. Hope is well worth the cost, and it never disappoints. I know this now. He lives.

THOUGHT FOR THE HEART

Hope can impact my life today in these ways.

— John Coulombe

●

GOD WANTS US HOME

"Do not let Your heart be troubled. Trust in God; trust also in Me. In My Father's house are many rooms; if it were not so, I would

have told you. I am going there to prepare a place for you. And if I go and prepare a place for you, I will come back and take you to be with Me that you also may be where I am." John 14:1-3

God wants us home. Hope is that simple. No passion is greater, no desire is stronger. God's greatest yearning is to see that we come home.

God is the shepherd in search of the lamb. His legs are scratched, His feet are sore, and His eyes are burning. He scales the cliffs, He traverses the fields, and He explores the hidden caves. He even cups His hands to His mouth and calls into the canyon below.

The name He calls is yours.

God is the housewife in search of the lost coin. No matter that He has nine others, He won't rest until He has found the tenth. He searches the whole house. He moves furniture, pulls up rugs, cleans out the shelves, and stays up late. He rises early to search again and all other tasks can wait. Only one coin matters — the one that is lost. He will not rest until He finds that coin again.

The coin He seeks is you.

God is the Father pacing the porch. His eyes are wide with the quest. His heart is heavy with passion. He seeks His prodigal child. He searches the horizon. He examines the skyline. And He yearns for the familiar figure — the recognizable gait — of His child coming home.

His passion is you.

It is only in light of such pathos that we can understand the incredible promise of Matthew. "If you believe, you will get anything you ask for in prayer."

Don't reduce this grand statement to the category of new cars and paychecks. Don't lower this statement of devotion into the short-lived pool of perks and favors. In fact, next time you hear someone use this verse to guarantee that God wants you wealthy and famous — turn them off. They are selling God short. God's dreams for you and for me are much greater than earthly wealth or promotions.

God wants us to fly! He wants us to fly free of yesterday's guilt. He wants us to fly free of today's fears. He wants us to fly free of tomorrow's grave. These are the mountains He has moved. And these are the prayers He will answer.

If in the process you are blessed with possessions and health, then thank God, for you have been blessed. If, however, you are not, thank Him still! For still you have been blessed. What really matters has been done for you.

I am aware that it is difficult to focus on the eternal when we live in the midst of the temporal. I am aware that it is hard to be thankful for the spiritual blessings when we are worried about the physical needs of those we love.

But I am also aware that hope is the best gift we've been given, and it is the only gift which will grant us an eternity of provision beyond all that we ask or think. Our Lord is home now, preparing a place for you and for me, and He longs to take us there. God has leveled the Everests which blocked our journey so that we can go where He wants us to go. God has provided the way so that we can go home. And such is the gift of hope.

THOUGHT FOR THE HEART

I am aware of God moving these mountains for me.

—Max Lucado

●

THE LAST WORD

"I pray also that the eyes of your heart may be enlightened in order that you may know the hope to which He has called you, the riches

H O P E

of His glorious inheritance in the saints, and His incomparably great power for us who believe." Ephesians 1:18-19

If I had to choose one word to describe the benefit of Christianity that means the most to me, that word would be *hope.*

No matter what kind of situation we are forced to deal with, it is not hopeless. No matter how deep our sorrow might be, it is never the last word. And no matter how rebellious and far from God we or a loved one might stray, "hopeless" need never be used to describe the situation. With God, there is always hope.

Gethsemane was a terrible and agonizing experience for our Lord. None of us will ever know the depth of His pain nor the agonizing loneliness that accompanied His choice. And if we were to view that situation from the human perspective alone, we would see "hopeless" engraved on every heart and every expression of life that day.

On that Friday we call "good," there hung One who claimed to be God's Son. Straddled between two thieves while hundreds looked on, any "hope" of His being the Savior faded as nails held His hands to the wood. Yes, all of the dreams once shared by the disciples grew pale against the dark death of "the King of the Jews."

What happened? What went wrong? How could things have ended this way?

As hopeless as everything seemed, God always has the last word. Nothing ended that Friday; in fact, hope really began. And I smile to think of the look on their faces as person after person inspected the tomb and searched for a body once dead.

God took the most hopeless situation we will ever face and removed its sting. His victory became ours that day. And in such hope, I find great relief.

Whatever you're facing right now, no matter how impossible or hopeless it may seem, just remember Easter. Easter put hope into our lives to stay, and nothing this world offers can ever change that provision.

There is now a bright light in the tunnel of death. There is now a great good in the well of our suffering. And there is now infinite hope in the heart of every believer, there simply for the taking.

I'll rely on hope today. Someone will call to share deep pain. Someone will confess a wrong that's still not right. And somewhere in the midst of it all, I'll feel my own loneliness, weariness, or frustration.

Yet hope will be my companion and my grateful reminder that we are His. The same power that raised Christ from the dead is at work in you and in me.

THOUGHT FOR THE HEART

Hope can have its impact on me in these ways today — not in spite of my struggle, but in light of God's power.

— David Lynch

●

GOD'S VERSION OF HOPE

"I remember my affliction and my wandering, the bitterness and the gall. I well remember them, and my soul is downcast within me. Yet this I call to mind and therefore I have hope: Because of the Lord's great love we are not consumed, for His compassions never fail. They are new every morning; great is Your faithfulness. I say to myself, 'The Lord is my portion; therefore I will wait for Him.' The Lord is good to those whose hope is in Him, to the one who seeks Him; it is good to wait quietly for the salvation of the Lord."
Lamentations 3:19-26

It is a dark day in my memory. I have no idea if the sun was shining or if it rained that day; I only know that the darkness crept around me and I could see no light. It was the day I was told I have cancer. It was the day I was told that I should expect to live for only a few months.

How does a twenty-eight-year-old plan to live for only a few months? And where is God in the midst of such news? Didn't He know I was hurting, afraid, and quite alone?

The word *hope* flickered through my mind time and time again throughout those long days. I wandered through the memories of my brief life and once again chased the trails of happiness, purpose, and love.

Where did I go wrong? Was God mad at me? Why had He removed all hope?

I'm not sure what conversation, book, daydream, or prayer began to change my perspective, but something started to work. Not long after I'd received "the news," God began teaching me about His version of hope.

To you and me, hope is often defined as a condition of life. "I hope it doesn't rain today." "I hope she doesn't forget what I said." "I hope he studied." "I hope they don't get married too quickly." The list could easily go on.

Hope, as we use it, is wish-fulfillment or desires turned into realities. Yet while we have desires and wishes, God's hope is much more than my longings for what life should hold.

Jeremiah had been called by God. He knew the conversation was real. He had no doubt that God had spoken. But he also had no idea how to interpret the truth that was laid out before him.

"Jeremiah, listen to Me," the young man heard. "I know you and I set you apart from birth. You will be Mine and you will tell the world what I want them to hear.

"Jeremiah, you will speak My words and you will be My prophet," God continued. "I appoint you over nations and kingdoms. You will tear down and you will build" (my humble paraphrase of Jeremiah 1). And with that our young friend was commissioned into service.

"All right, Lord," Jeremiah finally uttered. "I'll do what You say." And with an almond tree and a boiling pot God prepared him for duty.

"Don't be terrified," were God's parting words. "They will fight against you but will not overcome you, for I am with you and will rescue you" (1:19).

There is no way that Jeremiah could have comprehended the grave nature of the years that followed. Jeremiah was despised by the people for telling the truth. He was plotted against, whipped, ridiculed, isolated, imprisoned, and dumped in a muddy well. He was anything but protected, by our definitions; and he was anything but the conqueror we dream to be.

Such was the setting for the Book of Lamentations. Jeremiah literally "lamented" a sad song of the heart. He had nowhere else to turn in his anguish, so he penned the words from the darkness of his own soul.

We lose "hope" when the conclusions of life are different from what we had planned. We lose "hope" when a loved one is afflicted with a threatening disease or a spouse is diagnosed with Alzheimer's.

We lose "hope" when we are terminated from a job or passed by for that promotion. We lose "hope" when a husband or a wife walks out the door. We lose "hope" when depression encases our minds and vows to leave no way out.

Yet in the darkness of a hopeless situation, there is Light. God's hope is not extinguished by those things that cause us grief. When we lose our definition of "hope," we gain God's true gift of HOPE.

Jeremiah saw that small light at the end of his own tunnel, and he called it God's faithfulness. He knew that even in his despair, God was still God. Yes, He visits us with hope in the quiet hours of our darkness.

Cancer has been my companion since 1982, and I have found true hope in its midst. I have learned about comfort, compassion, and joy. I have learned about heaven and peace and faith. And I have learned to reach a hand to another in pain and have more of His love to give.

Hope is a gift that is given to us through Christ. Hope is firmly fixed in place, and no divorce, death, cancer, pain, ridicule, or despair can change that reality.

Hope is the assurance that I will live with my Lord eternally. And hope is the assurance that He will be with me each step of the way.

Follow the journey that is all your own. Cry your own tears, laugh at your own predicaments, walk through your own sufferings, and ask your own questions. For this one thing I know. Your journey with Christ will take you to the same place we are all going; the same place that was revealed to Jeremiah in the very heart of his anguish.

Your journey will lead you straight to the faithfulness of God.

███████████ THOUGHT FOR THE HEART

I've been getting true hope confused with my "hopes" in recent days. Lord, help me to focus on Your point of view rather than my own.

—Shelley Chapin

●
PASSING THROUGH

"If it is preached that Christ has been raised from the dead, how can some of you say that there is no resurrection of the dead? If there is no resurrection of the dead, then not even Christ has been raised. And if Christ has not been raised, our preaching is useless and so is your faith. . . . If only for this life we have hope in Christ, we are to

H O P E

be pitied more than all men." 1 Corinthians 15:12-14, 19

This world is not my home I'm just a passin' through
My treasures are laid up somewhere beyond the
blue.
The angels beckon me from heaven's open door
And I can't feel at home in this world anymore.

O Lord, You know I have no friend like You.
If heaven's not my home, then Lord what will I do?
The angels beckon me from heaven's open door
And I can't feel at home in this world anymore!

This is a familiar song to my generation, one that we call a Negro spiritual. It was sung when slavery was still in force, and it is part of the American heritage. What we don't often realize is this: it is a song about the nuts and bolts of the Christian life. It is a song about hope.

My basic opinion of hope is this: there is no hope without the eternal. It is that simple. If hope is defined in terms of material accomplishments or bettering our positions in this world, then we are to be pitied. There is no race like the one I've just described and there is no reward for the one who has the most. Hope is known in the breadth and scope of eternity.

As I age, I am dealing with my own mortality. And I must admit this subject is a difficult one, as friends grow ill or lose their physical abilities or die. Mortality is usually a tough reality to face.

What about you? Have you stopped to think about your own mortality? Has it occurred to you that, compared with eternity's span, life is short, no matter how many years one lives? It is hope that gives purpose and meaning to life. It is hope that sets us free from despair.

The slaves of our history knew more about hope than

we do. They couldn't fathom a time when they would be free to travel, to choose, to protect and take care of their families. They couldn't conceive of a world in which they would be honored and sought after and considered as equal members of the citizenry.

Their solution to such a bleak realization? They sang with one another and they focused on the future that is sure.

I've heard people ridicule the faith of the persecuted. But what those people don't realize is that we have hope. Those who accept a life with Jesus Christ have hope, regardless of their situation in this world.

Pascal summarized this perspective quite well in his renowned wager: If there is no God, then I have lived a lie and we both die like dogs. But if I am right and there is a God, then I have eternal life and you will have to stand before Him. In both cases, you have everything to lose and nothing to gain. In both cases, I have everything to gain and nothing to lose.

I don't know where you stand on the message of the Gospel, but I do know this: the hope that is offered by Jesus Christ gives life its only true meaning.

▬▬▬▬▬▬ T H O U G H T   F O R   T H E   H E A R T

I find that at times I place my hope in the things of this world. Lord, remind me of my true hope — eternal life with You. And let that hope give my life shape today and every day.

— Jay Kesler

●

KEEPING THE BALANCE BETWEEN HEAVEN AND EARTH

"I press on toward the goal to win the prize for which God has called me heavenward in Christ Jesus." Philippians 3:14

H O P E

Christian writer John White observes that few believers are really spurred on by hope. He says that we opt for earthly reward rather than heavenly treasure because we don't really understand faith. The question he raises is thought-provoking: "If we really believe in heaven's treasure, who will be so stupid as to buy gold?" (my summation)

John White has a point! We don't spend much time preparing for the eternal, but we spend a lot sorting through that which will fade. Heaven will be our permanent resting place, but it's hard for that reality to sink in.

One of the most fascinating debates in Scripture is found in the Book of Philippians. It is a debate, though only one man is involved. His name is Paul, and he is facing the high probability of death at the hands of his persecutors.

"For me, to live is Christ and to die is gain," he said. And he was not just being glib or "spiritual." Paul genuinely longed to "depart and be with Christ," and this longing enabled him to see the circumstances he faced and the people he knew in an unearthly light. It is not that he was so heavenly minded that he was no earthly good. Quite the opposite.

Though Paul desired to depart and be with the Lord, his heavenly-mindedness caused him to consider the cost of such a change. Paul had learned to invest in the most important thing on earth—people. In fact, he esteemed these relationships so highly that he was willing to postpone the fulfillment of his deepest desire (to be with Christ) for the benefit of others.

I doubt you or I will be called upon any time soon to make this choice, but at many points in our lives we are faced with a longing to give up when the going is tough. We are faced with the choice of keeping on or resting, and sometimes the latter is quite enticing.

Still, Paul teaches us that further opportunities to be involved in this world mean further opportunities to enrich the lives of others. When he finally saw the "trade off," he became convinced that he would remain here just a little bit longer.

It is helpful for every believer to feel this "tug" at the proverbial heartstrings. We have practical responsibilities and roles to flesh out in providing for our families and participating in the community at large. We have jobs to do and meetings to attend and goals that we haven't yet reached.

The problem is, we often get so wrapped up in these activities that we forget who we are—pilgrims, sojourners, aliens, strangers in this world. And when we forget that which is unseen by being preoccupied with that which is seen, we tend to miss those wonderful moments when we are reminded that "for me, to live is Christ and to die— that's going home!"

▬▬▬▬▬▬▬ T H O U G H T   F O R   T H E   H E A R T

Lord, I would love to be more aware of hope . . . of my eternal relationship with You . . . of my eternal dwelling place. Help me to keep the balanced perspective, to not spend too much energy purchasing the gold.

— Ken Boa

●

A MATTER OF LIFE AND LIFE

"Now we know that if the earthly tent we live in is destroyed, we have a building from God, an eternal house in heaven, not built by human hands." 2 Corinthians 5:1

I'll never forget the day I learned that a close friend of mine had been diagnosed with terminal cancer. How does one deal with such devastating news? How does one begin to cope when time is no longer an expectation?

Though the news sent all of us who love my friend reeling, it was the man himself who taught us how to see this suffering. When discussing whether or not to take chemotherapy and radiation treatments, he said to me, "Dave, this isn't a matter of life and death; it's a matter of life and life!"

He is right! Imagine such a thought coming from someone who's actually facing that reality. Either way my friend wins, but such hope is difficult for us to grasp.

Paul describes the journey of hope in his second recorded letter to the Corinthians. In summary the apostle said, "If we die, we're really trading in this earthly body for a heavenly one!" What a testimony to the hope of the Gospel! Christians don't surrender life for death, we exchange earthly life for eternal life!

What crosses your mind when Paul writes the word *tent?* Security? Comfort? Permanence? No! Tents are none of these things. They were never intended to be permanent dwellings. And neither are these bodies of ours!

Paul likens our earthly bodies to temporary tents in order to remind us that living here is not the grand finale. Death, for the Christian, is the point of "exchange." Once we move into our new house, we can unpack and throw away every encumbrance we've ever known.

In short, death for the believer is a continuation of the life we have found in Christ. Our Lord said, "I have come so that you might have life"—and the life that He offers never ends. This is the essence of hope.

You may be struggling now with all kinds of difficulties and losses. Try to remember hope. No matter what we face, the choice is life and *life.*

H O P E

I have been focusing on my losses lately. I would like to begin focusing on the realities of my hope.

— David Lynch

●

LORD OF THE IMPOSSIBLE

"What is impossible with men is possible with God." Luke 18:27

As if in flight, she sat forward on the edge of the couch twisting her hands. Unable to maintain eye contact she stared vacantly at the floor. When she did manage a furtive glance, I saw eyes pregnant with fear and confusion.

"My boyfriend sent me here," she stammered. "He thinks I need to talk with someone." As I sat down beside her on the couch, the smell of alcohol was unmistakable.

The day that Mary entered my house forever changed my life! Over the following weeks and months Mary and I began to slowly and carefully forge a relationship she could trust. I discovered a bruised and used young woman who drowned her pain in drugs, alcohol, and dysfunctional relationships.

Divorces and abortions have ravaged Mary's life. The damage was obvious. And more than once in that period of time Satan mocked me, reminding me that women less damaged than Mary remain in his possession.

What made me think I could help her? What made me think she'd be interested?

When I returned from vacation, Mary's voice was waiting for me on my answering machine. The tone was vibrant and full of joy. She wanted to know if I'd come to her baptism!

The next time Mary sat forward on my couch, it was

340

with eager anticipation. No longer did the smell of alcohol permeate the room. She had a miracle to share! And as eyes full of hope made contact with mine, she talked about life for the first time.

Together with a pastor, Mary had simply and thoughtfully repented and acknowledged Christ as her Savior. She traded in the dungeon of despair for the kingdom of light, and now she had hope for the very first time.

Mary celebrated Christmas sober this year. And you may be wondering about her boyfriend! He finds it hard to accompany her rapid spiritual growth at times, but he's still there! And when he lags behind, she teasingly reminds him that all of this was his idea in the first place.

Mary's new life in Christ constantly reminds me that the words Christ spoke to the rich, young ruler still hold true: "What is impossible with men is possible with God."

Do you feel like Satan is tempting you to give up on that spouse, friend, child, parent, parishioner, or student? Is he tempting you to give up on yourself?

Do you feel ineffective and discouraged? Does the damage seem irreparable? Does your God seem too small for the task?

As I accompany the ongoing healing of Mary's life, Satan's mocking is silenced. Changes we as human helpers, friends, or loved ones could never achieve in a lifetime, Christ miraculously accomplishes.

Assist His work! Empower those around you with love and concern. And remember, nothing is impossible with God!

THOUGHT FOR THE HEART

I am realizing that no person is irredeemable and no damage incurable in the hands of the Great Physician. Help me, Lord, to keep my focus on You.

—*Bonnie Sloat*

H O P E

•
PLANNING A LEGACY

"Even when I am old and gray, do not forsake me, O God, till I declare Your power to the next generation, Your might to all who are to come." Psalm 71:18

One of the greatest gifts we give to the next generation is hope. Though we may not notice the significance of this gift from day to day, it is such an important part of our legacy.

We tend to worry about the tangible gifts we leave to our families. We plan for the education of our children. We plan for the financial well-being of those we love. We even plan our own funerals so that no one will be burdened by any unnecessary duties after our demise.

But do we plan the legacy of hope? Do we think about the greatest gift we have to offer our children and their children and the myriad of other children in the generations to come? A grandson's words capture the essence of hope for all of us.

"Dear Grandpa,

It's been so hard to let you go. I keep remembering the times we've shared. I remember sneaking out of bed when I was a kid to have breakfast with you before the sun came up—just you, me, and the Grapenut flakes. We'd talk for a while about anything, and then you'd go to work. 'See ya at lunch, Snickalfritz,' you'd say, and I'd sneak back to bed with a dream to be just like you when I grew up.

I still have that dream. When my wife and I spent a week with you and Grandma last summer, I noticed things I had never noticed before—the love and respect you had for Grandma, the inner strength you knew from your walk with Christ, your commitment to daily read God's Word, and your ability to keep your eyes on heaven no matter how much pain you were in. Each night, when we went to bed, my wife and I would pray for the same dedication and devotion you and Grandma have known for each other and for Christ.

Well, Grandpa, today you are with the Lord, and it is hard to let you go. The night you went home, I was a mess—one of my best friends, gone from this world. But I'm going to see you again! I'm so happy for you, Grandpa, because I know you don't have to suffer now. Yes, I am happy for you. And I can't wait to see you again.

Love, Snickalfritz."

████████████ THOUGHT FOR THE HEART

The real essence of hope is expressed in my life in these ways.

—*John Coulombe*

RHYTHMS OF MY HEART

JOY

JOY MIXED WITH SORROW

"When Herod realized that he had been outwitted by the Magi, he was furious, and he gave orders to kill all the boys in Bethlehem and its vicinity who were two years old and under. . . . Then what was said through the prophet Jeremiah was fulfilled: 'A voice is heard in Ramah, weeping and great mourning, Rachel weeping for her children and refusing to be comforted, because they are no more.' "
Matthew 2:16-18

It is somewhat surprising to find, in the midst of joy and the singing of angels, weeping and mourning so great that comfort is not possible. When God gave His best, man revealed his worst. That which God intended to be the greatest of all blessings, man turned into a nightmare. God proclaimed good will to men; man fostered jealousy and hatred. With the birth of Christ came the true love of God, and the true depravity of man.

Not much has changed in the centuries since our Lord lived on this earth. Pride, jealousy, and greed are as ugly as ever—just a bit more sophisticated. Evil is still imposed on people, regardless of their station in life or their goodness.

For some, marriage promises give way to hurt and chaos. For some, the innocence of childhood suffers abuse and great neglect. For some, sweet success becomes the bitter soil for greed and ingratitude. And for some, a gracious heart must bear the burden of a world still ravaged by sin.

The birth of Christ held greater joy than any moment man had known since Creation. Yet with the birth and life also came some of the deepest pain we have known. Evil is alive and well, and we grieve at the price it exacts in the hearts and lives that it touches. Lest we live in our despair, we must remember that the murderous act of Herod is not recorded to rob us of the joy and glory of Christ's coming. Instead, his selfish deed underscores for us how desperately we need the ringing of the bells and the angel's song. I come in contact with hurting people every day, and such paradox brings to mind the reality of Joni Eareckson Tada's words, "In every event of this life, both heaven and hell participate."

Life can and often does bring hell, yet we are not consumed. Life can and does rob us of relationships and stabilities that form the fiber of our hearts. For a little while we grieve, but then there is relief. For a little while we grieve, but then, heaven.

By God's grace, it is my lot to do all that I can do to bring heaven to the grieving. If I am going to bring heaven to those who weep, I must see the light of His coming. I must embrace the totality of His incarnation. And I must experience the presence of His joy.

Some are not able to hear the bells ring or the angels sing for now. For some, the grief of depravity and pain is weighing heavily upon the soul. And so I will listen to their mourning. I will share in their weeping. I will help their pain become their joy.

███████████ T H O U G H T   F O R   T H E   H E A R T

I can reach out to the grieving with this little bit of heaven.

— *Buck Buchanan*

●
DON'T BE A JOY STEALER

"If you have any encouragement from being united with Christ, if any comfort from His love, if any fellowship with the Spirit, if any tenderness and compassion, then make my joy complete by being like-minded, having the same love, being one in spirit and purpose. Do nothing out of selfish ambition or vain conceit, but in humility

consider others better than yourselves. Each of you should look not only to your own interests, but also to the interests of others."
Philippians 2:1-4

I don't quite know how to say this, but people can threaten our joy. Yes, it's true! All of us encounter people who are hard to get along with, and this can lead to anger, frustration, hate, resentment, bitterness, and disunity. Left to our own devices, we can lose our joy very quickly when surrounded by someone who is critical or abusive or simply pessimistic.

It is easier to talk about the importance of loving people than it is to get along with those we see on a daily basis. As some wise sage once said,

> To live above with the saints we love,
> Oh, that will be glory!
> But to live below with the saints we know —
> Well, that's another story!

The New Testament frequently underscores the importance of unity among brothers and sisters in Christ. Our Lord said that the unity of God's children would demonstrate to the world that the Savior had come! Yet there are times when I'm fairly certain we are not a living demonstration.

When Jesus was preparing the disciples for His own death, He prayed the prayer that we all dream about yet find such difficulty living: "That all of them may be one, Father, just as You are in Me and I am in You" (John 17:21).

It's not surprising, then, that Paul was distressed when he heard from Epaphroditus that there was discord among the believers in Philippi. While he rejoiced in their steadfastness, generosity, and continued interest in his welfare, he knew that the seeds of disunity, once germinated, could undermine the cause of Christ in their city. Such concern prompted Paul to appeal to their hearts.

It is so important that we live with internal harmony. It is certainly critical that we unite against external opposition, but sometimes the worst battles are waged within the unit. It is those internal battles which choke out the joy and leave us with discouragement in its place.

The closer you and I come to our Lord, the closer we come to one another. This is true in marriage, in friendships, in relationships at work, or in the body of Christ. The more focused we are on the Savior, the better chance we have of supporting and understanding one another. And the more we understand and support one another, the more joy flows within and between.

It is hard to always be supportive, encouraging, forgiving, and kind. But the price we pay for not living this way is far more devastating. When we are critical or bitter or jealous or dissatisfied or disinterested, we sow a seed of sadness in the heart of someone else our Lord loves.

Beware of stealing another's joy. And hold tightly to your own. Joy is something to be shared, not destroyed.

THOUGHT FOR THE HEART

I tend to take joy from this person or these people, and I tend to lose my joy when I am with this person or these people. I want to commit myself to learning more about the meaning of joy and to encouraging such a gift in the lives of those I love.

—Ken Boa

●

OVERTAKEN BY JOY

"Was it not You who dried up the sea, the waters of the great deep, who made a road in the depths of the sea so that the redeemed might

cross over? The ransomed of the Lord will return. They will enter Zion with singing; everlasting joy will crown their heads. Gladness and joy will overtake them, and sorrow and sighing will flee away." Isaiah 51:10-11

At first glance it is difficult to connect joy with grief, yet so often the two are beautifully intertwined. It is as if the paradox creates the awareness itself. If I had never felt grief, would I recognize joy?

John Strom went to be with the Lord in March of 1993. I did not know him long, but I knew him well. I do not know what foods he liked or what colors were his favorites, but I know a part of John that means more to me than the preferences: I know a little portion of his heart.

I have the rare opportunity of visiting families when their lives are turned upside down. That is how I first came to meet John and his lovely wife, Marjorie. John had been diagnosed with cancer and God brought us all together to experience the process of "letting go." For a few months of my life, I shared in the privilege of their final journey together. And I count myself among the fortunate people of the world for such a rare gift.

On Friday, March 12th, we celebrated John's homecoming. I watched as a lifetime companion, five sons, one daughter, six spouses, and an array of grandchildren bid farewell. And I was filled with an inexpressible joy.

Joy and grief go hand in hand. We will miss John here. We wanted him to stay. There will be sleepless nights, lonely waves of emotion, longings for a time gone by; and there will be thanksgiving.

Memories of a loving husband, father, and friend will fill the air in years to come. Stories of laughter and family frenzy will be told to the next generations. And a legacy of faith and love will be shared for as long as there is breath in this world.

JOY

"O Lord, how I thank You that there is joy in the midst of grief. How I thank You that John is at home now with You. He sees things we long to see and he understands the mysteries which we long to comprehend. How I thank You that we have hope in a faithful Redeemer."

Joy comes to us in the ever-present reality of our Savior. Joy comes to us in the reminder of hope and eternal life. Joy comes to us to bring peace in the midst of our storms.

As I penned the first words to a song for John, the sorrow turned to great expectation . . . the weeping turned to joy.

> John is alive, feeling no pain.
> John is alive, he has been born again.
> In the twinkling of an eye
> He was captured by surprise —
> Born on angel wings to heaven's light!
> John is alive!

THOUGHT FOR THE HEART

Lord, I am often well aware of my grief. Open my eyes to the joy that gives purpose to our pain. Open my eyes to life!

— Shelley Chapin

REMEMBER CARMEN

"Until now you have not asked for anything in My name. Ask and you will receive, and your joy will be complete." John 16:24

I sank into the sofa as the door closed behind them. Them . . . a Hindu professional and his Christian wife. I was incredulous! In an attempt to dissuade his wife from her faith in Christ, this Hindu professional and concerned husband had unknowingly brought her to a Christian counselor!

J O Y

Carmen is a lovely young woman and as she and I got to know one another I learned of the miracle which had pointed her to Christ. Her son had been ill as a toddler and he had been dramatically healed. Born into the priestly Brahman Hindu caste, Carmen's long search for meaning and significance ended at the cross of Christ.

Carmen was open with her husband about her conversion, and at first he took little note, thinking it another of her many passing fancies. When he realized this was not a passing commitment, Carmen's husband became alarmed and frantically and fanatically rekindled his own Hindu religion. He made life unbearable for his family.

The story is a tragic one. The husband's efforts to dissuade his family from Christianity resulted in persecution and isolation. He even went as far as to exile Carmen to her native India in hopes that she would see the folly of her faith and once again embrace Hinduism. His efforts were to no avail!

Today, years after her conversion, Carmen is a radiant and joyful Christian. To know her is to love her. In the eyes of the world she renounced wealth, social status, and spouse for the sake of Christ. In the eyes of God she will receive a hundred times as much in this world and in the age to come, eternal life (Matthew 19:29).

I see Carmen often. After years of struggle her marriage ended in divorce, but she hasn't lost her joy! Carmen is a source of encouragement and hope to other hurting women. Just recently a woman expressed to me how much meeting Carmen and seeing her joy has given this woman hope for the first time since her own painful divorce.

"I want just what she has," I heard this woman say. Carmen's deep joy and contentment give witness to God's unfailing love as other women experience the pain of rejection and violated vows.

Perhaps broken promises and life's hurts have caused

your own joy to flicker and wane. Adverse circumstances tempt us to doubt the reality of the joy Christ promises in John 16.

When you are hurting, think of Carmen and others you know like her. Hold on for joy! For as Nehemiah reminded the weary Israelites, "The joy of the Lord is your strength" (Nehemiah 8:10).

████████████ T H O U G H T   F O R   T H E   H E A R T

Happiness hinges on happenings, but the Lord is the source of my joy. Lord, let no one and no circumstance take my joy away.

— *Bonnie Sloat*

●
BETTER THAN DISNEYLAND

"Let all who take refuge in You be glad; let them ever sing for joy. Spread Your protection over them, that those who love Your name may rejoice in You. For surely, O Lord, You bless the righteous; You surround them with Your favor as with a shield."
Psalm 5:11-12

While my family and I were visiting in Southern California one year, we went by the world-famous Disneyland. I was struck by the message on the huge billboard outside the park's entrance. It read, "The Happiest Place on Earth."

The "happiest place on earth" is quite a claim, even for Disneyland! Is it true? Could this place of rides and attractions, food and fun, be the "happiest place on earth"? A lot of children would probably agree that it ranks right up there at the top. Even some adults would second the motion. But what is happiness? And what makes Disneyland the happiest place on earth?

For most people, happiness focuses on a way of life

rather than a specific location. The consumer mentality so prevalent in our society dictates that happiness is directly related to the accumulation of things. You know, "the one with the most toys wins."

The position with the company, the neighborhood in which we live, the kind of car in the garage, and the designer labels in the closet are symbols of happiness in our society. Anyone who has all of the "stuff" of the dream is in the happiest place on earth. And Disneyland certainly has much of the "stuff" in a child's dream!

The Bible, however, paints an entirely different picture of happiness for us. Jesus gave us what we know as the Beatitudes. And they contain God's formula for real happiness. They give us the true nature of what believers know as "joy."

Guess what? None of the symbols we cherish so highly make the list for truly joyful living! For the believer, joy is found in receiving God's forgiveness. Joy is found in living a life in which we acknowledge Christ as Lord. Joy is found in pursuing righteousness. Joy is found in giving, in humility, in sensitivity and mercy, in seeking truth, and in being refined. Joy is found in the lifestyle and attitude of the follower of Christ.

I guess it boils down to who we want to believe — Disneyland or Jesus!

The happiness Disneyland provides will fade once the rides are over. But giving our lives to Christ and living by His priorities and values will produce an increasing sense of joy and fulfillment. There is no joy like the joy of living with our Lord.

▰▰▰▰▰▰▰▰ THOUGHT FOR THE HEART

I sometimes confuse "joy" with the "happinesses" of this world. Right now I find I am searching for happiness in these areas.

— David Lynch

J O Y

●

AWARE OF HIS PRESENCE

"Sing to the Lord, for He has done glorious things; let this be known to all the world. Shout aloud and sing for joy, people of Zion, for great is the Holy One of Israel among you." Isaiah 12:5-6

I will never forget the feelings I experienced in the summer of 1963. In many ways it was one of the most significant times of my life. I came to know Christ and began that journey which has since been the focus of my existence. The joy that began back then has continued to flood my heart, literally through thick and thin, laughter and tears, celebration and sorrow.

I still remember walking into the small, wooden cabin that would be my home for the week. The exterior walls were mere screens that served to separate us from the gifts of nature. And the only privacy to be found was in the shared bathroom, some fifty yards from our cabin door.

"Welcome to camp. My name is Judy and this is Jane," I heard as I entered the cabin. "We're your counselors and we are so happy you're here."

The smiles were genuine and warm, and I immediately felt at home with their kindness. My cabin mates seemed friendly and equally as excited. And thus began my encounter with joy.

I had only been at camp for about eight hours when the Gospel was presented in words, but it had been presented in action since my first step on the premises. I don't know how to explain this next statement, but I knew even then that God had sent me to this place and to these people for a very important reason.

The first night at camp found me in the upper bunk, closing my eyes to the sound of tree frogs singing their songs to the world. The place was a wonderland for me and would be my resting place for many years to come.

Joy is not one moment of happiness, though I enjoyed many such moments through the years at camp. I loved horseback riding and canoeing and rodeos and testimony campfires. I loved arts and crafts and swimming and singing and all of the other activities we shared.

To me, joy is the presence of love and purpose in the midst of all the events. Joy is the love which holds us together no matter what life brings. Let me see if I can explain.

Jane, Judy, Don and Fonnie, Bob, Doc and Janelle, Trice, Chip, Eileen, Howard, Duane, Rick, Kerry, Bev, Susan, Brent, Suzanne, Ron, Mike, Greg, Steve, and literally hundreds of others like them impacted my life through the early years of my Christian growth. They modeled love and well-being, commitment and growth for me. They taught me heart-lessons that I never knew I would need. God used them to build upon the foundation of my parents' love and faithfulness so that my cup would be full whenever I have need.

God set me apart to receive His mercy. And He personally led me through years of purpose and preparation. And He continues to do as I've described, reminding me daily of His commitment and devotion. This is the meaning of joy to me.

I have known periods of intense sorrow, moments of almost paralyzing fear, situations of confusion and disappointment, but none of the pain I've known can begin to compare with the love I've been given and the purpose I've seen and the presence of God made abundantly clear through His people and His Word.

I pray I do not seem "out of touch." I simply want to share with you that joy cannot be captured or measured by one circumstance or one sorrow. Nor can it be measured by the absence of pain.

Joy is the presence of our Heavenly Father. And we have that presence throughout our lives in this world and certainly throughout eternity.

I am guessing that you need a touch of joy right at this very moment. Simply close out the world for an instant and reflect on the presence of God—that presence you have come to know through His Word, through His movement in your life, and through all who have loved you.

Joy is the presence of the One who knows us fully.

THOUGHT FOR THE HEART

I have experienced joy through these people, these touches of God's grace, and these awarenesses of His presence.

—Shelley Chapin

●
CAUSE FOR JOY

"But even if I am being poured out like a drink offering on the sacrifice and service coming from your faith, I am glad and rejoice with all of you. So you too should be glad and rejoice with me." Philippians 2:17-18

Have you ever noticed that the word *joy* is not often used in our secular, conversational language? Think about it for a moment! The word *happiness* is used often enough, but rarely do we hear people on the street or friends in conversation talk about "joy."

In the Christian community, "joy" is used a bit more often. When we talk about joy, however, it is generally in a worship setting or in response to a leader asking, "What joys can we share with one another today?" Rarely is the word *joy* used in and of itself.

J O Y

Part of the beauty of Paul's epistles is that they are models of the very things they exhort their readers to practice. In the first sixteen verses of Philippians 2, Paul encouraged the believers to manifest the attitude of Christ in their lives. He wanted them not only to believe in Christ, but also to live like He lived. And Paul was willing to be a model of such a lifestyle himself.

The remarkable thing about Paul's letter to the Philippians is that he was imprisoned at the time of the writing. He was clearly in danger, and he considered martyrdom a very real possibility. Yet against that backdrop, he was willing to say, "Rejoice!"

If I were writing a letter to you now, aware of the distinct possibility that I might die for the cause of Christ, I very well might sound discouraged or angry, frustrated or panicked. And I'm not suggesting that Paul didn't feel those emotions from time to time.

Yet what Paul chose to convey to the Philippians was not an attitude of anger or discouragement, but an attitude of joy! He did not tremble at the thought of death nor did he seem fainthearted. Paul saw death as being just as much a reason to rejoice as living.

It is hard for us to wrestle with the issue of joy. It seems easy to rejoice when *we* feel we have reason to, yet hard to rejoice when God guides our path into something painful or difficult to bear.

The central principle that motivated and guided the apostle in every situation he faced can be summed up in one short expression. "For to me to live is Christ, and to die is gain" (Philippians 1:21). This was the foundation for his joy. And as we lay hold of this truth, we become less and less controlled by the circumstances around us and more and more empowered by the Spirit of Christ.

Rejoice and have joy! We are redeemed. And any path God leads us down moves toward the same destination.

J O Y

Our joy lies in our hope, and our hope is found in Christ.

████████████ T H O U G H T   F O R   T H E   H E A R T

I do not often use the word "joy" but I would like to be more aware of that condition. Even in the midst of my pain I can see that my hope lies in the Lord, and in that I can rejoice.

— *Ken Boa*

RHYTHMS OF MY HEART

LONELINESS

THE VOICE THAT TALKS BACK

"My heart is not proud, O Lord, my eyes are not haughty; I do not concern myself with great matters or things too wonderful for me. But I have stilled and quieted my soul; like a weaned child with its mother, like a weaned child is my soul within me. O Israel, put your hope in the Lord both now and forevermore." Psalm 131

There are times in the life of every individual when loneliness sets in. No matter how many friends one has or how happy a marriage or how connected to the children, there are times when we all feel lonely.

Man has a soul! It's true. It is one of the great mysteries and masteries that separates us from other living things. We have a soul, and that soul is shaped for relationship with the Creator. Nothing else can fill that void, and nothing else can possibly give any greater satisfaction.

For the most part, *we* attempt to fill the gnawing void. We have work activities and family activities and "life" activities which keep us going. We have dreams and goals and achievements that keep us focused. Yet still, in the quiet place of the soul can be found that sense of loneliness, that sense of "I'm not sure I fit," of "I don't feel understood." And that place can only be soothed by one relationship.

I know that there are many ways in which loneliness sets in. Sometimes the death of a husband or wife will leave the surviving spouse with loneliness enough for a decade or two. Sometimes the loss of a parent or significant mentor will leave a hole a mile deep in our hearts. Sometimes being away from the world in which we feel safe can give way to that gnawing loneliness. But there is a healing balm. It is found in our relationship with Jesus Christ.

Now, you may be thinking, "Jay, I'm already a Christian. I know this stuff. I know about a personal relationship with Christ and that's fine, but that isn't going to help me right now." I might respond, "I know what you're saying, but stay with me a moment. I'm not talking about the initial invitation or time spent in the Word, I'm talking about listening to the voice that is within and responding to that voice."

I don't believe we can fill the emptiness inside of us without God. When Jesus Christ is not in residence in the inner soul, then we only hear an echo when we cry out to Him. But for the believer, there is no echo. We cry out and we get a response. We really do! You might give this a try.

No matter how many people are around us, no matter how much music is playing, no matter how much activity there is, no matter how many accomplishments we've achieved and so on, we are lonely without a regular, growing, vital relationship with God. We are lonely without the dialogue that exists for the believer.

For me, one of the greatest proofs of the existence of God is the fact that there is this voice that talks back to me when I care to listen. Sometimes He doesn't speak in ways that are pleasant. Sometimes He convicts and reminds and challenges me to grow.

But always the voice talks back! We simply need to develop our ability and our willingness to listen.

You may be feeling really lonely right now. Try to cultivate that voice—the inner voice that talks back. God is there, and He will answer.

THOUGHT FOR THE HEART

I've never really thought before about God talking back to me . . . about God filling up that void that I feel inside of me. Lord, help me to listen for Your voice. And help me truly hear what You say.

—*Jay Kesler*

L O N E L I N E S S

●
GODLY GUESTS

"No one who has left home or brothers or sisters or mother or father or children or fields for Me and the Gospel will fail to receive a hundred times as much in this present age (homes, brothers, sisters, mothers, children, and fields — and with them, persecutions) and in the age to come, eternal life." Mark 10:29-30

Since the early 1980s I have had the privilege of traveling to Poland on a number of occasions. I was first invited there to teach Bible to college students, and that has remained my privilege through the years.

During one of my teaching trips I found myself feeling extremely lonely. I had contracted my customary nausea and diarrhea and I just wanted to be home where I could be safe and warm again. Teaching was a joy, but I began to suffer from a good case of martyrdom. I informed God, "I have given up so much to do this and the result? I am completely miserable."

One evening I returned to my room and did something I do not often do. I let my Bible fall open and I said, "Lord, I need to hear from You." I looked down and read the Scripture that began this reading. It was as if it were written directly to me, and I thanked the Lord for my time with Him. I was already in bed, though the evening was not late, and I thought about that passage as I attempted to fall asleep.

A short while later I heard footsteps on the stairs leading up to the room where I was staying. It was a very simple house with only curtains for doors, and the sounds of the night were easy to hear.

The steps approached my room and I thought, *O Lord, I'm weary and I'm already in bed. . . .* But before I could complete my plea, a young man entered.

LONELINESS

"Could we come in for a moment, Dr. Hook?" he asked. As I nodded, three young women and one young man quietly pushed the curtain aside and entered my room. They said they were there to say good night to me.

"You have no one to sing to you here and no daughters to kiss you good night, so we have come to sing and to kiss you good night."

They stood around my bed and sang for about ten minutes, and then, in the custom of their country, each one kissed me three times. They hesitated only a moment before leaving as quietly as they had entered. And that room which had felt so empty and lonely before was now filled with the marvel of God's presence.

God gave a simple gift to a martyred heart that day. He gave my lonely soul a gentle reminder that I belong to a wonderful family that spans all nations, all languages, and all time.

THOUGHT FOR THE HEART

I have been feeling lonely these days, and I am grateful that I have a place to belong in my loneliness.

— Phil Hook

●

ALONE WITH THE SAVIOR

"He withdrew about a stone's throw and prayed this prayer, 'Father, if You are willing take this cup from Me; yet not My will but Yours be done.' An angel from heaven appeared to Him and strengthened Him. And being in anguish, He prayed more earnestly, and His sweat was like drops of blood falling to the ground." Luke 22:41-44

One of the most helpful books that I have read is called *The Road Less Traveled* by Scott Peck. I was first introduced to this book in 1981 when I began a personal journey toward maturity.

I was lonely in 1981, more lonely than I had ever felt before. And it was the kind of loneliness that you feel even when people are around. It was an internal loneliness, an unsurety about the future, an uncertainty about "me." I was ready to listen to what God has to say.

Peck says that there are two kinds of loneliness: one that we feel when there is literally no one around and one that we feel when we are with people but unable to really communicate the longings or struggles of the heart. It was the latter type of loneliness that I felt back then, and I wanted to understand its purpose.

We have such a gracious God. He literally stepped into our world in order to experience all that we experience. He went through the birthing process. He went through the helpless years of infancy. He went through the trials of growing up. He went through the adjustments to being out, all on His own. And He went through the pain of being misunderstood and, ultimately, murdered.

Our Lord experienced each step because He loves us and He wants to feel our feelings. One of the feelings He knew quite well was loneliness.

The day was fast approaching for His death. He knew all that He would face and why. He knew that His back would be lashed and that His disciples would flee in fear. He knew He would suffer the jeers of soldiers and Pharisees. He knew everything, yet knowledge didn't cancel out the loneliness.

Our Lord decided to go to the Mount of Olives to pray. His moments of solitude had been few, so this one would be particularly treasured. The disciples followed Him and He asked them to stay awake and pray. He needed some time alone with the Father, and He needed the support of those He loved (see Matthew 26:36-46).

LONELINESS

I am certain that Peter, James, and John intended to stay awake for their friend and teacher. They loved Him. But they had no idea what He was truly facing in His loneliness. Jesus had prepared them as much as possible, but they did not fully understand.

Jesus withdrew a stone's throw from His friends and He began to pray to the Father. His heart was anguished and His pain was deep, but He bore that pain without the disciples' support. His friends had fallen asleep. We are told that their sorrow kept them from bearing His. He understood.

The next step in the process was the arrest. Before their very eyes, Jesus was betrayed with a kiss and then taken away. The disciples could only run, hide, and weep from fear and concern. They did not know how to walk in Jesus' shoes.

I think the heart of loneliness lies in its very meaning. There is no one around who can actually feel what we feel or bear what we must bear. Though we might be well-loved and heartily supported, there is still only one way to walk through the pains that God allows: alone, so to speak, with the Father.

I see aloneness a bit differently these days. It has taken time, but now I sense that loneliness is part of maturity. No one can "grow up" for us, so by definition we must face certain changes alone.

Aloneness for the believer is not the same as loneliness for the man or woman who has no relationship with God. For you and me, loneliness means being alone in the company of the Savior. It means having the ear of the only One who can truly meet our need.

I do not ask that we pretend to enjoy loneliness, only that we see our times on the Mount of Olives as times of real connection with God. Loneliness helps us listen to a different voice, a deeper message, a higher purpose.

L O N E L I N E S S

I have been feeling lonely of late. Lord, thank You for being in my garden. May I learn to open my heart's song to You. May I take solace in the assurance that You are here.

— *Shelley Chapin*

●

PLANTING A GARDEN

"And the second [great commandment] is like it: 'Love your neighbor as yourself.' " Matthew 22:39

Paul's realities have far exceeded his dreams. He is chairman of a large company and he is wealthy now. His money is wisely invested and he is proud of a career carefully calculated and planned. Over the years, he has become more and more interested in the growth and preservation of his wealth. He sees himself a success.

Paul has a new wife now. After fifteen years of marriage, he called it quits. While there are moments of remorse, he rationalizes them away and is convinced that his first wife simply didn't share his ambitions. She didn't fit with the people he admires, and now that problem is resolved. Paul's new wife is young, stylish, and socially in vogue. They are at the top of their social world.

Over the years, Paul has learned to weed out those people he does not need. He is aloof with subordinates and suspicious of people with smaller net worths. He is annoyed by those who seek funds for charities and community projects. The early characteristics of generosity and concern have gradually diminished, but he is not aware of missing them.

There is only one problem. As the last guests leave a party hosted by him and his wife, Paul sits in his study with a strange sensation of loneliness. There were people at the party, but no real friends. And he doesn't share anything of importance with his wife. He goes to bed wondering where things have gone wrong.

We could write this same story dozens of ways. Men and women of all ages and nationalities who reach a plateau, only to realize that they have much and yet little. While they avoid the feeling as much as possible, there are always those moments when the true sense of loneliness cannot be denied.

What has happened to Paul? We might say that he is reaping what was sown. The connection is simple. When we are planting a garden, what we want to grow dictates what we plant. We must water and cultivate, weed and care for the garden. And if we leave part of the land unplanted, we do not expect flowers there.

The same is true with the garden of the heart. If we want love, we have to plant love. If we want friendship, we have to plant friendship. Compassion begets compassion. Kindness begets kindness. And the story unfolds.

Part of the balm for loneliness lies in our seeing people as people. They have feelings, concerns, dreams, and ambitions just as we do. They have families and friends. They laugh and they cry just like we laugh and cry. They are our neighbors.

Regardless of our age or where we are in life, it is never too late to care about people, and the rewards can be amazing.

If loneliness is a major factor in your life and you feel as if you have no one to care, then reach out and care for others. Plant a garden you'll be pleased to harvest.

THOUGHT FOR THE HEART

I would like to sow seeds of love, caring, kindness, and compassion in the garden of my heart.

— Frank Beaudine

LONELINESS

●
BUILDING BRIDGES

"Deep calls to deep in the roar of Your waterfalls; all Your waves and breakers have swept over me." Psalm 42:7

It was 1948. The church my father pastored was a separatist church, and among its many rules was a strong stand against divorce. In all of the years of my youth, I only remember one divorced person being active in the church.

I was tall, young, and began to play basketball at school. Like all of the boys, I enjoyed the practice and the games, and I watched my confidence improve as we all worked together toward a goal.

At the beginning of my sophomore year of high school a new coach arrived. A coach is a very important thing to a ball player and to a young man. The coach is hero and mentor. He is also enemy—he has the power to control your ability to play. Great feelings of admiration and great feelings of fear affect every player about his coach.

When the new coach arrived, I began to observe and take note. I wanted to know this person who would be so much a part of my world, and as I observed, two things quickly came to my sixteen-year-old attention.

The first observation was a great surprise for me. Our new coach was the owner of a brand-new, metallic green "woody" Ford station wagon, which is one of the most beautiful cars ever made! I love to look at cars, so this endeared me to him quickly.

The second observation was a painful one. Our new coach was divorced—and that was horrible news for me. This created enormous crisis in my thinking. After all, how could anyone good be divorced?

I remember walking around his car and admiring its beauty. And I remember wishing that I could get to know him better. Yet somehow I knew that he could never be my friend. As a divorced man, he would not be welcome in the "inner circle" of my family's world. That's a very sad commentary on the thinking of a young boy.

I look back from mature years and realize how lonely that coach must have been in our town. He lived alone. And as far as I know he had only teaching and coaching to fill his life. Our world wasn't big enough for him to belong.

We never did become friends, though I regret that to this day. He always seemed to expect more of me than I could deliver. In fact, I frequently felt like a failure. During my senior year our team never won a basketball game, although three years earlier we were expected to be champions.

Great expectations . . . great disappointments . . . and much loneliness in between. An ugly word that could not be accepted or forgiven kept boys from knowing a man and a man from belonging to his team.

Loneliness is part of our world, even when we don't exclude or judge one another. How sad it is when we allow the gulf between us to remain unbridged.

THOUGHT FOR THE HEART

I am aware of the pain of exclusion in these relationships and I would like to work on building a bridge of acceptance and communication.

— Phil Hook

●
EXTENDED "FAMILY"

"But Jesus often withdrew to lonely places and prayed." Luke 5:16

Why would a person go to a lonely place if another choice

were available? Why would a person go *often* to that lonely place? And why did Jesus choose a lonely place to talk to the Father?

I'm intrigued by Luke's observation. Jesus was surrounded by crowds as well as by His beloved disciples, so why would He want to go to a lonely place? Do you suppose He felt lonely, at times, even in the midst of the multitudes?

I have personally experienced this seeming paradox—at a party with friends, in a church congregation, or lost in the midst of a concert with thousands of people, I've been acutely aware of my loneliness. And I hate feeling alone! Loneliness makes me feel very small, like an insect in the path of someone's foot.

Loneliness frightens me. And I can't imagine someone wanting to be alone. But then I realize that being alone is very different from feeling lonely.

When was the last time I sought to be alone? I could not recall such a choice, so I decided to follow the model of Jesus and withdraw to a lonely place to pray. I settled on a public park with no one around, and this is what I discovered.

I am not ever alone. Oh, sure, I felt alone in the park at first, since there were no human beings around. And believe me, I was well aware of the pain of loneliness. But at the same time the pain and fear put me more in touch with what Jesus must have felt at critical times during His ministry. I am particularly sensitive to the loneliness He experienced at His trial and crucifixion.

Jesus had to feel the ultimate loneliness of being separated from the Father so that I need never be separated from Him at all. I may feel alone, but He has promised to be with me "to the very end of the age" (Matthew 28:20).

So how do we choose "alone" and still cope with loneliness? The psalmist says that "God sets the lonely in fam-

L O N E L I N E S S

ilies" (Psalm 68:6), and that's been the lifesaver for me.

Besides my family of origin, I have a "family" of co-workers, a church "family," a "family" of friends, a "family" of teenagers that I work with, and a "family" of business associates. All these people care about me and are willing to spend time with me, but I need to share my loneliness with them and ask for their help.

Perhaps you might look around and discover the "family" God has given you. Perhaps your "family" members are waiting for you to share your need for companionship. Perhaps your friends are standing by, ready to reach out if only you ask.

Perhaps your companions in church or at work are willing to be a support system for you in your loneliness. And perhaps a brief withdrawal to a lonely place might give a sense of God's presence in your life.

Though it isn't always easy to recognize the company, we are not alone. God is with us.

▬▬▬▬▬▬ THOUGHT FOR THE HEART

The name "Immanuel" means "God with us." I am aware of His presence in my life in these ways.

—*Pam Campbell*

RHYTHMS OF MY HEART

LOVE

SERVANT LOVE

"Love is patient, love is kind. It does not envy, it does not boast, it is not proud." 1 Corinthians 13:4

I wish I could introduce you to Jadwiga—"Jadzia" to her friends, though I am certain that the combination of letters looks strange to most readers.

Jadzia is a pediatrician in Poland. She is tall with dark hair and very striking cheekbones. She is intelligent, not satisfied with easy answers. She is highly dedicated to her job and to the children who depend on her. But best of all, Jadzia has a smile in her eyes which quickly betrays a heart of love. Jadzia is my friend.

I first met Jadzia when I was speaking to a group of college students in the Polish seaside town of Leba. We were there in August, but it was already cold and rainy. During my two-week stay we only saw the sun two times—and even then it only shared its warmth for an hour or so.

Our lodgings were nice for the Polish standards at the time. There were twenty rooms in each boarding house with two or three students to each room and two bathrooms for the whole group to share. Needless to say, there was little hot water available for baths and little time when both bathrooms were unoccupied.

Jadzia and I were roommates during the two weeks. I was told some time later that she requested to be in my room, but I did not know that at the time. God knew exactly what He was doing by placing us together, and I am grateful for the gift of a friend He began giving me that summer. Let me tell you about my time with this gentle lady.

Each morning I awoke to a hot cup of tea and to Jadzia's voice telling me that my bathwater was warm and ready. While I went to take a bath, Jadzia cleaned my part of the room, made the bed, and laid out my clothing for the day. Then, when all the morning preparations were complete, my roommate got the Polish and English Bibles out so that we could read to one another. Every morning was a joy for me.

The evenings held more of the same generosity. I came into a room where the bed was turned down and ready for my tired body! Another hot cup of tea awaited me before I drifted off to sleep, and Jadzia insisted on praying for me as I let my eyes close so that my sleep would be "with God."

I could continue for pages, but I think you get the idea. Jadzia is a servant of God and of man. She is filled with kindness, and I have been privileged to receive a portion of her love while traveling through this world. Jadzia is my friend.

Though I had not known this young doctor long, she chose to treat me with a kindness and concern that have rarely been equalled in my lifetime. She truly cared about my well-being—and not just the part she understood from her own experience.

Jadzia took the time to get to know me. She decided (long before I'd met her or she'd heard of me) that people are worth loving.

Love someone today. In whatever way you are able to show your love, reach out and let someone know that you care.

████████████████ **THOUGHT FOR THE HEART**

I will reach out with love today and let people know that they are worth the effort.

—Shelley Chapin

L O V E

●

BACON AND EGG SANDWICHES

"Though the mountains be shaken and the hills be removed, yet My unfailing love for you will not be shaken nor My covenant of peace be removed." Isaiah 54:10

It seemed like I was allergic to my mother. From the time I reached puberty, she and I did not "mix." Somehow we struggled at even the basic communications of getting along with one another. I chose a typical teenage solution to the problem — I chose silence.

There is a sense in which I moved out of my parents' home in those years. I ate there, I slept there, but I didn't communicate at home. I rarely talked. I would leave for school in the morning, I would come home to eat, but I wouldn't come home to stay until the town had rolled up for the night — the last ball game finished or the last chance to play exhausted. When I was finally home, I read books.

A teenager is always hungry — especially teenage boys who are active. Our home was not an affluent home and I don't know how my parents afforded to feed us, but they did. I remember many times when my plate was empty and I was still hungry, Mother or Dad would take food from their plate and put it on mine. I remember thinking, *You must not get as hungry when you're older.* But I did not realize how much love was in that act until much later.

Late in the evening, my mother would come downstairs and ask me if I wanted a sandwich. I would be reading and I suppose I grunted my assent and the answer was always the same. I loved sandwiches.

A sandwich, back then, consisted of bacon, cooked not quite done, with one or two eggs, cooked not quite hard, on top of homemade bread with butter fresh from the farm. To this day, that sandwich is still the food of angels to me. Mother cooked for me night after night until I left home.

Years later and my own family well underway, I was visiting at home when Mother asked if I wanted a sandwich. It seemed I was still hungry and this was one of those happy memories of home.

"Yes, Mom, I'd like a sandwich," I said. Only this time I was a much more talkative son.

"Do you know why I made all of those sandwiches, Phil?" she asked.

"No, Mom," I replied. "I suppose because I was hungry."

"That was one reason," she said, smiling. "But the primary reason was this. If you would ever talk, you would talk while I made the sandwich."

Mom and I had our problems, but I marvel at the love of a mother who just wants to talk to her son. Night after night and year after year, she reached out in love toward me.

Love does not have to come in complicated packages. It is found, instead, in that consistent display of interest, commitment, sacrifice, and affection.

▬▬▬▬▬▬▬ THOUGHT FOR THE HEART

These memories and these realizations help me to realize how I have been loved.

— Phil Hook

●

LOVE OTHERS FIRST

"If I speak in the tongues of men and of angels, but have not love, I am only a resounding gong or a clanging cymbal. If I have the gift of prophecy and can fathom all mysteries and all knowledge, and if

L O V E

I have a faith that can move mountains, but have not love, I am nothing. If I give all I possess to the poor and surrender my body to the flames, but have not love, I gain nothing." 1 Corinthians 13:1-3

I'll never forget my first year in Africa as a "tentmaker" missionary. I was a young, single woman, afraid and very uncertain. My British heritage had prepared me to be "proper" and "respectful," but nothing had prepared me for the fact that those two words hold entirely different meanings in Nigeria than they do in my little corner of Great Britain.

In my world, "proper" had to do with dress, posture, manners, and clear boundaries. In my world, "respect" had been measured in tone of voice and choice of words. In Nigeria, none of my definitions fit. I was to learn the power of love — power that could mask the fears, undo the mistakes, and yield a harvest of friendship.

Where should I begin? Each story would, in itself, provide a chapter in a book, but there are a few memories I immediately call to mind which illustrate the point I would like to make. They are simple stories, but true.

I arrived at the hospital for my first day's work. I arrived early intending to get settled, but when I arrived there were already well over 100 people lined up for a visit. I had to walk by the long line of sick in order to enter my office.

I don't know if my face betrayed the horror, but I'm fairly sure that it did. I saw illnesses I had never seen before except in textbook illustrations. Men with large tumors growing out of their backs, necks, and stomachs. Children emaciated from hunger and diarrhea. Women coughing with sounds of tuberculosis. Sickness was rampant. How could I just walk by?

"Marie" became my interpreter for the months that followed. Every patient I saw she saw. And she showed me their world through the eyes of one who knows them. Without her, I would not have known most of what I learned in that first year. She served as my eyes, my ears, my heart—and together we learned much about loving.

One day after at least a year in service she arrived on the scene looking ill. Her eyes were clouded over and her voice was hoarse from coughing. Immediately I began to examine her, but she would not allow me entrance.

"We have work to do," she said. "There are more people today than ever before. There is a sickness in a nearby village and they have come to us for help." She began to gather supplies.

I am convinced we worked harder that day than we'd worked in the year since I'd arrived. Marie had been correct in her diagnosis. There was a sickness in the village and most had been exposed. Their drinking water was contaminated. They bathed in the watering hole together. There was no such thing as "sanitary," so disease spread fast.

Finally, at nine in the evening, we completed our last exam. Many had been admitted to the clinic so we made a final round. And as I turned to say good night to Marie, I *looked* at her for the first time in hours. She could barely stand.

How had I missed her pain that day? I asked myself. *She had worked so diligently and so lovingly. I had dismissed her need. She was ill. She needed my help.* The thoughts rolled over in my mind. Simply put, I had been so busy letting Marie be my eyes that I missed the symptoms entirely.

I apologized for my insensitivity as I took Marie in my arms. I'll never forget what she said.

"You have honored me today," she said, smiling faintly. "You have allowed me to work with you. Before you came here, I focused only on myself. Now that I have worked with you, God has taught me to love others. Today I needed to love others first. God will take care of my needs."

I wanted to argue that we must care for ourselves, but the Lord stopped my tongue from its errant ways. Instead of talking, I held my dedicated friend as another doctor began treatment. I held Marie and committed her words to memory.

"Today I needed to love others first. God will take care of my needs." Oh, that we all took loving to heart.

THOUGHT FOR THE HEART

I would like to love others today. And I would like to love them as they need to be loved, not merely as I might want.

—Pamela M. Reeves

AN ORCHESTRA OF LOVE

" 'Of all the commandments, which is the most important?' 'The most important one,' answered Jesus, 'is this: Hear, O Israel, the Lord our God, the Lord is One. Love the Lord your God with all your heart and with all your soul and with all your mind and with all your strength. The second is this: Love your neighbor as yourself. There is no commandment greater than these.' " Mark 12:28-31

It was my first trip out of the country alone, and I had scheduled myself for seven weeks of speaking engagements! After four weeks in Poland, I was weary and homesick and wishing I could cancel the remainder of my work.

I had been riding the train all night, luggage high above my head and clothing soiled from the long trip. I had not slept well. No matter how I tried to convince myself that I would wake when the train reached my destination, my mind was not convinced. Every time the train slowed or came to a stop, I was at the window surveying my surroundings.

I had to change trains in Frankfurt. A nice man helped me pull the luggage down from the rack and lift it off the train onto the platform. I had never seen anything like the size of the Frankfurt train station. People everywhere, trains departing with great precision. I was fascinated, yet the strange faces and bustle of the crowds made me feel even more alone.

I found my place for the connecting train and waited patiently until time to board. I remember looking at faces, hoping to find someone with whom I could share a moment's connection.

The conductor called for our departure, and I quickly lifted my belongings onto the great train and began the search for the right car . . . the right compartment . . . the right seat. The train was already quite full, and so I prayed to find a place where I might feel welcome.

Just then I saw her. She was an aging woman with lovely white hair and sparkling blue eyes. The corner of her mouth turned slightly with a smile as I entered the compartment to claim the last seat.

No one said a word for a while, but I found myself sneaking glances at this lovely woman. I couldn't help wondering what her life was like. Who was she? Where did she live? Did she speak English? Did she know I was curious?

Not long after the train left the station, the young man next to me engaged my older friend in a conversation. The German was fluent and the topic apparently light as they both smiled and seemed to speak freely.

"You want to know what we are saying, yes?" She was speaking to me! And I guess I hadn't given her much choice.

"Yes," I replied, and I'm certain my tone betrayed both

my eagerness and my loneliness.

"I do not speak English well. I have not spoken since the Second World War. But I will try. I must speak slowly."

Maria is a German physician who has lived through the deepest of sorrows and the greatest of joys. She has a husband still living and a home in the country and several children of whom she is very proud.

Maria opened her heart to me that day. She made me feel welcome. And she never seemed to tire of trying to speak my language in order to meet my needs.

She asked questions about me and my family. She was interested in my work. And she never once betrayed the severity of her own pain. Maria was there that day to love me, and I knew I'd encountered one of God's gifts of grace.

I don't know who in your world needs love today, but I imagine that you will encounter someone who is lonely or confused or in pain. Pray to be an orchestra of love. Pray to play the instruments of caring and listening, of kindness and compassion. Pray to give someone else the gift that God has given you.

Maria knew nothing about me, yet she read my needs with ease and has remained my treasured friend through the years. She simply took time to love.

We sometimes bow out of our calling to love under the auspice that it is too much work or that it takes too much time. Maria didn't think so.

She took a moment of life she was already living and she shared it with me. She did just what Jesus did so many times and in so many ways.

My life is far richer since meeting this orchestra of love. And I know your life will be full as you give your love away.

L O V E

I'm not sure where my love is needed today, but I will pray to be aware and to take the time to give.

— *Shelley Chapin*

●

WASHING FEET

"It was just before the Passover Feast. Jesus knew that the time had come for Him to leave this world and go to the Father. Having loved His own who were in the world, He now showed them the full extent of His love." John 13:1

In the thirteenth chapter of John's Gospel, Jesus is seen doing a very strange thing. Instead of acting like a leader in the traditional sense, He takes the role of a servant. We are told that He demonstrated the full extent of His love by washing the feet of His disciples.

Why did Jesus wash their feet? Why was this act so important to His loving?

Jesus left His disciples not only with teachings to follow, but with an example to live by. He didn't want to just tell them to love one another, He wanted to show them how. And He wanted them to experience the privilege of servanthood. He wanted them to know their worth in His eyes.

Leona is one of the faithful servants of the world. She and her sister Elsie were members of the first congregation we pastored. I was new to the ministry and anxious to exhibit the love and servanthood of our Lord, but I wasn't too sure just how such love and servanthood should be exhibited!

Leona and Elsie lived in a small frame house with none of the modern conveniences. Water for cooking and washing had to be carried in from the pump. But Leona was a gracious host and insisted we sit at her table. Both Wanda and I counted it a joy to be served by this loving woman.

Elsie was mentally handicapped and she needed a caring guardian. Long ago, Leona had chosen to be that person. She never married. She never pursued her own dreams. She chose, instead, to devote her life to caring for her sister.

Sometimes the road got rough and she would call for help or comfort, but most of the time Leona simply loved her sister, literally "washing her feet" and caring for her needs. Such love is hard to come by.

Jesus could have chosen a more visible role. He could have insisted on obedience and a powerful position. He could have demanded that the disciples wash *His* feet. But that is not the path our Lord wanted to walk.

Jesus had a message to share and to live, and that message was simple: "Love one another as I have loved you. Serve one another as I have served you." The two go hand in hand.

Leona didn't write a book or lead a conference or serve on many committees. And I doubt if she's *ever* had many of the modern conveniences. Leona spent her whole life washing the feet of one she loved. And few even noticed. She showed the full extent of her love each day as she set aside her own rights for those of an unaware sister.

▬▬▬▬▬ THOUGHT FOR THE HEART

There are people in my life who are in need of a foot washing from me. Help me to be like Jesus and show the full extent of my love.

—David Lynch

●

OUR GREATEST AND HIGHEST PRIVILEGE

"Though you have not seen Him, you love Him; and even though you do not see Him now, you believe in Him and are filled with an

L O V E

inexpressible and glorious joy, for you are receiving the goal of your faith, the salvation of your souls." 1 Peter 1:8-9

There are many ways to talk about love: the love of a husband for a wife, the love of a parent for a child, the love of a boy for a girl or a friend for a friend. We can also speak about the ingredients of love and glean insight from 1 Corinthians 13.

All in all, there is much to learn about love. But there is someone who needs our love more than we generally know. That someone is our Lord.

You might know something about sunspots. Through telescopic photographs of the sun we have seen massive areas on the solar photosphere which we have come to call "sunspots." They are temporary cool regions which appear to be dark because of the hotter photosphere which surrounds them.

If you and I could see a sunspot by itself, we would see that it is brilliant! A sunspot is hotter and brighter all on its own than anything you or I could witness on this earth. It is only against the backdrop of something even brighter that the sunspot appears to be dark.

We are called to love others. And this is such an important command that Jesus spent many of His final days and moments with the disciples reminding them of this fact (John 13). As He knelt to wash their feet, we are even told that Jesus intended to show the disciples the full extent of His love. With that in mind, He washed even the feet of the betrayer.

Our love for others should shine! But that love is to look as a sunspot compared with our love for the Lord. Although we have not seen Jesus, we can love Him and hope in the One who first loved and delivered Himself up for us.

Our highest calling is to grow in our knowledge and

love of Christ and to make Him known to others. Our love for Him should make all other relationships pale.

Loving one another is a critical ingredient to the Christian life, to our families, to our workplaces, to our ministries. But loving God is our greatest and highest privilege.

████████████ THOUGHT FOR THE HEART

It seems easier to love my family and friends than it does to love God, simply because He isn't here in "the flesh" right now, responding in a way I'm accustomed to. Lord, I want to love You. I want to know You, love You, and share You with those who are important to me. Help me to love You sincerely.

— Ken Boa

●
ALWAYS AVAILABLE

"When Israel was a child I loved him, and out of Egypt I called My son. But the more I called Israel, the further they went from Me. They sacrificed to the Baals and they burned incense to images. It was I who taught Ephraim to walk, taking them by the arms; but they did not realize it was I who healed them. I led them with cords of human kindness, with ties of love; I lifted the yoke from their neck and bent down to feed them." Hosea 11:1-4

The picture painted here by Hosea is such a spectacular portrait of God as Father. It is easy to go back in our mind and see the helpless, enslaved people in Egypt rescued by our God. God began to teach them to trust again, and Scripture records the outpouring of His love.

Mighty deeds, heroic acts, and the triumphal departure through the Red Sea marked God's outreach to His people. The Red Sea meant grief for the Egyptians who lost their oldest sons, yet it meant the beginning of freedom for the people of Israel. Once again, they were well aware of God's love. Once again they felt like His people. A cloud by day and a fire by night, God provided for His people in every way.

A problem arose, however. In the midst of God's provision, the people became unfaithful. As in days gone by, they began to take matters into their own hands. They grew disgruntled with God's provisions and they used His law to segregate themselves. Slowly but surely they pushed away from God's love. Slowly but surely they forgot His provision.

When I read these stories, I am reminded of the dilemma we earthly fathers experience. God the Father is always available. Man as father is not so good at availability.

My father was very busy doing "the Lord's work," and for that reason it was difficult to criticize him. Surely that work was more important than the wishes of a young boy.

My father got up early to study. And he pastored small churches where he did everything from printing the bulletin to emptying the trash. In the evenings he visited families. Needless to say, he was rarely at home.

Dad wanted to play ball when he was young but he was never allowed to—he had to tend the farm from the time he was a boy. I wanted to play ball, and I wanted my dad to play with me. But he had learned early in his life that work comes before fun.

I remember a day when I asked Dad to play catch with me, and he promised we'd play when he got home. I came home from school that day, grabbed my ball and glove, and sat on the steps to wait for my dad. Gradually it grew darker and finally the sun went down. I still had my ball and glove, and I still had no Dad.

It's strange how many times we can read about a Father God who has time, yet we who are human fathers do not have time. I can remember with my own children when the newspaper seemed more important than they did. Mary, Barb, or Brenda would come running in and dive through the sports page, and I would be upset for the interruption.

Thankfully, the love of our Heavenly Father is a constant. Even when the Israelites decided to turn their own way (again), God's love remained unfailing. Even when they betrayed Him, His love never ceased. He never stopped spending time showing His children love.

God teaches us to walk, marks our every step, never lets us out of His sight, and never fails us when we need Him. His love is truly perfect, beyond our ability to grasp.

Though you and I fail those that we love, God does not fail. Though you and I have limitations to our patience and faults in our priorities, God's love provides exactly what we need. He never lets us out of His sight.

THOUGHT FOR THE HEART

I need to be reminded of Your love, Lord. This life can be very confusing and demanding. Help me to remember Your cords of kindness and ties of love.

— Phil Hook

RHYTHMS OF MY HEART

OBEDIENCE

FULLY ACCEPTED

"Abram believed the Lord, and He credited it to him as righteousness." Genesis 15:6

I grew up in a home with many rules, and most related to "keeping the Sabbath," as we chose to celebrate, on Sunday. There were other related rules like "no drinking, no smoking, no dancing," but the Sunday rules were always the hardest for me to keep.

Not only were we not allowed to shop or go out to eat (this would have caused others to work!), we weren't allowed to play ball or even listen to the Sunday games on the radio. In short, Sunday in our home was a pretty bleak day for little boys.

Outwardly we kept most of these rules, but I'd always break them "a little." I'd turn the radio on for a really quick check on the score or I'd throw the ball for just a moment while no one was looking.

I wanted to change the rules, but I could not. Instead, I just tried to keep them and to choose carefully which ones were worth breaking.

Many years later, while attending seminary, I returned to my parents' home for a vacation. I was working as recreation supervisor for First Baptist Church at the time. A woman in Dallas had given the money to build one of the first recreation buildings in the country, and it was wonderful! The center included bowling alleys and a skating rink and everything else to make a child's play spectacular.

I'd never told my parents about the bowling alleys or the skating rink before, because both of these were prohibitive behaviors. While visiting, however, I had a slip of the tongue. I started a sentence with the phrase, "When I was skating" and the eyebrows lifted almost on cue.

OBEDIENCE

"When were you skating?" my mother asked, an obvious concern in her voice. I recognized the familiar sound of disappointment. I said nothing.

"Phil, you haven't been skating, have you?" she continued. I knew now there was no avoiding the confrontation. I had kept many of the rules most of the time, but roller skating to music, even in a church recreation building, made me a failure and a disappointment.

When God called Abram, He said, "Leave your country, your people, and your father's household and go to the land I will show you." Abram was the man of faith in Scripture—but he really obeyed only two parts of the directive.

Abram left his country behind, but he took with him his father, nephew, all their possessions, and everything else familiar and portable!

Fortunately, God is perfect, but He is not a perfectionist. He honored Abram's incomplete obedience, and He continued to bless and guide His servant each step of the way. It is you and I who expect perfection of one another.

It is hard for us not to want others to comply with our "rules and regulations." All the way from parental rules of the house to what we expect from one another in a relationship, we have standards and expectations of one another.

I do not object to my parents' expectations and standards, but I was hurt by the importance placed on those standards and by the way I felt when I fell short. When I did not fully obey, I did not feel fully accepted. Instead of feeling able to talk with them about our differences, I hid the differences between my life and theirs and cringed when they discovered the variance.

God loves and accepts you and me. He wants us to obey, but He also well understands our struggles, limitations, needs, sins, and simple lack of commitment at times.

He understands and He wants us to share our confusion with Him.

Be careful to accept others even when they fall short of your expectations. And be aware that you are accepted fully and completely by our Lord. Whether you're struggling with the rules of someone else or the guidelines set by our Lord, remember that He is there to help and guide.

God loved Abraham and Sarah — sarcastic laughter, doubts, fears, and all. God loves you and He loves me.

■■■■■■■■■■■■■ T H O U G H T   F O R   T H E   H E A R T

I have been struggling with obedience in these areas. Instead of avoiding the struggle, I would like to open up the lines of communication and talk with God about my need.

— Phil Hook

●

OBEDIENCE FOR THE RIGHT REASONS

"And this is His command: to believe in the name of His Son, Jesus Christ, and to love one another as He commanded us. Those who obey His commands live in Him and He in them. And this is how we know that He lives in us: We know it by the Spirit He gave us."
1 John 3:23-24

It's never easy to be obedient. Obedience takes real discipline and a whole lot of inner direction. Obedience requires choice and trust and self-confidence and a certainness about where we belong and why.

Most parents want children to obey simply because it is convenient. If a father says, "It's time for church!" and everyone in the house lines up by the door, it's convenient! If a mother says, "You need to apologize to your sister" and the errant child says, "I agree. I know I was wrong!" that's convenient! If a college student majors in what the parent thinks is best, that is convenient. Obedience makes a parent's job much easier!

The problem is, we often opt for obedience simply because we're bigger or older or more authoritative or . . . because it's convenient. We demand obedience rather than modeling such an attitude. We require obedience rather than encouraging it. And I readily admit this is a tough distinction. It takes great creativity and patience to teach a child to obey because that's what he or she really thinks is best.

Let's move to our relationship with God for a moment. We generally associate obedience with having to do something we do not want to do! We associate obedience with God requiring us to behave or respond in some certain fashion. In most scenarios, obedience almost feels like a trial or tribulation in and of itself.

What about obedience growing out of significance? What about obedience growing out of a trusted relationship? What about obedience being our individual response to God?

When we feel comfortable with our place in God's family, we tend to find that obedience is not such a hard pill to swallow. God doesn't ask that we do everything "just right" or that we "match" in all our relationships or goals or plans. God simply asks that we do our best to listen to Him and respond accordingly.

God wants us to have some comfortable shoes and a few things out of place. He well understands our world and the struggles we have living here. Obedience is not immaculate perfection; it is a response to God that grows out of His love for us and our love for Him.

Look around at your life for a moment. Are you trying to get everything "just right" before you make God happy? Are you trying to fit in just the right minutes of prayer each day or just the right time in the Word?

See if you can relax a bit and allow your heart to respond to God's love. That is where you'll find obedience.

Though it might be more convenient to have a house full of children who never make mistakes and always do exactly as they are told, that isn't what family is all about.

In families, you know who doesn't get up well in the morning and you know who needs extra time in the bathroom. You know who cries easily or who is a bit more stubborn. You know who needs an extra hug and who wants to be left alone for a while.

Living obediently with God isn't exactly the same for everyone. It is responding to God's purpose as He has designed you—in your unique way, and in His time.

████████████ THOUGHT FOR THE HEART

I tend to be impatient with some of the people in my world. I want them to respond in the way I think best. I also tend to be impatient with me. I would like to begin to set myself and others free to be who God has designed us to be.

—Jay Kesler

●

THE PURPOSE OF OBEDIENCE

"Whoever has My commands and obeys them, he is the one who loves Me. He who loves Me will be loved by My Father and I too will love him and show Myself to him." John 14:21

My two-year-old is fascinated with the upright piano. After all, it is big and it makes noise. But I've tried to make the piano "off limits." I can't begin to say how many times I've spoken the word "no" as he climbs up to have his fun and test my limits.

How hard it is for children to believe that we have their best in mind! Our "no's" and "wait's" and "this is for your good's" seem so dissatisfying when all they want to do is live and have fun and test the limits a bit. It is difficult to be a parent . . . and a child.

It is hard to see obedience without seeing rules. I have had those moments in my relationship with my parents when I fought the rules and missed the whole idea of obedience. I wanted things done my way, and I couldn't even hear their reasons for saying "no" or "wait." I thought I knew best, and I resented their involvement.

Yet I'm learning, as I grow older and have children of my own, that obedience is about relationship—not limits, perfection, or competition. The rules are important, but true obedience is part of a growing relationship with those we trust and love. I never quite understood that concept as a young child in my parents' home.

It is unfortunate, but many of us view God as a grumpy old man, intent on preventing us from having any fun. At the very least, many of us view Him as a bit out of touch with our current lifestyles and needs. After all, the Bible was written a very long time ago!

As years go by, however, I am learning that a much more realistic picture of God is that of a loving parent. He knows it is best that His small child not climb on top of the upright piano, but there aren't many ways of communicating that knowledge such that the child wants to hear. Our obedience is desired, not in order to eliminate pleasure, but so that we can live our lives to the fullest.

For the believer, the key word in talking about obedience is *love*—both God's love for us and ours for Him. It is from love that He instructs us, and it is for love that He desires us to obey.

I love my little boy, more than words can say. And I know that my God loves me. How I long, then, to grasp the relationship of obedience. How I long to be able to offer God my love.

OBEDIENCE

Though it's hard for me to listen and obey, I can see God trying to take care of me in these ways.

— Mark Hoffman

●

THE COST—AND REWARD—OF OBEDIENCE

"Without faith it is impossible to please God, because anyone who comes to Him must believe that He exists and that He rewards those who earnestly seek Him." Hebrews 11:6

I have never liked the word *obedience*. It conjures up all kinds of memories or stereotypes in my own life or in the lives of school friends. Obedience is one of those words that we usually associate with resignation, struggle, and just plain lack of fun.

Sometimes obedience isn't fun, but I continue to learn just how important obedience is in the life of the believer. The key is the reward or gratification that we focus on, not the act of obedience itself. Anyone *can* obey if he wants to, but obedience without willingness holds very little reward or value.

When Paul wrote to the Philippian church, he encouraged them to live with the same attitude as Jesus Christ (see Philippians 2:5-11). Paul had lived that way himself and found such purpose that he wanted those he loved to follow in the steps of the risen Lord. Lest they not know where to begin, Paul willingly gave direction.

Paul wrote of a Savior who was willing to step into this world. He wrote of God become man. He wrote of our Lord taking the form of a servant. And then he wrote of obedience.

"He humbled Himself and became obedient to death on a cross." Somehow that statement reflects a level of obedience I have not yet struggled with and never will.

OBEDIENCE

It has been observed that only a divine being can accept death as obedience. For ordinary men, death is a necessity. How true that statement is for you and for me.

Our Lord came to do the will of His Father, and that will included obedience to death on a cross. For all of us, obedience includes a certain sacrifice. Yet for our Lord, the reward was greater than the sacrifice. He was exalted by God after all was said and done, and He still retains that seat of honor. Someday every knee will bow and every tongue will confess His glory. There are no more majestic pictures painted for us in Scripture than the portrait of eternity with Jesus Christ.

Our Lord's reward also includes His children being united with Him once again. The price for sin has been paid, once and for all, and we are no longer separated from Him. Such is joy for us and for our Creator.

As those who put their hope in Christ, we must understand that obedience is always costly. It may involve the sacrifice of serving others and being rewarded with abuse or cruelty for the effort. It may mean being misunderstood or humiliated. It may require giving up a cherished dream or enduring failure as the world sees the word. The cost can take on many different shapes.

Yet in the midst of the cost is glory. God rewards those who seek Him, and His reward is great! In fact, God's reward is always better than man's.

There will be times we are called to obey at great price. Just keep in mind the cost and the reward of our Lord. There is nothing He asks of us that He hasn't accomplished Himself—in our place, for us, for eternity.

███████████████ THOUGHT FOR THE HEART

I struggle with obedience in these areas of my life. I want to learn to accept the cost and to focus on the goal God has set before me.

—Ken Boa

OBEDIENCE

●

RIVER CURRENTS

"Paul, a servant of Christ Jesus, called to be an apostle and set apart for the Gospel of God — the Gospel He promised beforehand through His prophets in the Holy Scriptures, regarding His Son, who as to His human nature was a descendant of David, and who through the Spirit of holiness was declared with power to be the Son of God by His resurrection from the dead: Jesus Christ our Lord. Through Him and for His name's sake, we received grace and apostleship to call people from among all the Gentiles to the obedience that comes from faith. And you also are among those who are called to belong to Jesus Christ." Romans 1:1-6

One of my favorite activities in my younger years was whitewater canoeing! I will never forget the thrill of riding those waves, screaming with exhilaration and a healthy dose of fear. Each trip was a challenge for me, a chance for me to test my own skills and abilities against the river. I looked forward to the challenge.

By 1982, I felt like a pro! I had made dozens of trips and I prided myself on the fact that, when I was in the stern, the canoe never turned over. No, I was in control while running the rapids! I knew just what I was doing! And I certainly never let myself get into a position of weakness. For me to ride with someone meant they had to claim the bow while I manned the stern. I trusted my leadership and mine only.

There is one little part of the journey I have not yet mentioned, and that part is called "exhaustion." Though I thoroughly enjoyed each canoeing trip, I would return to Dallas completely depleted of all my resources. The river took every amount of energy I could muster! After all, I had to stay in charge. I couldn't let down my guard. I had to plot every move. I'd return home, hit the bed, and sleep for at least twenty-four hours.

I can still remember the morning a light turned on in my mind. I had awakened early, before the rest of the group, and I was already dressed and prepared for the day. I placed a pot of coffee on the slow-burning coals and walked down to the river.

We were camped near the rapids. I love the sound that the water makes—current rushing to and fro over boulders and fallen trees. I watched as the sun began to peek its head over the hills and I reveled in the moment.

With a simple, unthinking gesture, I picked a stick from the ground and hurled it out into the midst of the running water. I watched as the stick bobbed, circled, and twirled its way through all of nature's trappings. I could see just far enough to watch my stick emerge in a quiet pool at the other end of the rapid. I felt a sense of security.

It was at that precise moment that God chose to teach me one of those profoundly important lessons. As if He were beside me, my mind embraced this thought: "The water knows exactly which route to take 24 hours a day, 365 days a year. Even when you aren't here, Shelley, the water knows exactly where to go."

The statement wasn't particularly sophisticated, but the message ran its course through my mind and heart. And I made a decision to "run the river" just a little bit differently that day.

Twenty-one miles down the river our last canoe hit ground and we began to pack our things. Our much-anticipated trip was over, and everyone was healthy and happy. And all the participants looked weary, as usual; all, that is, except me.

My new discovery had worked! I knew without even a hint of doubt. That day, I had done only one thing in the river: I had kept my canoe "straight." Yes, that was the secret. Instead of choosing the "perfect" way to go through each rapid, I merely kept my canoe straight on its course and I allowed the river to guide my boat. God had taught me a lesson of life I would not easily forget.

I can say with certainty that the river led me toward the biggest rock in the rapid at times, but I can just as certainly attest to the fact that the water made its way around that rock and led me into safety each time. I only needed to keep the canoe straight on its course.

It is hard for us to be obedient to God. We are not built for obedience, so to speak, but for a touch of rebellion. We feel that desire to "do it my own way" from the time we are young. "Do not touch" becomes an invitation to "touch." "Let me help you" becomes a commitment to "do it myself." And various other tasks like "brush your teeth," "go to bed," and "don't fight with your sister" become predictors of how we are *un*likely to behave.

Obedience does not come naturally and we make it all the harder! Just like my method of canoeing, we want to be in the stern. We want to be in control. We want to carefully choose our own way, and we like life best when God is doing things according to our plan! We want to obey, but only when obedience is comfortable or otherwise rewarding.

When a stick tossed and turned in the river that morning, I learned a lesson I long to recall every day. I learned that staying in the stern only makes my trip exhausting. Demanding control only keeps me void of the privilege of God's being in the seat of honor. If I'll simply toss the stick into the river and trust that river to know where to go, my life will be far more healthy and fruitful.

God does know what He is doing. He has already pledged His love and commitment to us. He has already promised that He will care for us through every situation of life. There are no exceptions to that promise.

To obey is to release control and allow God His way. To

obey is to "step aside" and trust the One who loves us as no one else. To obey is to place our stamp of confidence on our Father, who was and is and will be.

THOUGHT FOR THE HEART

I tend to try to pilot my own canoe. Just lately, I've been wrestling God for control in these areas. I want to begin to learn how to release control and allow God His privilege of parenting this child that He loves.

— Shelley Chapin

●

SHEPHERD OF THE HEART

"My sheep listen to My voice; I know them, and they follow Me. I give them eternal life, and they shall never perish; no one can snatch them out of My hand." John 10:27-28

Of all possible animals to offer as comparison to man, our Lord chose sheep. Sheep . . . those curly-haired animals with a bleating voice . . . and why? Because sheep need a shepherd, and our Lord is willing to accept that job.

The optimum scenario offers a sheep that follows the shepherd's lead, but just as real a scene is the sheep who wanders away from the flock and needs to be brought back home. Never is the sheep more vulnerable than at that moment of departure from the shepherd's watchful eye. For the aimless, wandering sheep there is always the impending danger of a wild animal, a hidden chasm, or a fatal fall. The most life-threatening thing that a sheep can do is move away from the shepherd.

People are the same. It is just about impossible to catch a person who chooses to wander away from a relationship. Yet if we examine the picture that Jesus paints of His shepherding and our wandering, we see Him follow each sheep closely. He rescues and He protects and His sheep have the assurance that no one can steal them away.

It is our wanderings from the Good Shepherd's presence that help us learn (the hard way) how dangerous and frightening life can be out in the wilderness of our own making. It is in the fearful or lonely times that we learn to listen to the voice we know.

Though lost, we faintly hear His call. Though discouraged, we long for His presence. And though alone, we fondly recall His nurturing ways and warm security. The voice of our Shepherd can penetrate any wilderness we have chosen to place between ourselves and His shepherding.

Are you in danger? The Good Shepherd is there to protect you.

Are you falling? The Good Shepherd goes behind and before.

Are you lost? The Good Shepherd is calling for your return.

Are you weary? The Good Shepherd will carry you on His strong shoulders.

Jesus is a strong voice in our wilderness. He is faithful to the sheep who stay close and He is faithful to those who wander away. And wander away we will from time to time. After all, didn't He say we are like the sheep?

█████████ THOUGHT FOR THE HEART

I find I am prone to "wander" in these areas of my life.

—Martha Hook

●
ARE YOU A WILLING PARTICIPANT?

"But Jonah ran away from the Lord and headed for Tarshish. He went down to Joppa, where he found a ship bound for that port. Af-

*ter paying the fare, he went aboard and sailed for Tarshish to flee
from the Lord." Jonah 1:3*

It is said that obedience and love go hand in hand. I think
this correlation exists because it's difficult to truly obey
someone we do not love or respect. We can obey external-
ly to avoid consequences, but obedience from the heart is
what God truly desires.

I cannot think of one time God has asked me to obey
without giving me the strength to follow through. I can
think of times I've been afraid or unsure. I can even think of
times I've pretended to be short on strength. But if I am
honest, I must say that God always provides the courage
and the ability to obey. God always supplies my true need.

If God supplies the need, why is it so hard to obey? If
we know that He will be there with our best in mind, why
is it so difficult to accept the paths He chooses?

The answers to that question are many, so let me simply
explore the answer that occurs most often in my life. More
often than not, I do not want to obey simply because I do
not agree with what God is doing. In short, I want Him to
choose *my* path.

Jonah was a man of God. He knew God and loved God,
and he was angry that so many dishonored God by their
actions and attitudes. One of the peoples Jonah felt angriest
with were the Ninevites. According to Jonah's experience, the
men and women of Nineveh were an abomination to God.

"Jonah, I want you to go to Nineveh and preach against
the wickedness." There was no mistaking the message of
God. And there was no mistaking Jonah's response. He
wasted little time in going exactly the opposite direction!

"But Jonah ran from the Lord and headed for Tarshish."

Why did Jonah choose the opposite direction? Why
wouldn't he want the job of preaching against those he
disdained?

Though we do not know the complete answer, one thing seems apparent as the story unfolds. God is always willing to relent. The Ninevites had sensitive members in their society, and God was willing to spare the wicked city due to those hearts that would repent.

My sense is that Jonah knew this about God. He knew that God would relent, and that made the prophet angry. Like me, Jonah wanted God to do away with "the enemy." He wanted God to destroy her, teach her a lesson, keep her far away from His fold. I am grateful God does not think like me!

Perhaps you struggle with obedience when you sense God leading you in a direction you do not wish to go. I understand. I feel the same battle within.

Still, in my old age I have learned that God always gets His way! Thankfully, His will gets accomplished whether or not we are willing participants.

Jonah went to Nineveh and preached the message God wanted him to preach. He simply went the long way around—by whale!

Go ahead and struggle with obedience. Just let God in on the battle. Ask Him to help you when you want to obey yet you don't feel like heading His direction.

THOUGHT FOR THE HEART

I can tell that I am wrestling with You, Lord. I do want to obey and yet I am afraid that You're leading me down a path I don't want to follow. Help my unbelief. Help me to trust Your leading.

—Phil Hook

●

GOING AGAINST THE GRAIN

"Does the Lord delight in burnt offerings and sacrifices as much as in obeying the voice of the Lord? To obey is better than sacrifice,

OBEDIENCE

and to heed is better than the fat of rams." 1 Samuel 15:22

Everyone awakened to the sound of hammering. No one knew what was going on, but most felt annoyed. Why would someone disturb the neighborhood this way? And why so early in the morning? Person after person pulled on their clothing to see what this noise was all about.

"What's going on here?" The first neighbor to arrive could barely believe his eyes. He'd already labeled this guy a "nut," and now he knew why.

There were boards stacked up all over the place! And they all were marked for the exact same length. One glance told this neighbor that there was enough wood there to build an entire coliseum. He would tell the city manager about this—nip the problem in the bud before it got one step further.

The builder noticed his visitor and went over to offer a greeting. There was no love lost between the two. The disgruntled neighbor turned briskly away, muttering promises and commentaries under his breath. This would not be the last meeting between the two that day.

Before noon, the whole town was up in arms. There were petitions to stop the project, petitions to hospitalize the builder, petitions to remove the wood from the land, and petitions about the petitions.

The neighborhood was filled with anxiety. Everyone had a story of their own and few of the stories matched. The city manager sighed as she went to lunch, eager for even a moment's break in the action.

"Can I talk with you a moment?" The city manager approached the builder after ignoring the problem as long as she dared.

"Certainly," he replied. "I'm grateful for the breather." He put down his tools and wiped his hands on an apron.

"Let me get right to the point," she started. She saw no

reason to engage in small talk. "You're causing quite a stir. I'd like you to put a halt to this project—right now!" She paused and studied the man, trying to gauge his response to her "request."

"I'm sorry," he said, with an obvious disappointment in his voice that made her feel uneasy. "I can't stop this project. I'm simply doing what God told me to do."

She knew he heard the heavy sigh escape her lips. *One of those,* she thought to herself. *I hate having to deal with people who say God told them to do something. This is going to require more diplomacy than I thought.*

"Well," she heard her own voice continue. "I certainly respect what God has told you to do, but perhaps you misunderstood His message." He shook his head rapidly in eagerness to reveal her mistake. "All right, then." She was too hot to be tactful anymore. "Did God tell you what to do with all your unhappy neighbors? Did He tell you what to do about a permit? Did He happen to mention that you cannot build whatever this is HERE?" The man's face fell and he turned to walk away.

"I'm not through with. . . ." She cut short her sentence. He was clearly hurt *and* clearly set in his ways. He went back to his tools and to the monstrosity in his backyard.

Noah continued with his project, though no one approved. In fact, he became the laughingstock of the whole region. Everyone flocked to see the "crazy man" who was building an "ark" for the coming flood. No one believed him—at least not until it was too late.

Sometimes obedience makes us look out of the ordinary. For instance, these days being a virgin by the end of college is a real oddity! Keeping honest records for taxes, caring more about people than the product, apologizing when you are wrong, and forgiving others just because you want to—all these are real oddities. They are fruit of a believer's life.

OBEDIENCE

Living the life of a follower of Jesus means living differently than those who do not know His voice. Sometimes the difference feels uncomfortable. And yet the reward is incomparable to anything this world could offer. The result of living obediently before the Lord is a transformed heart and mind for eternity.

Noah received a reward his neighbors could not even fathom. He grew in grace and in knowledge of our Lord. He grew in love. He grew in peace and joy and purpose and perspective. He gained the only benefits that truly matter.

THOUGHT FOR THE HEART

There are times I behave like Noah's neighbors. I make it hard for others to obey or I try to avoid God's reality. Lord, help me to honor You and to find great pleasure in doing so.

—Shelley Chapin

RHYTHMS OF MY HEART

PEACE

MASTER OF THE SEAS

"Peace I leave with you; My peace I give you. I do not give to you as the world gives. Do not let your hearts be troubled and do not be afraid." John 14:27

It had been a long day. The preaching was different than it had ever been before. Jesus had used stories in His messages that day, and truth had been hidden. Always before the message was simple and clear; now, the truth was disguised. It would only be known and understood by seekers and believers. For the disciples, this was both a privilege and a puzzle.

When all the mental activity was over, Jesus invited His disciples to go to the other side of the lake. They were relieved at the thought and began to make preparations immediately. Before He knew it, an interesting change took place.

"They took Him in the boat," Mark records. The disciples were back in charge.

Now we can do something, they thought. *We know sailing. We'll get the Teacher safe to the other side. Come on.* They worked together steadily as the boat crossed the lake.

Almost smiling at the confidence and competence displayed by His young companions, Jesus took a pillow to the back of the boat and went to sleep. It had been a long day, and He had some resting to do.

The captains of the fate did just fine until a storm began to blow in. In the marvelous irony of God, a squall arose and grew in intensity until the disciples were certain they would drown. The boat became unsailable and keeping it from sinking became their primary task.

"Someone wake Him—and be quick!" said a voice in the midst of the storm.

The disciples woke Him immediately. And they woke

the Teacher not with a request for a miracle and not with concern about His welfare, but with a question.

"Don't You care?" they accused. "Don't You care that we are about to drown?"

The men didn't expect a miracle; they simply wanted protection from the ravages of the storm. When Jesus stood up, He spoke peace to their world.

"Peace, be still," said the sleepy voice. And in an instant everything changed. The creation responded to its Creator with calm.

The disciples had a bit of a different response. They were terrified. "Who is this man who can make even the wind and seas obey Him? Who is this person who was sleeping in the back of our boat?"

The power of the storm was overwhelmed by the power of the peace of our Lord. What a remarkable truth. One writer has put it this way, "With Christ in your vessel, the storm won't last forever and the boat will never sink." Peace in the midst of the storm continues to be one of the greatest gifts of God.

Life always has its storms, and God can provide peace in the midst of the raging waters. He does care. And His peace will reign.

THOUGHT FOR THE HEART

These storms are threatening my lifeboat right now. I will welcome the Prince of Peace into my wind-blown ship.

— Phil Hook

●

A PIECE OF THE ROCK

"I have told you these things so that in Me you may have peace. In this world you will have trouble. But take heart! I have overcome the world." John 16:33

PEACE

When a child in our church had outpatient surgery one day I learned something about praying with young children and I learned something important about peace.

I remember trying to pray in terms I thought my young friend would understand. I thanked Jesus for being David's friend. I prayed for the doctors who would be performing the surgery. And then I prayed that God would give David a peace while he waited for the surgery to begin.

What I did not know until later was this. When I prayed for "a peace," little David opened his eyes, looked at his mother standing near, and mouthed, "A piece of what?" As his mother related the story to me, we both had a good laugh.

Later, after the surgery had gone well and David was resting, I pondered the misunderstanding which had earlier clouded my prayer. Two things occurred to me.

First, I decided not to pray that prayer with a small child again! But, second, I realized that when we trust our lives to the Lord we have both "peace" and "a piece"! This is what I mean.

When we trust our lives to Jesus Christ, we have "a piece" of the Rock! God's grace lifts us out of the kingdom of darkness and places us into the kingdom of light. A piece of everything that belongs to Christ belongs to us — everything!

Is that fantastic or what? You and I own a piece of heaven! We have access to God's storehouse of riches! We belong to God's forever family. And if I read Scripture correctly, our rooms in God's mansion will be debt-free. There will be no taxes, no utilities, no repairs, and no mortgages. Hallelujah!

We also have peace when we trust our lives to the Lord. And we don't have to wait for heaven to experience this part of God's gift. Peace is a promise from God, a deep reminder of our eternal belonging. Peace reminds us of the ministry and love of our Lord.

As Jesus prepared the disciples for His own death, He described the eternal blessings that would be theirs. And then He ended with a simple statement of purpose. "I tell you these things so that you might have peace."

I pray that as David grows older he will accept a piece of the Rock. And I pray that he will experience the peace that only the Rock can give.

■■■■■■■■■ THOUGHT FOR THE HEART

These promises are mine! I want to take the time to focus on all God has in store for His beloved.

—David Lynch

●

WHERE PEACE BEGINS

"Glory to God in the highest, and on earth peace to men on whom His favor rests." Luke 2:14

For a long time I thought of this biblical statement as strictly a "Christmas verse." The reasons are obvious. The verse is found in the middle of the story about Christ's birth, and the only time of year when "peace" and "good will" show up on cards is during the Christmas season!

As a person who unlearns stubborn habits of thinking and acting slowly, it took far too long to dawn on me that this is a verse for all seasons. After all, even though the Prince of Peace was born into His earthly existence at Christmastime, Christ's birthday is certainly not the only time of the year when mankind needs peace. The peace that is graciously given by the glorious God of heaven is in demand all year long, at least in the Luter household!

Admittedly, most of us long for peace at two primary

levels. We desire the absence of outward hostilities, and we long for an inward peace of mind. What we don't realize is that both of these aspects of peace, plus an even more basic foundational sense, can only be realized on an everyday basis because of the Lord's Christmas peace initiative. Yes, spearheaded by the babe of Bethlehem, the possibility of true peace now lives.

Open your mind and heart to receive this encouraging and comforting truth: Christ is the peacemaker who provides peace with God. For all who will trust Him, the once fractured relationship is restored. And that is the real foundation of peace.

Yes, we want other evidences of peace as well, but they begin with the birth, the life, the death, and the resurrection of our Lord. Peace can only come about and flourish because of Him. Promises of peace based on any other foundation are but shortsighted cease-fires in the larger battle.

Signing your own personal peace treaty with God is the beginning! And as we come to know Him better, we can consistently gain the "peace of God which passes all understanding" (Philippians 4:7). Even in the midst of anxiety-producing circumstances, we can experience the gift of peace.

Peace in our relationships and peace of mind begin with our own peace with God. Together let's give peace, through Christ, a chance!

THOUGHT FOR THE HEART

These are the areas where I feel a distance between myself and God right now, and I would like to experience His peace in these aspects of our relationship.

—Boyd Luter

P E A C E

●

AN INSTRUMENT OF PEACE

"You will keep in perfect peace him whose mind is steadfast, because he trusts in You." Isaiah 26:3

"Peace" is one of those illusive words. It is always easier to define what I want by "peace" rather than to see all the sides at work and address all the conflicting needs.

I've been thinking about the affairs of our country — the angers, the injustices, the hurts, the lack of forgiveness, the apathy. These are not for me to judge, but they are for me to explore and to feel and to do all I can to try and understand. People are desperately searching for peace and we Christians have a peace which is eternal. But peace is hard to grasp these days. There is so much anger and resentment. I have written a letter to express the hunger as well as the conflict I feel.

"My pen will not engage the paper. Words will not come. God, allay the pain I feel and help me say what needs to be said.

"I know the suffering out there. It wrenches my heart. Sometimes I find it hard to breathe and my hands clench tightly when they need to be confident. Dear God, I do feel the pain. Perhaps I *am* the pain. Acid fills my throat and dulls my appetite. Food is no longer a comfort.

"There are those who have no hope. Their children have no hope. I know their circumstances. I have lived them. That was years ago, but I have not forgotten the groping for basic needs, the day-to-day existence with little time for growth. Tomorrow could be just like today. It could be worse.

"Even through hard times I was sustained by a feeling of hope. I could work hard and study and make my life better. I had Your peace inside, but others do not. By

419

themselves, they cannot better their lives or achieve their hopes.

"Others suffer too. The beauty of their lives is threatened. Wonderful traditions, years in the making, will be altered. They know that, and they defend their place with blood and anguish. What none of us seems to realize is that we cannot move forward while trodding on the spirits of other human beings. Peace is not found in resentment and revenge.

"Why have You placed me at this moment? What the world needs is a tough guy, someone who does not feel so terribly, terribly alone. I know that You are with me, but I feel overwhelmed and vastly underqualified. I hope I am hearing You correctly.

"Now I must rely on You, Lord. You alone bring peace. I must deliver a speech at 'Gettysburg,' and it's time I got it written."

THOUGHT FOR THE HEART

I know that we are all in need of the peace that passes understanding. Lord, help me to be an instrument of Your peace, not merely an apathetic bystander.

— Sally Dobbs

●
JESUS IS OUR PEACE

"For He Himself is our peace, who has made the two one and has destroyed the barrier, the dividing wall of hostility, by abolishing in His flesh the law with its commandments and regulations. His purpose was to create in Himself one new man out of the two, thus making peace, and in this one body to reconcile both of them to God through the cross, by which He put to death their hostility. He came and preached peace to you who were far away and peace to those who were near, for through Him we both have access to the Father

PEACE

by one Spirit." Ephesians 2:14-18

One of the hardest benefits of peace to enjoy is that between fellow believers. Because Jesus Christ is our peace, Christians can live in peace, but the working out of that possibility is not easy to accomplish.

How many church splits have you read about in recent years? How many families do you know that are torn in two by the ravages of hatred, accusation, sin, or silence? How many friendships grow stale after once pledging undying faithfulness? How many statements are made about someone else that fall short of "keeping the peace"?

No matter how well we diagnose the problem or prescribe the cure, one fact is certain to remain true as long as we live in this world. Peace among believers is not easy to make or to keep.

Jesus is our peace. Paul described the scene beautifully to the Ephesian church. "He is our peace, who has broken down the barrier so that the two can become one." The picture is miraculous. But if we stop to examine the life of our Lord, we realize that "peace" is hardly a term many would have chosen to describe His final days.

Our Lord was mocked, He was spit upon, He was stalked and maligned. Our Lord was betrayed, He was abandoned, He was treated as a criminal and murdered. Does that sound much like peace?

Yes, Jesus is our peace. But it takes work, wisdom, and eternity to realize the fruits of His sacrifice. He brought peace to all who will receive, but it takes a heart open wide to accept the benefits. And it takes work on our part to flesh out the peace that He offers.

Peace is a fruit of the Spirit that begins as an internal spring. From within, we accept the gift of life that our Lord offers and we allow that spring to begin to run deep. We read His Word, we hear it taught, we talk to Him about our needs or our pains or our questions, we observe our relationships and the patterns of our lives. And we begin to make peace with the very essence of who we are in Christ.

Our spring of peace then overflows into our external behavior and, thus, our relationships with other people. Those truths that we've begun to understand for ourselves become the foundation for our relationships, and we attempt to reach out to others the way our Lord reaches out to us.

Love, joy, peace, patience, goodness, kindness, and the other fruit of our relationship with Christ become the avenues by which we express our needs, our angers, our frustrations, our thanksgivings, and our expectations. We no longer find the old patterns of relationship satisfying or valuable. Instead, we are able to treat others in the way we long to be treated.

Now, we are fully aware that we are painting a picture we would all like to experience yet find nearly impossible to uphold. And it's simply because we are not perfect nor do we live in a world which supports our desire for peaceful living.

We have all been hurt and we all experience fears and we all struggle with how to relate to that person who seems unapproachable or unkind. And some of us have been scarred in deep ways from abuse and control and unbridled anger. Thus, our dilemma.

Such wonderful, internal, and interpersonal peace will only occur in limited supply until the Prince of Peace returns for His climactic peace initiative. Then, and only then, when the Lord Jesus flexes His omnipotent muscles as King of kings and Lord of Lords, will all threats to internal and external peace be curtailed.

Until then, we are asked to follow His example as best we can and be peacemakers in an otherwise contentious world. We can offer peace for those who will receive, as we allow the Author of peace to touch our lives.

████████████ T H O U G H T   F O R   T H E   H E A R T

I need to invite peace into these relationships in my life.

— *Boyd Luter & Shelley Chapin*

●
PUTTING PEOPLE ABOVE PLANS

"Sing about a fruitful vineyard: I the Lord, watch over it; I water it continually. I guard it day and night so that no one may harm it. I am not angry. If only there were briers and thorns confronting me! I would march against them in battle; I would set them all on fire. Or else let them come to Me for refuge; let them make peace with Me, yes, let them make peace with Me." Isaiah 27:2-5

I dare not boast of much wisdom in this matter, but I can speak from a year of experience and at least provide food for thought. I'd like to let you in on a moment in time when peace was sought after and rudely denied.

I had been a physician on the mission field for many years when this situation occurred. I had seen new missionaries come and go, I had seen new mission organizations come and go. But rarely had I witnessed a struggle so vividly opposed to my whole concept of Christianity.

A man in his late twenties arrived in Nairobi with a band of young men and women. They would be missionaries, or so they were inclined, and their stated mission was to bring peace among the various tribes of the region.

It seems that the leader had some familial ties in the area. He wanted to return and make things better. He even had a well-thought plan of how to unite them all into one cooperative state. He was certain they would see his vision and embrace this better life he had to offer.

PEACE

I liked the young man's spirit very much. He was vivacious and tireless, and he volunteered his help in our makeshift hospital. It was clear that he wanted to help, and so we became friends.

The young group listened to their leader as if he knew all the answers. I remember feeling, at the time, that he liked their devotion, but it was not my place to pass judgment. His goal was to "fit in" to the society, infiltrate the tribes, and then bring them together. Each evening they shared strategy.

"Here's the problem with you, Pamela," he often said as we worked. "You're too conservative with sharing your views. You are a good physician, but there are more important things at stake here. You should speak up more. All you're doing now is repairing bodies. What about the future of these people? Doesn't their future need repairing?" As I recall, I would simply smile and keep working to bring relief.

To spare you a year of details, let me move ahead to the heart of the matter. After his people had worked for one year in the different tribes, the leader determined it was time for the reckoning. He called a meeting of key men from each tribe and they were to convene that evening, just before dusk.

I can tell you what I did that night. I prayed. I knew what would likely occur and I had warned my young friend from time to time (when I thought he might be listening). His response was always the same. "You play things too safe," he would say. "You have to be willing to get dirty."

The following day dawned and talk was all over the town. The young missionary and his group had met well into the night and they had gotten nowhere. He tried to argue from his experience in the United States and they answered from their experience in African tribes. He tried to present the plan he thought best and they presented their own goals and ideals. The two perspectives never wed, and the meeting left most with a bitter taste in their mouths.

My friend was embarrassed and his followers soon grew discouraged. It was only a matter of time until they all went back home, back to the land where their own dreams could be heard. And, sadly, the tribes in Nairobi went on as if little had happened. My friend stayed on for a while, but without the zeal which had once served to feed his vision.

Sometimes we know what is best for others. Sometimes we don't understand where they are coming from or what they need. Sometimes we reach out through genuine concern. And sometimes we fail to hear those we're trying to serve because our minds are already cluttered with our own determinations.

Making peace isn't deciding what's best, telling the person, and then walking away. Mothers, fathers, teachers, and counselors have all learned this lesson from time to time. Making peace requires sacrifice on all parts and a willingness to "hold on," even when no one is willing to listen.

Jesus lived here for years of life. He didn't send a note with the plan or give the people a money-back guarantee. He rolled up His sleeves, lived His truth, wept with the suffering, ate with the sinners, and walked with those who would be saints.

Jesus lived peace, He did not merely make an offer. And He stays with us, even when we spurn His plan. Though perfect, He respects our histories, our needs, and our slowness to accept change. Though He possesses the perfect plan, He does not demand that we accept that plan "now or never."

I have treated certain illnesses for years, knowing full

well that clean water, a bath, an inoculation, or a healthier diet could come close to alleviating the problem. For those who are willing to hear, the ideas for change are always presented.

But I cannot require that the other person change before I am willing to serve. I cannot link the peace I offer to another person's unequivocal and timely support of my plan.

Making peace is a process. And that process involves care and a genuine outpouring of love.

My young, zealous friend had a plan, but he did not offer peace. True peacemaking is a matter of the heart.

███████████ THOUGHT FOR THE HEART

It is quite easy for me to nag those I love. After all, I often know what is best! I would like to learn to place people above my plans — to put their well-being above my own need to change the world.

— *Pamela M. Reeves*

●
YOUR CORNER OF THE WORLD

"But the wisdom that comes from heaven is first of all pure; then peace-loving, considerate, submissive, full of mercy and good fruit, impartial and sincere. Peacemakers who sow in peace raise a harvest of righteousness." James 3:17-18

I had a great idea for peace when I was nine. I remember it well. Though I understood little about what was then "the Cold War," I knew enough to realize that the world was in trouble. I knew enough to believe that we had to find a solution. Mine was at least a place to begin.

We were sitting outside on the steps of our red porch when I first broached the subject with my father. I wanted Dad to send me to the Soviet Union! Yes, he heard correctly.

PEACE

I explained matter-of-factly that I was certain I could help bring peace. I thought that the reason we weren't friends with the Soviet Union rested in the fact that adults were all trying to control one another. With my idea, such a notion would be disbanded.

I felt certain that those in charge of peace in the Soviet Union would be willing to participate in peace with the United States if we would all agree to appreciate our differences and leave one another alone. The idea made perfect sense to me. After all, isn't that what brothers and sisters do in a family? We keep peace by respecting one another's space.

I still remember my father laughing quietly to himself. He was genuinely pleased with my efforts, but he also knew that such a simple idea would never be accepted. My father understood about mankind. He knew that war would be "in the wings" as long as there were nations, religions, neighborhoods, and families. What I wanted was not the goal of those in charge of keeping peace.

Paul described Jesus as a peacemaker. Paul even wrote that Christ *is* our peace. He Himself broke down the dividing wall and brought the two together — Jew and Gentile, slave and free, man and woman, you and me.

Christ is our peace, but I wonder how many would have called Him "peacemaker" on that day when He hung on Golgotha's tree . . . or that day when He drove money changers out of His Father's house . . . or that Sabbath when He healed the crippled man . . . or that day when He dared to confront the Pharisees.

Christ is our peace, but the peace is often hard to determine. The peace that He offers doesn't necessarily make nations end their wars or husbands return to their wives or children stop suffering. The peace that He offers doesn't necessarily feel peaceful. The peace that He offers doesn't always feel good.

PEACE

When I became a Christian at nine, I wanted the world to change. I wanted people to love one another and respect one another and make this world a safe haven for individuals to survive. Instead, I found that "the world" didn't change at all from my conversion.

What has changed, through the years, is me. I represent the peace that Christ died to make possible. I live the peace that He lived and modeled for all who would see. I offer the peace that can take even the darkest hour and fill it with light.

The peace that passes understanding is a condition of the heart and soul. Christ did tear down the wall that divides, but He doesn't force us to cross over the old barrier and become one with the "other side." Christ did tear down the wall that divides, but He doesn't guard the territory to keep us from erecting walls once again.

Peace takes work! Peace takes commitment. Peace requires understanding and a willingness to do some self-sacrificing. Peace requires that we keep in mind the "bigger picture" of what life and love and relationships are all about. Peace requires letting go of control and embracing God's truth.

I don't think a quick trip to Russia today will bring peace between nations. And I'm fairly certain that this world won't become that safe haven for everyone anytime soon.

Still, I believe that a commitment to peace on each individual's part will change lives. Our corner of the world will be healthier, more truthful, and far more inviting if we live and model "peace."

Take a look at your world today. Examine your plans and relationships, attitudes and actions, through the glasses of peace. And please remember, you do make a difference.

PEACE

Lord, help me to remember that I represent life in this world. I stand for hope and acceptance, love and truth. I go in the name of Jesus and offer His peace. May my corner of the world honor You today.

— Shelley Chapin

●

EXTRASENSORY PEACE

"Do not be anxious about anything, but in everything, by prayer and petition, with thanksgiving, present your requests to God. And the peace of God, which transcends all understanding, will guard your hearts and your minds in Christ Jesus." Philippians 4:6-7

There are those who claim to have extrasensory perception or "ESP." In layman's terms, this is the ability to communicate mysteriously across the miles. Those who claim the ability may know what is happening to someone in another part of the world. They may dream that a certain person has died and then wake the next day to discover that the dream is indeed a reality. Or they may reveal the location of a lost article.

I don't know how to explain ESP except to acknowledge that there are experiences beyond our understanding. But there is another form of ESP I do understand because I have known its benefits time and time again.

I am talking about "Extrasensory Peace." It is a gift from God and it comes at just the right moment to fill our need. It is a peace that truly passes understanding and comes from a source way beyond our own senses.

Jesus promised us His peace when leaving this world and He kept His promise. He spoke peace on all who came to find rest, love, and healing, and He continues to speak peace. His is a supernatural peace that transcends understanding and it is constant, even in the midst of life's most difficult circumstances.

Peace comes to us in times of grief when we have suffered the loss of someone very dear to us. Though the tears fall and the loss seems overwhelming, a deep sense of peace and comfort are also available to our hearts.

Peace comes to us in moments of crisis. Suddenly we are facing surgery or an unexpected bill we cannot pay or the loss of a job. Fear grips us, but God's peace overrides the fear and enables us to move on by faith.

No matter what the situation, God's peace is available and constant. It becomes our anchor in the storm, our security in the midst of uncertainty. When everything else fails us, His peace reigns in our hearts.

Extrasensory perception may serve a select few who find it comforting. But it is only one more of this world's substitutes. Christ gives us peace—true peace, His peace, peace that passes all explanations, peace that gives us calm, even while the storm is raging.

I marvel at the number of people who will call a hotline to hear some unknown person offer encouragement for the future. They're in search of something and they just do not know what God has to offer.

The real plan of peace rests solely in our Lord. Regardless of the circumstance, God speaks peace.

■■■■■■■■■■■ T H O U G H T   F O R   T H E   H E A R T

I need God's peace in these areas of my life, but have been afraid or too uncertain to ask. Visit Your peace upon me, Lord—that peace that surpasses all comprehension.

—David Lynch

RHYTHMS OF MY HEART

SHAME

LASTING EMBARRASSMENT

"Look upon my affliction and my distress and take away all my sins. See how my enemies have increased and how fiercely they hate me! Guard my life and rescue me; let me not be put to shame, for I take refuge in You. May integrity and uprightness protect me, because my hope is in You. Redeem [me], O God, from all [my] troubles." Psalm 25:18-22

I had never heard the word *shame* as a descriptor of my pain until 1987. I was attending a medical conference in Europe at the time and was drawn to a workshop covering "Adult Children of Alcoholics." I don't know why I was pulled toward that workshop—at the time I told myself it was curiosity. Within moments of entering that room I knew that God's intervention led me there.

I did not grow up in a home where alcohol was present, so I had never linked myself to such a label. After a few descriptions of what "ACA's" look like, though, I changed my mind!

For years I felt shame. It is a burning sensation deep in the pit of my stomach. It was there most of my growing up years, and it would dramatically increase if I was called upon in class or if I thought I had done something "wrong."

I distinctly recall an evening when we were in the library at home. It was only my father, my mother, and myself growing up. And my parents were both quite serious.

I was seven at the time of this incident, and I had learned a song from a gregarious child at school. She taught me the words to the song and a little dance, and I wanted to share my fun with my parents.

I dressed up and offered my number right in the middle of the living room floor, and the only response I got was a blank stare from my father and a look of sympathy from my mother. As I saw their empty faces, I felt that burning sensation course through my veins. I felt embarrassed somehow—out of place.

My mother and father had no idea how to enjoy the antics of a young child, and that was the last time I would attempt to share those antics with them. When I finished the song I slipped silently out of the room as they continued their reading. I stopped to listen on the stair, but nothing was said.

My parents did not drink alcohol, but they were "holics" all the same. My father was addicted to work and my mother, to pleasing my father. I was well cared for physically, but I felt like a stranger in their home. The only thing that linked me to my parents was obedience. As long as I met my father's expectations, all was well.

I hung on every word of the seminar that day and for the first time I felt that there is hope for those who feel shame. Just learning the word *shame* gave a sense of release to a feeling that had long gone unaddressed.

I have since worked hard on uncovering the pain and allowing God to minister to that little girl who simply wanted to belong. I have found a resting place in Him.

THOUGHT FOR THE HEART

I too have a burning sensation deep inside. I have wondered for years if any relief is possible. Thank You, Lord, for offering hope to the brokenhearted.

—Pamela M. Reeves

●

OVERCOMING INADEQUACY

"Again I looked and saw all the oppression that was taking place under the sun: I saw the tears of the oppressed—and they have no

comforter; power was on the side of their oppressors — and they
have no comforter. And I declared that the dead, who had already
died, are happier than the living, who are still alive. But better than
both is he who has not yet been, who has not seen the evil that is
done under the sun." Ecclesiastes 4:1-3

It is easy to feel Solomon's pain in the words that he
wrote. I think we overlook, at times, the legitimate struggles of God's people. Solomon shares openly from his
heart so that you and I can uncover our own wounds.

One of the most obvious struggles in our world today
relates to the issue of shame. People doubt their worth.
They sense that they are unlovable. They feel broken in
their very core, broken and irreparable. All of us who play
some role in ministry hear the painful stories of sexual
abuse, incest, physical traumas, eating disorders, and inadequacy. At the root of these struggles runs a common
thread — shame.

I will leave therapy to those who are trained in its art,
but I do have some insights which might serve as reminders and encouragements. As I hear the stories I am reminded again of a God who touches even our shame with
His healing. I am reminded of a God who offers love and
acceptance to His people.

All of us have built-in needs for personal worth. Love
and acceptance are so crucial to our sense of well-being
that we can barely function if we are convinced that no
one loves us. Though no earthly love can completely fulfill
our need, the lack of earthly love can cause us to feel
shame.

So many of us find our identity in what others think or
in what we think of ourselves. Certainly this is true within
the framework of our families. When we feel valued at
home, it is easier to value ourselves and to see ourselves as
valuable in God's eyes. When we feel valueless at home, it

SHAME

is likely that we'll see ourselves as useless, insignificant, unimportant to the world.

There are other pressures which threaten to cause shame. We often focus on sexual or physical abuse, but artificial performance standards can also cause damage. A perfectionistic attitude can be devastating to a child's self-image: "Why didn't you get all A's?" can be interpreted "You're not measuring up" to the child who is suffering from poor self-worth.

Inadequacy is difficult to live with. Some who feel inadequate withdraw. Some compensate by formulating an alternate plan for success. The variations are virtually limitless.

Sadly, plans to achieve self-worth on our own are virtually unattainable. The only way to conquer shame is to begin to see ourselves through the eyes of our Creator.

Though this is hard to believe when we live with shame, the truth for the believer is this: we belong to a healthy, spiritual family; we are created in the image of God; we are gifted specially by God and needed by Him and by others; we belong to Him for eternity.

It takes time to work through the abuse, the shame, the inadequacies, and the pain that are residuals from our suffering, but healing can occur! God can take the memories and bring light out of the darkness.

Many live with shame. Many hunger for relief. Try to remember that God, in His love and mercy, will use our needs to drive us from futility to fulfillment.

THOUGHT FOR THE HEART

I still search for my identity in what others think of me, in what I accomplish, in relief from my pain. Lord, I want to shed the shame, but I need Your help. Help me to see myself through Your loving eyes.

— Ken Boa

S H A M E

●
SOOTHING THE SHAME

"I offered My back to those who beat Me, My cheeks to those who pulled out My beard; I did not hide My face from mocking and spitting. Because the Sovereign Lord helps Me, I will not be disgraced. Therefore I have set My face like flint, and I know I will not be put to shame. He who vindicates Me is near. Who then will bring charges against Me? . . . They will all wear out like a garment; the moths will eat them up." Isaiah 50:6-9

Wanda was nine years old and a third-grader at Henry Wadsworth Longfellow Public School in Dallas. I was an older and wiser ten-year-old and already comfortable in my role of peacemaker and counselor to those in search of a listening ear.

The setting was 1963 and our nation had just begun to integrate the public schools. My grade remained entirely Caucasian, but from the third grade down, the world became a different place that year.

"Shelley!" My name echoed down the long, empty hall. In just a few moments the bell would ring and betray the quiet. I was late that day, and I clutched the doctor's note in my hand.

"Shelley! I'm down here!" I looked around for a moment before I saw her, but I knew from her voice there was something terribly wrong.

"Wanda? Is that you? What's wrong?" I asked as I finally reached her side.

Wanda was crying hard and my presence caused the tears to flow more generously. I waited for a moment before asking again.

"What's the matter?"

It took a few verbal nudges to get the whole story, but Wanda's reply went something like this.

SHAME

"They call me 'Locomotive.' They say I weigh 200 pounds but I don't—I swear I don't." And with that, the heart of a young African-American child fell just a little bit farther away from confidence and well-being.

We all make mistakes. We all fail. We all hurt those that we love. We all need correction and reproof at times. And we cannot expect to like and be liked by everyone. But to shame someone is to take away a piece of the beauty God has created in that person and replace it with self-doubt, fear, and discouragement.

Wanda was a treasured young child, created and loved by God and appreciated by anyone who would take the time to know her. But other children who didn't feel good about themselves found in her someone they could tease and belittle. The rest of the story is a familiar one.

I have chosen to tell you about Wanda for several reasons. First, she is often on my mind. I was Wanda's friend, and I've never stopped wondering how she fared. She was mistreated, as are so many young people who don't "fit in" to the status quo of the moment.

I've also chosen this story because shame comes in all shapes and sizes. We are fairly aware of the ramifications of the extreme end of shame, but we often dismiss pain such as Wanda's. In reality, that kind of shaming demands a terrible toll and sets a pattern for years of self-rejection.

Shame says, "There is something wrong with me— something fundamental." Shame says, "I am flawed—not good enough, disabled in some basic way." And shame can't be soothed by the "don't pay any attention to them" advice of a ten-year-old.

Be careful with words. Moms, dads, husbands, wives, teachers, and friends have so much influence on the way we see ourselves. Give the gift of kindness and acceptance. Give the gift of understanding. Give the gift of love.

S H A M E

I can remember feeling shamed when . . . and I would like my memories to have this influence on the way I treat others.

— Shelley Chapin

●
A CHILD OF THE KING

"See to it that no one takes you captive through hollow and deceptive philosophy, which depends on human tradition and the basic principles of this world rather than on Christ. For in Christ all the fullness of the Deity lives in bodily form, and you have been given fullness in Christ, who is the head over every power and authority." Colossians 2:8-10

Many years ago I received an invitation to participate in a debate on a university campus. The invitation was extended by a young woman I had never met before, and she spoke with an authority and confidence I will never forget.

"You don't even know me," I said to her the night before the debate began. "How did you get the courage to assemble this debate in the first place?"

"That's easy," she replied. "I'm a daughter of the King."

"A daughter of the King?" (I'm sure my tone betrayed the surprise.) "Of course!" I responded. And I was hooked! Who could argue with reasoning like hers?

That phrase, "a daughter of the King," played through my mind throughout the entire debate. After all, I am a son of the King, but I had never let that thought sink in and give me courage or opportunity. In fact, if the truth be known, I had always felt like the flawed child of a perfect and slightly unreachable King.

I grew up the middle child in a preacher's home. My sister was the "perfect child," my younger brother, the "willing child," and I—I was the rebel. I was the one who seemed to live with an internal anger, who seemed to struggle with all of the rules, regulations, and requirements.

It is not that my parents attempted to shame me. They were committed to the Lord and to their children. And they fully believed everything that they taught and stood for. If there is any one word I could use to describe my parents, it would be *consistent*. They were predictable and very disciplined, and the rules rarely changed.

Yet in the middle of all the messages taught and lived in our home, I grew to feel shame. I thought there was something fundamentally wrong with me. I felt flawed, and the feeling was devastating.

As most who have felt the core of shame, I never told anyone about my pain. Outwardly I looked like the great athlete, the popular young man, the one who had it "all together," but inwardly I was anything but those descriptions of confidence.

Shame has a terrible message. It says that we, as individuals, are flawed. It says that there is something wrong with the way we feel, with the way we think, with the way we perceive the world. Shame says that we do not fit and never will, and that others are not burdened by this malady. Shame says that no one else will understand, so keep the pain to yourself. Shame feels hopeless.

You may have grown up with some messages of shame in your family. Even well-meaning parents can make shame statements or implications to a child.

"Good Christians don't watch television (or, in my family's case, listen to radio) on Sundays." "Good Christians don't think thoughts like that." "Good Christians don't go to movies or listen to jokes that others tell." "Good Christians don't think about sex or sexuality."

"Good Christians don't want to stay out late or otherwise worry their parents." "Good Christians like to go to church on Sunday and don't become bored with the sermon." "Good Christians behave and obey and never struggle with unexpressed anger or jealousy with siblings or thoughts of running away from it all."

In one form or another, we are all overwhelmed by the do's and don'ts of others. And some of us walk away from those messages with the thought, *There is definitely something wrong with me.*

I have felt shame for much of my life, so my simple prayer is this: that you and I will embrace the truth that we are not fundamentally flawed. We are purely and simply children of the King!

THOUGHT FOR THE HEART

These are some of the do's and don'ts which have sent their messages of shame my way. I can replace those do's and don'ts with these healthy messages.

— Phil Hook

●
THE POWER OF THE PAST

"My soul is weary with sorrow; strengthen me according to Your Word. Keep me from deceitful ways; be gracious to me through Your law. I have chosen the way of truth; I have set my heart on Your laws. I hold fast to Your statutes, O Lord; do not let me be put to shame. I run in the path of Your commands, for You have set my heart free." Psalm 119:28-32

My world is but an illusion;
My life—a secret.
In darkness I live in the depths of shame.
I am hidden from a world I love so dearly—
And silence is my mask.

SHAME

This bit of prose was offered to me by a young woman in pain. Her life was torn in two, and as far as I could tell, it had been in pieces for a long, long time. On the outside she had everything together, but on the inside she was a lost little girl.

The more I began to listen to her pain, the more I realized the incredible power of the past. The relationships which are part of our lives, the way we react and respond to those relationships, the way we handle our experiences and the way we process other people's responses all work together to either help or harm, build up or tear down.

I readily admit that such is true for all of us. There is no one who has an unencumbered yesterday. Each of us has our own private pain that we try to hide, avoid, or otherwise cover. But there are some who experience the deepest griefs and, thus, their suffering is increased. This young woman has endured a deep and abiding pain.

I am reminded of the story of a young, forgotten girl in Scripture. Her name was Tamar, and she was the daughter of David, king of Israel.

We know little about Tamar's background. We don't know what she liked to eat or where she liked to go. We don't know about her friends or her favorite pastimes. We don't know much about her at all except that she was lovely enough to attract her half brother, Amnon.

Amnon wanted to sleep with Tamar. It was that simple and that terrible. I imagine he dreamed about her and created a fantasy in his mind — a fantasy that would not die down until fulfilled. Through deceit he finally raped her, and then all fantasy was gone.

We're told that Amnon hated Tamar after his abuse was finished. She was left in anguish and shame, and he went on. Sadly, both would be destroyed — she through seclusion and he through death at the hand of his brother, Absalom. Both were running from a dreadful secret and both were caught in the depths of shame.

Our lives are affected by our yesterdays. The way we see ourselves is closely aligned with the pains we have suffered, the love we've been given or denied, the lessons we've been taught. The shame that people feel is not born in a momentary decision or a bad day; it is an abiding reaction to a series of events which add to the mistaken belief, "There is something wrong with me."

My young friend will be "working" on her pain for quite awhile. She has much to overcome, but she has hope. She is already learning that she is worthwhile and that God considers her valuable. Tamar was not so fortunate.

Shame tears down, but love builds up. The love of God can remove the mask of silence and replace our secrets with truth.

THOUGHT FOR THE HEART

In time, perhaps my heart will say,

My world is real,
My life — a gift.
In light I now live, no longer in shame.
I am part of the world I love so dearly
And life is my reward.

— Shelley Chapin

●

WRESTLING WITH SHAME

"O Lord, we and our kings, our princes and our fathers are covered with shame because we have sinned against You." Daniel 9:8

"Shame" is a word that has been largely absent from my personal vocabulary for most of my life. I recall hearing people say, "Oh, what a shame!" in response to a sad story or situation, but I don't believe I ever even uttered that sentiment myself.

It wasn't until I was studying Daniel that I began to wrestle with shame. And I would have rather done just about anything else! I had always associated the word *shame* with "shameful"—something to be denied, covered up, or at least very embarrassed about. My study of shame literally felt like a scene from *Showdown at the O.K. Corral.*

In the process of exploring shame, I began to sweat bullets. I just knew I'd feel terrible in my discovery. I thought of failures to feel shameful about and stories I'd never told anyone. Yet, in the midst of it all, I also learned more of the truth about me.

All shame is not the same! Some is contrived, but much shame is legitimate. Some shame is our personal responsibility, but much grows out of our tragic, neglectful, or traumatic inheritance. Some shame is shared, but much is held deep in the dungeons of our pain.

The more I studied shame, the more I became aware that I had been unwittingly playing "the shame game" for most of my life. Much of it had landed on my shoulders like light rain, and I hadn't even noticed. Some had arrived through my own persistent unwillingness to face recurring issues. But there was also shame that grew out of my own family relationships. Yes, I needed to deal with both my own personal shame as well as that bequeathed to me through the family tree.

I was greatly encouraged to discover I have something in common with Daniel. There is no clear personal sin identified in Daniel's writings, yet the long prayer of chapter 9 reveals Daniel's confession of personal responsibility. The bottom line: shame does not just "go away." Whether personally induced or inherited from someone else's sin, shame must be unearthed, discussed, and understood for healing to take place.

There may be some deep cellars of shame in your heart, and I would urge you to begin to unloose their hold upon you. Shame is weighty, and it is not easily satisfied. It requires daily allegiance to the lie: "There is something wrong with me."

We need not live alone in our shame. There is help available to teach us about the pain and to remind us of our value in the midst of discovering the dungeons.

We are worth too much to God to live with unbearable shame.

■■■■■■■■■■ THOUGHT FOR THE HEART

There is something deep in my heart that is causing me to feel shame. I would like to invite God and others to help me sort out the emotions.

— Boyd Luter

●
WORTHY MESSAGES

"In the year that King Uzziah died, I saw the Lord seated on a throne, high and exalted, and the train of His robe filled the temple. Above Him were seraphs, each with six wings: With two wings they covered their faces, with two they covered their feet, and with two they were flying. And they were calling to one another: 'Holy, holy, holy is the Lord Almighty; the whole earth is full of His glory!' At the sound of their voices the doorposts and thresholds shook and the temple was filled with smoke. 'Woe to me!' I cried. 'I am ruined! For I am a man of unclean lips, and my eyes have seen the King, the Lord Almighty.' " Isaiah 6:1-5

I don't know if you've ever stopped to consider what you would do if you saw the Lord in the way Isaiah saw Him. It might be interesting to ponder that scenario for a moment.

S H A M E

One of my favorite places to play as a child was outside. I loved to be outside! Playing hide-and-seek with the neighborhood children, climbing trees, roller-skating down the drive, or riding my bicycle were favorite activities. And at least once each week we all got together to play football. (As the only girl in the neighborhood I "hupped" the ball for both teams! You know, "Down, set, hup!")

"Wash your hands and comb your hair," Mom would say when I entered the house to eat dinner. I never quite understood the purpose of those directives. I never considered myself "dirty" when I got home. What's a little bit of grass in the hair or dry mud on the hands? That isn't *dirt*.

When we view ourselves against the backdrop of this world, dirt is a relative term. I was generally much cleaner than Mark, for instance. He used to make mud on purpose and jump in and out of the puddles. "Dirty," in this world, is a relative description.

It is only when we stand next to someone who is immaculate that we begin to see dirt. I would have known I was dirty had I been standing next to a bride in her lovely white array. But I wasn't. I was comparing myself to my friends, and with them, I was the clean one!

Isaiah had a similar "problem." Next to the other men he came in touch with from day to day, he was a saint. After all, Isaiah was a prophet and a sought-after adviser. He knew God and he served as God's spokesman. Few men or women exhibited more righteousness than Isaiah the prophet.

Then one day, Isaiah confessed, "I saw the Lord," and we are invited to view the transformation.

When we feel shame, we feel "unworthy" or "dirty." We feel as if we do not measure up to some arbitrary standard. And we tell ourselves we aren't worthy to want or accept more.

In the world in which we live, shaming is a pastime. Parents send these messages to their children: "What's wrong with you?" "Why can't you obey like your brother?" "You're a disgrace to this family." "I can't believe you'd want to hurt us like this after all we've done for you."

Employers send similar messages to their employees: "If it weren't for you, we would have made that big sale." "I've told you a hundred times." "What are you trying to do, ruin me?" "Do I have to do everything myself?"

And husbands and wives send similar jibes back and forth: "We never should have gotten married." "I could have done a lot better." "I can't believe you're this stupid." "What were you thinking?" "You never choose me over the kids."

Can you hear what I'm talking about? Direct and indirect, these messages exist all around us all of the time. They are messages of shame, designed to make the hearer feel guilty, inferior, ashamed, and just plain subhuman. Messages of shame say, "You don't measure up, and you never will."

Isaiah expected to hear such a message from the Lord. He even tried to make it easy on God by jumping right ahead to the punch line. "Woe is me, I am a man of unclean lips." In short, "I am not worthy."

The great news? God does not shame His children. He didn't agree with Isaiah. Instead, He played along just long enough to make Isaiah think that his lips were about to be burned with fire. But instead of fire, Isaiah found healing. His guilt was atoned for, and his sin was removed.

I can only imagine the joy that Isaiah experienced when he realized that God had made him whole. Isaiah was overjoyed! And his immediate response was a longing to serve this God who unconditionally loves.

Parents, husbands, wives, employers, friends—please listen to the words you use and the messages you convey. Be careful not to send messages of shame. Send messages, instead, of love, acceptance, forgiveness, and worth.

We don't have to shame to get our feelings across. In fact, shame widens the gap of misunderstanding and mis-communication. We can let others know what we feel and what we need without threatening their very character.

"I saw the Lord!" And I found peace and belonging there with Him. There is no room for shame in God's family.

████████████ T H O U G H T   F O R   T H E   H E A R T

I tend to send messages of shame when I am with these people or in these situations. I am willing to work on changing those messages to expressions of honesty, worth, forgiveness, and love.

—*Shelley Chapin*

RHYTHMS OF MY HEART

SIGNIFICANCE

CHILDREN OF THE HEAVENLY FATHER

*"The body is a unit, though it is made up of many parts; and
though all its parts are many, they form one body. So it is with
Christ. For we were all baptized into one body — whether Jews or
Greeks, slave or free — and we were all given the one Spirit to drink.
Now the body is not made up of one part but of many."*
1 Corinthians 12:12-14

If I asked you to name the ten most significant people in
human history, who would you choose? What if I asked
you and a group of friends to name the ten most important people in human history? What if I asked you and
your graduating class from high school to come up with a
list of the ten most significant people in human history?
Where would you begin? What would be the criteria?
How would you agree?

I imagine that most Christians would put Jesus Christ
on the list, but from there we would have differing opin-
ions. Some of us would choose well-known men and
women; some of us would choose a mother, father, or
significant adult in our lives; some of us would choose a
person we respect or seek to emulate; and some of us
would choose men or women from Scripture to whom we
feel connected in some way. Of one thing I am certain,
our lists would be different!

What makes a person significant?

I really feel that significance is tied to being children of
the Heavenly Father. The creative activity of God brings
us significance. We may gain a certain temporal significance from writing or from lecturing or from our positions
or discoveries here in this world, but that kind of significance is tied to a moment in history. It is not a significance
that forevermore gives us security, belonging, peace, and
affirmation.

SIGNIFICANCE

Think for a moment of those who are tied to an histori-
cal event. Lee Harvey Oswald was held accountable for
the death of John F. Kennedy. Neil Armstrong and Buzz
Aldrin walked on the moon. Martin Luther King had a
dream and shared it with humanity. John Wilkes Booth
shot Abraham Lincoln. Helen Keller transformed communication for those born deaf.

I chose just a few of the "significant" men and women
of United States history to prove a small point. For some
of these people, "significant" meant helpful. For some it
meant tragedy. And we know nothing about the actual
day-to-day life, happiness, purpose, or success of these
who are marked by an event in history.

We can enjoy significant moments. We can impact the
world in significant ways. But true significance is born out
of a relationship with Jesus Christ. Finding our significance in response to God's creative purpose results in a
lasting and vital "connection" with this world and with
eternity.

Our significance lies in the fact that God has made us
and we are part of His plan. It is His plan that is significant. We are a "drop in the bucket," to use a biblical
phrase, or a blip on a screen without His purpose. But
with His purpose, we are part of an eternal plan.

I often end a prayer with some variation on these
words, "God, help us to be the kind of people You had in
mind when You first created us." And in that prayer is my
longing that we all find our significance in relation to our
Father.

If we can learn to see ourselves as children of the Heavenly Father—children who glean our significance from
Him, perhaps we will begin to enjoy the privilege of our
creation. We are significant because we are His.

SIGNIFICANCE

I tend to look for significance in these accomplishments. I would like to become more aware of my place in the family of God.

— *Jay Kesler*

●

OUR SOURCE OF IDENTITY

"The Lord will fulfill His purpose for me; Your love, O Lord, endures forever — do not abandon the works of Your hands." Psalm 138:8

My father was a minister. He knew the exact day when he first sensed God calling him into service. My dad immediately switched gears, left everything behind, worked his way through seminary, and then set out to pastor for the remainder of his days.

"Reverend Hook" is what everyone called him. And he fit the title. Once the farm work was behind him, he shed the overalls in which he'd grown up and donned the coat and tie of the pastorate. My dad was never happier than when he was in the clothes of "Reverend Hook."

Many things happened to our family during my growing up years. My father was struck with osteomyelitis in his thirties and remained quite ill for a time. Those days were difficult on us all. But my dad always had his work to go back to. His purpose as "Reverend Hook" pulled him through.

My dad weathered just about everything. Though battle-scarred at times, he managed to keep moving and keep serving the God he believed in. But one day, everything changed for Reverend Hook.

My dad's backbone had always been my mother. She was his strength, his support, his reminder of what family is all about, his communicator to the children. And one day she died. Before my dad was ready to let her go, God took her home.

My dad continued in his daily routine, but nothing was ever the same again. All of the children tried to help, but he was lost without a church and without my mom.

Toward the end of his days, while visiting our home, I tried to fit my dad with my clothes for living.

"Take off your tie, Dad," I urged. "You're no longer Reverend Hook. You're Ernie." And my fingers unloosed the tie around his neck.

My father graciously humored me, but almost as soon as I turned my back, the tie was once again in place. Reverend Hook did not feel complete without the attire. His significance had always been in his purpose. Instead of losing Mom and the pastorate, my dad lost himself.

It is hard not to identify ourselves as "pastor," "teacher," "mom," "dad," "husband," "wife," "president," "administrator." It is hard not to see our significance in light of that which has always been important.

Try to remember that your significance comes from God alone. Before we even step foot in this world, He has stamped His wonderful design on our very soul.

My dad was Reverend Hook, but he was so much more. My dad belongs to the Lord.

■■■■■■■■■ THOUGHT FOR THE HEART

I am prone to define my own significance by these titles or achievements. I will try to remember, instead, that I am significant simply because I belong to God.

—Phil Hook

●

THE "SUPER" SYNDROME

"But you are a chosen people, a royal priesthood, a holy nation, a people belonging to God, that you may declare the praises of Him

who called you out of darkness into His wonderful light." 1 Peter 2:9

One of the best stories I've heard recently concerns the former heavyweight boxing champion of the world, Muhammad Ali. It seems he was on a flight one day when the attendant said, "Please fasten your seat belt."

"Seat belt?" Ali replied. "Superman don't need no seat belt!"

And the attendant's reply was priceless. "Superman don't need no airplane! Now, please, buckle up!"

Our friend, Ali, is not the only one suffering from a superman or superwoman complex. Many of us have the urge to step into the nearest phone booth and come out with cape flying!

Some feel the pressure to be "Supermom." You know, work eight hours, fix the meals, do the laundry, spend quality time with the kids, serve on the PTA, and then be ready for bowling and pizza with the husband. Supermoms never tire, never get depressed, and they never, under any circumstances, get sick!

Then there is "Superdad." You might recognize him. He puts in seventy hours a week so that his family can have all the good things they deserve. He heads up the Scout troop and coaches Little League on Wednesday afternoons. He has the best manicured lawn in the neighborhood. He keeps both cars clean. He leads family worship, takes his wife on a date once a week, never sounds grouchy, and never watches Monday night football (at least not in its entirety!).

Know anybody who does all those things? Neither do I. But I know plenty who think they should and even more who keep trying. Why? Because we are performance oriented. We find our worth in what we do, the degrees we earn, the awards bestowed upon us or our children, and the services we render.

SIGNIFICANCE

It is no surprise that we carry that behavior into our Christian life. We strive to be "supersaints." We serve on several church boards, we sing in the choir, we lead a Bible study, we spend at least three nights at the church, and we never, never, never say no when asked to do one thing more.

We are not supersaints! And God never intended us to be. We didn't earn our salvation, and no amount of works will make us holy. Salvation is a gift offered us by a loving Father. He has already paid the price, and the gift is offered free of charge. We are not accepted by God for all of the good we do; we are accepted on the merit of Christ's work on the cross.

God doesn't love us more if we do more — He loves us even if we can't do anything! His love is truly unconditional, and our significance grows out of that love.

We will make mistakes. We will fail. We will miss the mark, and we will need to ask for forgiveness more than once on lots of issues.

Forget about being a supersaint. Yes, stop before you are ahead. Be the person God intended you to be, and rest in the storehouse of love that will not let you go.

THOUGHT FOR THE HEART

It is difficult for me not to evaluate my significance in the things that I do. I would like to begin to realize that God's love is what makes me significant.

— David Lynch

●

PRECIOUS IN HIS SIGHT

"O Lord, You have searched me and You know me. You know when I sit and when I rise; You preserve my thoughts from afar. You discern my going out and my lying down; You are familiar

with all my ways . . . I praise You because I am fearfully and won-
derfully made; Your works are wonderful, I know that full well."
Psalm 139:1-3, 14

A young boy went to a pet shop looking for a puppy. The
store owner showed him a newborn litter in a box. For
a long while, the boy looked at the dogs. He picked
each one up, examined it carefully, and put it back in the
box.

After several minutes, the boy walked back to the owner
and said, "I picked one out. How much do they cost?"
The man gave him the price and the boy promised to be
back in a few days with the money. "Don't take too long,"
the owner cautioned. "Puppies like this sell quickly." The
boy turned and smiled knowingly. "I'm not worried," he
said. "Mine will still be here."

The boy went to work cutting grass and cleaning yards.
He worked hard and saved his money until, after a few
weeks, he had enough for the dog. The boy returned to
the pet store, walked up to the counter, and placed a
pocketful of wadded bills on the top.

The store owner hadn't forgotten the boy. He sorted
and counted the cash and when he had verified the
amount, he smiled at the boy and said, "All right, son, you
can go get your puppy." The young man walked over,
reached into the back of the box, and pulled out a skinny
dog with a limp leg. Then, as he started to leave, the store
owner stopped him.

"Don't take that dog," the owner objected. "He's crippled, son. He'll never run with you. He can't fetch. He
can't play. Get one of the healthy dogs." But the boy
shook his head in quiet protest.

"No thank you, sir," the boy replied. "This is exactly the
kind of dog I've been looking for." And the boy turned to
leave. Suddenly the shopkeeper understood. Extending

from the bottom of the boy's trousers was a brace — a brace for the boy's crippled leg.

Jesus loves people. He knows how people feel. He knows that people are special. We are, each of us, precious in the sight of God just as the puppy was precious in the sight of his young keeper.

Are you under the gun at work? Jesus knows how you feel. Are you pushing the limits of your strength? Jesus experienced the same. Do you have children who make a chaos out of your dinner hour? Jesus did too. No matter what you are experiencing, Jesus knows how you feel and He cares.

Try not to forget how precious you are. So precious that Jesus became like us so that we could come to Him and receive love. Like the boy, Jesus picked each of us out and decided to take us home. Remember your significance today.

■■■■■■■■■■ T H O U G H T   F O R   T H E   H E A R T

Sometimes I allow these pressures or these responsibilities to cloud the awareness of my own significance.

— Max Lucado

●
GAZING IN GOD'S MIRROR

"On that day you will realize that I am in My Father, and you are in Me, and I am in you." John 14:20

Most of us, in varying degrees, have experienced direct and indirect rejection. The rejections can come in a look, in a sentence, in physical violation, in an attitude, or in direct statements which tear down the fiber of our beings.

Comments like "No daughter of mine would do that," "Why can't you be like your brother?" "You are so stupid," or "Look what you've done" can quickly steal the confidence of young, impressionable children. When children hear these things, it is easy for them to conclude that they are not worthy of being members of a family.

We can be more subtle about our rejections. With every intention to do good, parents can whittle away at the confidence of a child through overprotection. Statements like "Let me do that," "You don't know how," and "Children don't need to know these things" can teach a child that he or she is incapable of making good decisions.

Short, disheartening experiences with our parents, trusted adults, and peers can seriously threaten our sense of identity and personal worth. And without a sense of significance, our lives are painful indeed.

Before the foundation of the world, God planned to meet our needs. And He planned to meet those needs of personal significance and identity. When Jesus stepped into this world, He stepped in to redeem us, not only from sin but from an untrue picture of ourselves.

But God has a tough task at hand. He must help us wade through the painful misunderstandings, broken promises, mixed messages, and even abuse. He must help us reach through the misinformation to the truth.

If we do not find our source of identity in Christ, we will inevitably turn to something or someone else to fulfill this basic need. Christians can easily succumb to the pressure of finding their significance and identity in possessions and status—the right neighborhood, the right house, the right car, the right clothes—rather than in Christ. We see this happen all the time, both in the lives of those we love and in the lives of other friends and families.

It is God's gracious intention to fulfill our needs and thus draw us to Himself. God longs for us to know that we have extraordinary worth and importance in His sight. God is the true source of our significance, even though it is hard for us to grasp this truth.

Our task is to begin to strip away the layers of untruth and discover the essence of our worth in Christ. Our privilege is to begin to gaze in the mirror of God's eyes and see ourselves the way He has designed us to be.

Reach out for true significance. Release the burden of unhealthy messages that have come your way. Allow God the fatherly privilege of loving you. For as hard as the information is to grasp, we are in Him and He, in us.

■■■■■■■■■■ THOUGHT FOR THE HEART

I am aware of having these painful attitudes and thoughts about myself. I would like to allow God to begin to show me my true significance.

— Ken Boa

●

UNIQUE BUT NOT ALONE

"Now you are the body of Christ, and each one of you is a part of it." 1 Corinthians 12:27

The letter arrived and as I finally pulled the page from the envelope, my eyes grew wide. Africa! I was invited to speak in Africa! Imagine that! Since those missionary conferences of my childhood, it had always been my dream to speak in Africa.

The date for my departure arrived, and I boarded the plane for one of the great adventures of my young speaking career. I even had an added bonus for the journey! I would be meeting some friends in Zaire. At least someone familiar would be around to show me some sights.

David was very busy with the work of the ministry, so his lovely wife Ann and I were left to explore the places tourists go. Since my friends were familiar with Zaire, the sightseeing was effortless and quite successful.

We visited a "traditional" family—one man with multiple wives. We visited the market where food had to be sold daily to compensate for the lack of refrigeration. We visited a clinic where people lined up for hours for the chance to receive some form of medical care.

It took awhile to adjust to the clothing and customs of a country so different from my own. Many people wore Western styled clothing, but most remained in the customary dress of their particular tribe of people. All in all, I was fascinated with everything I saw.

For most of the women, the customary dress included only a loin covering accompanied by extensive jewelry. Women wore jewelry around the neck, jewelry around the waist, jewelry around the ankles and feet, and the pieces themselves adorned these women with a uniqueness all their own.

I thought it would be interesting to purchase some of the jewelry for my wife back in the United States, so I asked Ann if this were possible. A short time later we met a woman whom Ann had known for some time, and Ann asked her to explain her jewelry to this traveler.

The woman explained the intricacies of her jewelry and the materials from which each piece was made. The more she told, the more fascinated I became with her story, until finally I asked Ann if the woman would sell her jewelry to me. The negotiations began!

When the transaction was complete, I paid the woman and asked Ann for the jewelry. Ann turned to me and smiled, indicating success, and said, "We'll have to wait for delivery until tomorrow."

"Why?" I inquired of Ann.

"That's easy," she explained. "No respectable woman will appear in public without her jewelry on. It would be immodest and improper for her to do so!" What a striking lesson about significance—about you and me.

We have so many different perspectives and definitions. Modesty and respectability are important in any culture, but their definitions differ from one to the next. In the United States, our modesty and respectability can be seen in our clothing. In Zaire, modesty and respectability are revealed through the jewelry.

We are all significant. In the story I have just told, each person played his or her own part. Likewise, each person plays a vital role in the world. God simply asks that we respect each other and encourage one another rather than offering each other judgment and condemnation.

We are all part of the same body, and all privileged to share the significance that makes each and every one unique.

■■■■■■■■■ T H O U G H T   F O R   T H E   H E A R T

I am significant! I belong to the Lord, I belong to the family of believers, and I am significant!

—Phil Hook

●

DESIGNER ORIGINALS

"For You created my innermost being; You knit me together in my mother's womb. I praise You because I am fearfully and wonderfully made . . . my frame was not hidden from You when I was made in the secret place." Psalm 139:13-15

Do you ever feel insignificant by comparison with the world around you? Do you ever wonder if you are really important?

We seem dull in the presence of television ideals of face, form, and athletic prowess. We lose significance in the video presence of nations and leaders on the evening news. What meaning or value can grace our lives, when, at best, we are minor-league successes?

In the world's eyes, we may be average people with average looks, average jobs, and an average tomorrow. But we do not live by the world's definitions.

For the believer, significance is not just new clothes, promotions, or good feelings about our successes. For the Christian, significance exists because we are held in high esteem by the God of the universe.

God's spoken truth about us gives meaning and definition to our lives and to our struggles. God's spoken truth declares that we are significant in spite of how we may feel, simply because God says it is so.

God crafted our bodies and our inner beings such that we are "fearfully and wonderfully made." The wonder is still in us, in spite of our fallenness or crippled forms.

We alone of all creatures on the globe possess a throat designed for speaking, a mind designed for thinking, and a heart designed for true love and value. We alone possess hands that create with needle and hammer, violin and pen. We alone in all the world have an eye for beauty and a heart for pain. We alone are never filled by the earth, but long for reality beyond our existence here.

Though feelings of insignificance will come, try to remember that God knows each of us individually. He crafted each body and each person for a purpose in the present, and He will resurrect and re-create us for a future too grand to speak about. We are creations from His image, and in such promise we are called to rejoice.

I know that it is hard to see ourselves in the mirror of God's image. It is difficult to choose to be uniquely gifted when we feel uniquely flawed.

Try to hold on to significance, even when the mirror grows dim. Try to hold on to what you know to be true about God and His love for you.

■■■■■■■■■■ THOUGHT FOR THE HEART

I would like to see myself through God's eyes, and I can begin right now in these ways.

—Mark Cosgrove

●
TRUE TREASURE

"Command those who are rich in this present world not to be arrogant nor to put their hope in wealth, which is so uncertain, but to put their hope in God, who richly supplies us with everything for our enjoyment. Command them to do good, to be rich in good deeds, and to be generous and willing to share. In this way they will lay up treasure for themselves as a firm foundation for the coming age, so that they may take hold of the life that is truly life." 1 Timothy 6:17-19

We tend to live with myths, and they start while we are very young. We dream of being the President or playing in the NBA or marrying the perfect person or living the life of a wealthy entrepreneur or being recognized as a famous physician. I see this all the time, and particularly in the academic setting which is now my own.

I see students who think that they must live up to some certain standard or expectation in order to be important. I hear echoes from their parents' perspectives adopted as their own. Or I hear shades of movie star images, contemporary artists, and sports figures. I hear dreams that often have little to do with who they are and much more to do with who they think they should be in order to really be happy.

The conflict is not confined to the student population! There is a certain synthetic or transitory significance which grows out of a degree. Some people can't finish a whole sentence without saying, "When I was in graduate school" or "When I was working on my doctorate"! This isn't much different than the statements I hear from the students.

Those who are more secure in life generally don't need to tell you what they've done or what they are doing. Those who feel significant generally don't measure their importance by lists or degrees. Perhaps another example will help.

When you enter the home of a family that's known wealth for generations, you tend to see an old armchair, a tattered sweater, or maybe a well-worn jacket or baseball cap. They are "the favorites," and it doesn't matter that a new one could be purchased without delay. Families who have known wealth for years are rarely in need of flaunting that wealth.

When you enter the home of someone newly rich, the scene is usually different. The furniture is brand-new and everything matches. The toys are the latest and they're all picked up. There is an air of "perfection" in the room that makes everyone feel a bit uncomfortable. The wealth was intended to bring significance, but money does not have that kind of power.

Paul made it very clear that he learned to be content in all circumstances, and that kind of learning doesn't come easy. Paul knew he was significant and that significance cannot be measured in earthly possessions or positions. He had already tried that route and found it lacking.

Paul's best encouragement to Timothy was not to achieve or collect or hold on to treasures. Paul knew those would not work. His young friend would never find significance in something that could be earned or bought. Paul's best encouragement was to lay hold of the real treasure: life with God.

Significance is this: it is you and me enjoying our position as children of God, accepting what He allows, and walking through this world responding to His love.

Significance cannot be bought, earned, measured, or tied down. It is not about "doing."

Take a lesson from Paul and from an old university president. Significance is not about myths or degrees. It is a God-given gift for you and for me. It is about "being" His in both this world and the next. It is about laying up treasure for "the life that is truly life."

▬▬▬ THOUGHT FOR THE HEART

I am aware that I tend to try to gain significance through accomplishments or the various wealths of this world. I would like to experience my own significance in Christ and to pass that along to others.

— Jay Kesler

RHYTHMS OF MY HEART

SUCCESS

THE LESSON OF THE PALM TREE

"The righteous shall flourish like the palm tree, they will grow like a cedar of Lebanon; planted in the house of the Lord, they will flourish in the courts of our God. They will still bear fruit in old age, they will stay fresh and green." Psalm 92:12-14

Ask a small girl how old she is, and with a gleam in her eyes and a toothless smile she will gladly hold up her fingers. Ask a teenaged youth how old he is, and with great pride (and a little exaggeration!) he will tell you. The young long for the success of growing older, while the older lose sight of the prize.

Something happens as we move upward in adulthood. We begin to think of aging as a curse instead of as a sign of success and achievement. We begin to try to roll back the clock and recapture years already gone by. It seems we fear "wearing out" our success.

God's view of success is very different from our view! From the heart of a sixty-six-year-old man of faith came these words. "Sixty-six isn't old, if you're a palm tree." He's got a point.

Palm trees can withstand great external abuse since the life of the palm tree is on the inside. Palm trees can survive drought because they send their roots deep into the soil. The fruit of the palm becomes sweeter with age. And palm trees can be transplanted any time of the year, as their aging produces flexibility.

When we're successful, we can withstand the pains of this world. Who we are is an inner quality of character, not an outer definition of beauty or strength. When we're successful, we can survive periods of drought because our roots go deep into the soil of God's nourishment.

When we're successful, we taste sweeter with age from

470

the wisdom that grows out of our experiences. And when we're successful, we are flexible. We can "move" with the Spirit's leading and literally bloom where we are planted.

Success lies in being committed to who we are and who we're becoming. Success lies in the character rather than the number of wrinkles or the balance at the bank.

Adopt a view of success that reaches far beyond your years! And when you feel like you can't carry on, hold on to the lesson of the palm tree.

▬▬▬▬▬ T H O U G H T   F O R   T H E   H E A R T

I would like to adopt a definition of success that includes who I am — at any age, and in any situation.

— *John Coulombe*

●
SEEING GREATNESS WITHIN

"Who are you to judge someone else's servant? To his own master he stands or falls. And he will stand, for the Lord is able to make him stand." Romans 14:4

A great big Buick with Iowa license plates drove up in front of the school. It was August and time for classes to begin. I was the Wheaton College Dean of Students at the time, and I was there to greet students and their parents. I even memorized pictures and biographies so that I could greet each family by name (hard to believe now, but true!).

I walked over to the Buick and a stocky Iowa farmer got out and extended his hand to me. I received the hand, introduced myself, and greeted him by name. His hand was thick and like sandpaper against my soft, professorial hands.

Somewhere deep inside I knew that this was a man of character and accomplishment in a world much different than my own. But he didn't understand my world and fell easily into the trap of admiring what he thought rather than what was real. The farmer seemed almost worshipful of me and of Wheaton and with great pride he said, "I've brought you my son to be a student here."

The back door of the Buick opened and I was immediately taken back. The boy who emerged was small for his age, with soft hands and a very shy demeanor. I knew, from that instant, that we were in trouble.

"I only got to the sixth grade in school," said the dad. "I am doing everything I can so that my son can be an educated man."

The son said nothing, and I looked with sorrow on that father. He didn't understand greatness, and he didn't understand what made him great.

Years of hard work and farming had made the man a very successful farmer, but it was obvious that he had protected his son from his own greatness.

This little boy won't last a year here, I thought. *He is not prepared for our world. His father hasn't given him the greatest gift of all — himself.*

In despising his own lack of education, the father had failed to give his son the great legacy of a man who knew how to work. The son was totally unprepared for life.

A few months later I called the father and told him he needed to come get his son. His son had been protected from greatness, and missed his opportunity for a true education.

We often fail to see our successes even though they are within us and with us all of the time. We tend to see other people's greatness, but rarely our own.

Success isn't living up to a certain dream or expectation; it is being the person God has designed you to be — anywhere and anytime.

God has made you great. He is making you successful in this very moment.

SUCCESS

I tend to define success in these terms or expectations rather than allowing God to define success in me!

— *Phil Hook*

●

A DIFFERENT MEASURING STICK

"The greatest among you will be your servant. For whoever exalts himself will be humbled, and whoever humbles himself will be exalted." Matthew 23:11

What constitutes greatness? In a world dominated by materialism, we tend to equate greatness with possessions, wealth, and power. Yet in the Old Testament, a man's importance was measured by how many cattle, sheep, and other animals he owned (remember Job?).

Are the cars in the driveway, the number of suits or dresses in the closet, the accumulation of electronic gadgets, or the titles on our door a measure of greatness?

When we think of "great" people, we tend to think of international leaders, super jocks, movie actors, or rock singers. We even dress like they dress, eat what they eat, and follow them around, waiting for an autograph or a glance in our direction.

It is not strange that the world would measure success this way, but I grow concerned when we allow that kind of mind-set to invade the church! When we do, we start thinking that the "great" pastors are the ones who have large congregations or television programs. We begin to think that big churches are better. Or we assume that those who write best-sellers and hit songs are the "successful" people in the kingdom.

Some are going to be blessed by God in these ways, but

the material blessings do not equal success. We can pastor large churches, minister to huge audiences, sell a million books . . . and fail miserably. All of that power and attention can turn even the most careful man or woman into a self-centered and self-reliant disaster. This is what happened to the Laodicean church described in Revelation 3:17.

Jesus measured greatness in terms of servanthood. That's what He tried to convey in the words recorded in Matthew 23 as well as in His daily life. Spiritual greatness is measured by humility, faithfulness, obedience, love, and many other qualities we tend to avoid. The Pharisees struggled with such a low-profile view of success and we struggle too.

I have a dear friend whose wife of many years became confined to a wheelchair. A woman who had once cared tirelessly for him suddenly needed constant care herself. Totally unable to communicate with her, my friend simply served his wife day after day.

Such is "success" in the kingdom of God. No possessions accumulated on earth can take the place of love and service, of mercy and simple heartfelt commitment.

This is the "success" which truly matters.

THOUGHT FOR THE HEART

I often confuse these definitions of greatness with God's definitions. I know it will take time for me to learn, but I want to embrace the success that has been modeled and taught by our Lord.

— David Lynch

●

STRETCHING EXERCISES

"You did not choose Me, but I chose you to go and bear fruit — fruit that will last." John 15:16

Getting beyond that which feels natural and comfortable is quite painful for any of us. For the runner, "breaking the wall" to go on to greater distances seems almost impossible. For the shy person, starting a conversation with a stranger is like pulling teeth. And yet, stretching beyond our comfort zone usually pays great dividends. For the runner, it means finishing the race. And for the shy person, it means enjoying relationships with people who were once considered strangers.

There is a woman in our town who is as normal as you and me. She is a growing Christian and she feels a burden for junior high and senior high students. She even teaches a Sunday School class at her church.

She also lives close to a junior high school. *Wouldn't it be great to start a Bible study there?* she thought. *No, that would be too difficult.* The idea seemed risky, and she resisted. One year later, she found herself in the middle of the lunch line at school, passing out fliers for a Bible study in her home. Even the principal who sent her outside with her invitations could not deter this woman from her goal. She now has a group of girls studying God's Word in her home every week.

We are often bound by our longing for the comfortable, but God moves us out of that boundary into places of growth and significance. Abraham was asked to pick up everything and go. Job was asked to turn loose all that was important to him. Mary was chosen to bear life and pain. And Paul was called from the world he knew into the great unknown.

What ridiculous idea is God placing in your heart? What is God urging you to do that you would never feel comfortable doing? What growth lies ahead that you long for, yet fear?

God stretches us to grow us up. And He grows us up to be like His Son. This is success.

SUCCESS

Step out of your comfort zone today and find the success that comes from stretching for God.

▬▬▬▬▬▬▬▬ THOUGHT FOR THE HEART

I can feel God stretching me in these areas of my life.

—Tim Hawks

●

GOD WILL MAKE UP THE DIFFERENCE

"There was a Benjamite, a man of standing, whose name was Kish. . . . He had a son named Saul, an impressive young man without equal among the Israelites—a head taller than any of the others." 1 Samuel 9:1-2

The description is clear. Saul was a young man who stood a head taller than anyone else! His family was prominent, his father was a soldier, he had all the normal definitions of success in his world. And he was about to be chosen for a very significant position.

The Bible begins its introduction of Saul by telling us an interesting story about this young man. His father sent him hunting for donkeys and the donkeys came home before he did! What did God want us to learn? Why was his search for the donkeys significant?

The story seems to be a commentary on Saul's entire life. He enjoyed a great heritage, he had great potential, but there was little realization from Saul's perspective of the greatness that could be his.

While hunting for the donkeys, Saul turned to Samuel for help. "You are the desire of the nations, young man." I am certain Saul looked surprised.

"Why do you say this?" Saul replied. "Am I not a Benjamite, and is my clan not one of the smallest of my tribe?"

"The Lord has anointed you leader over His inheritance." And with that, Samuel blessed Saul and Saul went on his way back home.

Israel wanted to be like other nations. They wanted a king like other kings. And so Samuel chose Saul for the job—a job that the young man had no ambition to fulfill.

God in His grace gave Saul a special measure of His Spirit. Saul was able to talk with prophets, even able to sound like a prophet. And finally the day came for his coronation. It was to be a great celebration.

Samuel lined the nation up by tribes and families. The tribe of Benjamin was chosen. The family of Kish was chosen. The son, Saul, was chosen . . . but he could not be found. Everyone was assembled and ready, but the king was nowhere in sight.

"Where has he gone?" "Is he here?" "Maybe he's ill." "What's going on?" The place was astir with everyone's best guess at what was happening to the king.

Then, the same servant who helped Saul find the donkeys was dispatched to help the people find the king. And you probably remember the conclusion: Saul was found hiding among the baggage.

On a day of joy and triumph, Saul was afraid of the responsibility and he chose to hide. Saul did not see himself the way God saw him. Saul did not know that he was great or a head taller or the one "set apart." Instead, Saul saw only his fear and inability. In his own eyes, Saul was anything but a king.

It is difficult to see ourselves through God's eyes. He has formed you and me as He desires, and from God's point of view He only makes successes!

For you and for me, however, the task of seeing ourselves from God's point of view is not always easy. We tend to see the flaws, the impossibilities, the imperfections, the failures, and the inadequacies.

Remember that God knows we fail. He knows we have

insecurities and weak spots. What He also knows is that He will make up the difference. He will provide all that we need to live out our success in this world — and in the one to come.

■■■■■■■■■■■ THOUGHT FOR THE HEART

I have trouble seeing myself as God sees me. This is what He sees. . . .

— Phil Hook

●

BE YOURSELF, NOT PERFECT

"With what shall I come before the Lord and bow down before the exalted God? Shall I come before Him with burnt offerings, with calves a year old? Will the Lord be pleased with thousands of rams, with ten thousand rivers of oil? Shall I offer my firstborn for my transgression, the fruit of my body for the sin of my soul? He has showed you, O man, what is good. And what does the Lord require of you? To act justly and to love mercy and to walk humbly with your God." Micah 6:6-8

"Sing your best today!" the worship leader says as she begins to lead the congregation in song. "Let's give our best voices to the Lord." And so we sing, most of us on key and most of us trying to be enthusiastic.

I've traveled quite a bit through the years and such a scenario is not unusual. I even understand the purpose of a statement like that or the goal of that poor worship leader who's trying his or her best to prepare the congregation for a significant encounter with God's Word.

Every time I'm in a situation like that, I pause for a moment to ponder what's been said. I'm not sure I know what "my best" is. I usually give my best for that moment, given my mood, given the church, given the song, and given the leader. What would my best sound like? And how would I know when I was giving that best to the Lord?

I think one of the biggest obstacles in our striving for success lies in equating success with that illusive ideal of perfection. There simply is not a perfect way to do most of what we are called upon to do in this world, but we try to find it most of the time! And we often send a message to those we love that tells them whether we think they've reached success or not.

It's debilitating to think that we must reproduce something perfectly in order for that something to be successful. And it's quite debilitating to equate our version of success with God's expectations.

For me, success has a lot to do with effort . . . giving the "old college try" in a situation. Perhaps that sounds a bit lazy or undefined, but I have learned through the years that success is me, Jay Kesler, competing with my own potential, my own opportunities, and my own gifts. It is me growing and learning and putting to use what I've learned.

On the other side of the coin, I do not equate success anymore with external standards around us. We've already seen, in recent years, how devastating such definitions have been to children from other socioeconomic or cultural environments or even those children with completely different gifts. If we judge all children based on one culture's standards, one institution's standards, or one family's standards, then we do those children a great disservice.

An artist does not sit down and create a masterpiece the first time he or she paints. Nor does a dancer dance impeccably the first time the shoes are placed on the feet.

Success is a process of growths and failures, the conquering of fears and the commitment to go just a little bit further tomorrow. Success is measured in years, not in one day or the next. And success relates solely to that person's gifts, abilities, and dreams rather than to one, universalized expectation.

It takes time and failures to grow a family. It takes time and failures to grow a relationship. It takes time and failures to grow a person. It takes time and failures to grow "success."

■■■■■■■■■■■ THOUGHT FOR THE HEART

I can see that I am growing and learning in these areas and in these ways and from these "failures." I want to see myself as a "success" rather than as one who never quite reaches "the mark."

—Jay Kesler

●
NOT A ONE-TIME THING

"Create in me a pure heart, O God, and renew a steadfast spirit within me. Do not cast me from Your presence or take Your Holy Spirit from me. Restore to me the joy of Your salvation and grant me a willing spirit, to sustain me." Psalm 51:10-12

It was springtime—the time when kings go to war. But this year, David sent Joab to lead his men in battle. They fought against the Ammonites while the king stayed home and grew restless. Though a very successful ruler, he was bored with his life.

There was another restless person in the city that night. Her name was Bathsheba, the wife of a soldier who had gone to battle with the other men. Bathsheba had no children and nothing to fill her life, so while the king walked the balconies of the palace, she bathed in the backyard of her home. Both seemed to be looking for some activity to fill the void.

SUCCESS

Success is both a necessary and dangerous process for men and women. I remember a night at basketball practice many years ago when I wore the blue shirt of the starting lineup. It seemed like every time I shot the ball it went in. I knew this was the beginning of a great career.

When the game was over I was ready to receive the accolades of teammates and coaches. I was ready to count myself a success, but I had one problem.

In the splendor of my shining moment, I had forgotten that this was a practice game. And I had forgotten that this was my first time to do well. I was ready to mark myself a success before there was any evidence for that reality. In fact, I did not enjoy any more successes that year. I scored points and played games, but never again did I experience the same level of confidence.

David too had forgotten that there was much life ahead. Some of the practice games were over and he had done well, but he hadn't prepared for a lifetime of living. Success is a dangerous word and an even more dangerous feeling.

I think this is why God labels us "successful" based on the attitude of our hearts. He isn't impressed by games where the score is high, nor is He left helpless by our failures and unwise choices. God works with the heart for a lifetime, and He sees the heart as He guides you and me through the course of our lifetime.

Success is an attitude. Success is a lifestyle. Success is personal. And success is a process.

Work with God on that process in your life.

THOUGHT FOR THE HEART

I have been bored or discouraged about my life lately. I am willing to look at the "bigger picture" of success that God is weaving in my heart.

— Phil Hook

RHYTHMS OF MY HEART

SUFFERING

• THE GREAT ENABLER

"Though the fig tree does not bud and there are no grapes on the vines, though the olive crop fails and the fields produce no food, though there are no sheep in the pen and no cattle in the stalls, yet I will rejoice in the Lord, I will be joyful in God my Savior. The Sovereign Lord is my strength; He makes my feet like the feet of a deer, He enables me to go on the heights." Habakkuk 3:17-19

Neva had been diagnosed with cancer and was experiencing a slow, terrible walk toward the end of her life. My friend told me how Neva phoned her each night, crying and asking my friend to pray with her for some release from the pain. I remember thinking, *I wouldn't know what to say or how to pray. I hope she doesn't call me!*

Then one week, Neva showed up at the Sunday morning worship service. As our pastor asked the congregation to share any requests or answers to prayer, Neva shakily stood to her feet.

"I don't understand why God is letting this happen to me . . . why He doesn't take away the pain . . . " she muttered. Then, in a stronger, more determined voice she continued, "I can't see any good in this, but I keep thinking of Habakkuk waiting and watching. So I will stand at *my* watch and see what God will say to *me*. And though my life is falling apart and the pain won't go away, 'I will rejoice in the Lord.' "

Neva's thoughts from Habakkuk have stuck with me since the day she spoke them. I've watched my friends lose children, my family members lose certain qualities of life, the teenagers I work with lose their innocence to abusive parents or coaches . . . the list of sufferers could go on and on. We all know people who seem to experience more than their share of loss or pain. And like Neva, we wait for a response to our cry of, "Why, Lord?"

It doesn't seem fair when bad things happen to good people, does it? But then, where did I get the idea that life is supposed to be fair? Why is it that, when I face any degree of suffering, I automatically question the justice of my Father? Can't I trust Him to manage my life regardless of the circumstances?

Like Habakkuk, I have had to learn the lesson of faith. Not once. Not twice. But over and over again with each circumstance of suffering, including my own.

At times my life has been reduced to such shambles that it seems as if I have had no choice but to trust the Father's work. Yet I have discovered that it's during those times of intense pain that I have felt most dependent on Him for strength and the power to go on.

Could it be that suffering isn't meaningless? That, in a sense, it actually drives us to our knees in search of the One who listens to our complaints, comforts our emotional pain, and gives us grace to continue on?

Habakkuk, anticipating the horrible results of the imminent Babylonian invasion of Judah, declared his trust in the Lord and expressed his confidence that the Lord would enable him "to go on." Neva, likewise, expressed her willingness to trust God, even though she could not understand the pain.

As you and I face suffering and the consequences of a depraved world, let us reaffirm our faith in our Father who loves us and cares about our suffering.

THOUGHT FOR THE HEART

Jesus felt deeply His aloneness during the Crucifixion. I have an Advocate who will never allow the Father to leave my side in times of suffering.

— Pam Campbell

●

EYES TO SEE ETERNITY

"My ears had heard of You, but now my eyes have seen You." Job 42:5

The word *cancer* was a total surprise to me. I was twenty-eight years old at the time and totally unprepared for that kind of news. And the type of cancer I have is rare — only found in men who are older and have been exposed to asbestos over a period of years. Needless to say, suffering has played its tune in my life since my first introduction to cancer.

Though people have tried to offer help through the years, I have found that most believers do not feel comfortable with the unknown. Instead of offering a kind word, a gentle touch, or a listening ear, they offer advice on how to cure the problem so that all can be "OK" again.

I easily understand the struggle. For much of my life I responded in the same way to other people's pain. I was afraid of things I could not control and horrified of "bad news." We are rarely prepared for suffering, and almost never prepared for the reality that suffering can happen to "me."

I'm not sure why it is so difficult for Christians to bear pain. Jesus was honest with us about the trials we would experience, and He certainly lived a life in which suffering was a regular occurrence.

In fact, those who have known God through the years have experienced great losses. I am reminded of Job — a man who knew God and had served Him well, only to lose all that he had worked for and enjoyed in this world.

Job was heartbroken. He could not understand why God would allow such loss, and his friends certainly didn't help. It was easier for them to blame Job for his lack of faith or hidden sins than to accept suffering's reality. And so Job was left alone in his pain, to hurt and to grieve and to wonder why.

I think one of the most important gifts Job gave to believers was his attitude. He openly grieved. He openly questioned. He openly despaired, even of life. And yet he also held on to the One who had always been faithful.

Christians who are eager to put suffering in its place often go too quickly to the end of Job's story. We cite the fact that God restored His servant and even gave him a new family, but in so doing we miss the very purpose of Job's pain.

"Once my ears had heard of You, but now my eyes have seen You," Job spoke quietly. Such humility from a man whose body and soul were in torment.

Job had learned an important lesson. He had been given eyes to see eternity even through his pain. And such a gift can hardly be despised.

I fully recognize how hard it is for us to bear our sufferings. No one likes to suffer grief, but our God is not absent in our pain, nor does He waste our experiences.

I am still learning to see God in the presence of my own pain, and I pray that He grants you the grace to see Him in your difficulties too.

▄▄▄▄▄▄▄▄▄▄▄ THOUGHT FOR THE HEART

I am struggling in these areas of my life, and I would like to see God at work—even in the presence of the pain.

— Shelley Chapin

●

ADVENT ECLIPSES ADVERSITY

"Yet it was the Lord's will to crush Him and cause Him to suffer, and though the Lord makes His life a guilt offering, He will see His

offspring and prolong His days, and the will of the Lord will pros-per in His hand. After the suffering of His soul, He will see the light of life and be satisfied; by His knowledge My righteous servant will justify many, and He will bear their iniquities. Therefore, I will give Him a portion among the great, and He will divide the spoils with the strong, because He poured out His life unto death, and was numbered with the transgressors. For He bore the sin of many, and made intercession for the transgressors." Isaiah 53:10-12

Adversity is a part of life. Sooner or later it knocks on all of our doors. Joseph and Mary were no exception. Their first Christmas was anything but festive and carefree.

Because of the uniqueness of Mary's conception, their reputations were in question. The young couple was faced with high taxes to pay. They were forced to make a trip they didn't want to make with the baby due any day. And to top it all off, there were no rooms in the motel for them. Even American Express couldn't help!

But that night, in a stable, something happened which made all of the adversities seem insignificant. A child was born—not just any child, but the Son of God! Mary became part of the miracle of Christmas! And adversity was eclipsed by joy.

The story doesn't end there. The same power that transformed the journey of Joseph and Mary can transform our journey as well. And our world around us desperately needs to know this truth!

To all the wounded, grieving, hurting, lonely, helpless, and hopeless people around us, God is announcing the good news:

ADVENT ECLIPSES ADVERSITY!

Christ is greater than any need we are facing. His grace is sufficient. His love is unending. His presence prevails.

People need to know this great truth about the Gospel.

People need to see this reality demonstrated in our lives. They need to know that Christianity is much more than a "prosperity gospel" in which everybody has plenty of everything that is desired materially or physically. They need to know Christ.

God never promises adversity-free living. I have never known a mature Christian who has not gone through adversity. Over the years I have watched dear saints deal with the worst that life can throw at us and, in the midst of the battles, demonstrate the grace of God.

We will experience tough times financially. We will suffer loss. We will not all "get well." We will not all be "delivered" from our problems. But we *will* become monuments to the power of God. We *will* prove that God is faithful and His Word is true.

To all of you who face adversity, take heart in the message that was born with the Savior: Advent eclipses adversity!

THOUGHT FOR THE HEART

I can see God at work in these adversities of my life, and I am willing to let God shine through me in the midst of my pain.

—David Lynch

●

WHEN SCARS RUN DEEP

"Your hands shaped me and made me. Will You now turn and destroy me? Remember that You molded me like clay. Will You now turn me to dust again?" Job 10:8-9

She would have been noticeable in any audience. She sat near the front and listened intently. Her large, brown eyes never seemed to leave my Bible or hers, and she looked as if every word meant life.

The thing that made this young woman particularly noticeable to me was the gaunt nature of her body. She looked as if she'd had no consistent nourishment at all.

She must not have enough to eat, I thought. *Maybe I can offer money to provide some relief.* But when I tried to talk with her after the engagement, she seemed unable to respond and ran away.

Throughout the days of my teaching, this young woman stayed close but never close enough to talk. I asked one of the missionaries about her and discovered she was one of the most faithful young people they had known. She came to all of the meetings, carefully studied the Scriptures, and participated in all of the events. I also learned that she was seventeen years old and lived by herself.

"Is that why she looks so thin?" I inquired. "Doesn't she have a family?" I could tell I was asking some privileged questions.

"She lives under several doors that are leaned up against the side of her family's house. It is the place she sleeps, the place she keeps her clothes, and she eats wherever she can," I heard.

"Why?" I asked. "Is her family too poor to provide?" The missionary seemed hesitant to speak further, so the subject was dropped for the rest of the day.

I kept my eye on this young woman throughout the week. I found myself consciously trying to slip messages of encouragement into my words to try to help. I knew she was hurting, but I didn't know why or how much.

Finally I learned her story. She came from a home where marriage played no meaningful role. The man who was living with her mother was not her father. He was abusive to the mother and, yes, he was abusive to this young, lovely girl. At the hands of one she should have been able to trust, she had suffered both physical and sexual abuse.

SUFFERING

As you might imagine, the young girl remained quiet throughout my stay. After all, who could she trust? She longed to reach out to me, but I was a man and a stranger—both signs of danger for her.

She has since become quite a leader in her church and community, but the marks of abuse remain. Her physical health is still poor, and to this day she is afraid of men and has not married.

Abuse is not unique to any culture, and the symptoms and consequences span both time and place. The suffering abuse brings is extensive and prolonged.

But we have a God who loves and heals and forgives, who hears and soothes, who comforts and walks by our side each step of the way. Let Him embrace your pain. He is here.

THOUGHT FOR THE HEART

I am aware of the suffering I feel as a result of some painful memories or circumstances. I am willing to allow God to embrace my pain and help me in the process of healing.

—Phil Hook

●

FLYING LESSONS

"Therefore, since Christ suffered in His body, arm yourselves also with the same attitude, because he who has suffered in his body is done with sin. As a result, he does not live the rest of his earthly life for evil human desires, but rather for the will of God." 1 Peter 4:1-2

I received a letter one day from one of the young families in our church. In it they shared some of the recent battles they had been facing. And as I read the letter I expected it to be signed by Job! Murphy's Law was indeed in effect—everything that could go wrong had gone wrong!

This father described physical pain, loss from fire, problems in the business, and substantial financial loss. Yet through all of these bitter experiences, this family had maintained their faith and were trusting God for the future. They were indeed holding on to faith, even in the midst of the refining.

One portion of the letter spoke volumes to me about God's abundant grace in our times of trouble.

"When Brooke, our oldest, was little, I used to throw her up in the air and catch her to squeals of 'more!' and 'higher!' After Daniel was born, I started doing the same to him. And he seemed to find like pleasure in the game.

"Brooke, when three years old, saw me playing the game with Daniel, and she wanted to be thrown too. But when I threw her up as I'd done so many times, she was afraid. She set rules for how high and how fast. She was no longer sure this game was safe. And she trusted her head more than her daddy."

How much this is like the way we trust God. Sometimes He plays rough, and we don't like it. But He has a purpose for throwing us in the air. He wants us to learn to simply trust Him. He's teaching us to fly!

Maybe you're finding yourself thrown in the air right now. The circumstances in your life threaten to become overwhelming. The pressures are intense. Anxiety is a constant companion. No relief is in sight.

Perhaps these are flying lessons! Though you might feel unprepared for the game, perhaps God is growing your faith. And perhaps, if you listen close enough, you can hear the voice of the Father saying, "Trust Me! I won't let you fall!"

Peter's message has become a source of comfort to most of us who are familiar with pain. He wrote to folks who were under attack and enduring intense persecution.

Learning to fly is never easy. After all, we didn't come

equipped with wings, and we certainly feel afraid when tossed high into the air.

But as we learn to trust Him, we discover that we've been safe all along. The Lord will not let us fall. Instead, He is teaching us to soar like the eagles.

████████████ T H O U G H T   F O R   T H E   H E A R T

Though I struggle with the pain, I sense that God is "teaching me to fly" in these areas of my faith.

— *David Lynch*

●

PURPOSE IN PAIN

"Now My heart is troubled, and what shall I say? 'Father, save Me from this hour'? No, it was for this very reason I came to this hour. Father, glorify Your name!" John 12:27-28

In 1989 cancer struck my body. I prayed fervently throughout the days of my illness, "Lord, let this cup pass from me." There were moments when my supplication appeared to transport me into another dimension, and I experienced God more profoundly than I had before.

In this state of altered consciousness, I sensed God returning me to the foot of the cross at Calvary. There, He reminded me that we could suffer and still be united in God's will. He had a purpose for me that went beyond a shallow and untested existence. He desired to perfect my faith. He wanted to change me into the likeness of His Son. Pain and suffering were not wasted in the process of purification.

Learning to trust God's ultimate purpose for my highest good and His glory does not remove the reality of cancer. I am human! I am afraid at times. And I grow weary with the pain that requires more than my body has to offer.

But knowing God has purpose in my pain does do something supernatural within me. His purpose transforms the nature of my suffering and it transforms the way that the suffering affects my life. Instead of being abandoned in my anguish, I have found His presence in my pain.

I find peace, even joy, in my affliction these days. And I have experienced the freedom to respond with the words that Jesus offered so courageously.

"Father, if You are willing, take this cup from Me; yet not My will, but Yours be done" (Luke 22:42).

■■■■■■■■■■ THOUGHT FOR THE HEART

It is difficult for me to find strength in my sufferings, particularly right now in the midst of this pain. I need God's perspective to find His presence in my pain.

—*Annette Richter*

•
A YOUNG MAN'S COURAGE

"For it has been granted to you on behalf of Christ not only to believe on Him, but also to suffer for Him." Philippians 1:29

I never imagined that I could see suffering as a gift rather than a curse. I never saw myself as a good candidate for suffering; in fact, I was certain that I was not cut out of the kind of mold that could endure real pain. And I felt that way until I met Bryan.

Bryan was just a little boy when he and I first met. He had an older brother and sister who attended a camp where I was counselor for the summers. Finally it was Bryan's turn to enjoy himself in a whole new world of horses and archery, riflery and canoeing.

Bryan had beautiful blond hair and lovely blue eyes,

and his smile gave everyone who knew him a burst of joy. He seemed at peace with the world for his age, and very much in tune with the God who had made him.

By the time Bryan turned twelve he was no longer running around in a happy, protected world. Bryan had contracted leukemia — and not just "any kind." Bryan was afflicted with the most serious type of leukemia that a young boy could have, and he was dying.

Like all families, Bryan's parents and siblings did all they could to support him. They tried every treatment available to man and every possible therapy that might bring relief. Bryan rallied at times and enjoyed brief respites from the disease, but finally we all knew he would not recover.

I remember my moments with this young man as if they were yesterday. Little did I know then that Bryan's bout with cancer was preparing me for my own. Within five years of his death I was well acqainted with cancer myself, and my memories of Bryan's courageous acceptance of suffering have remained a real stronghold for me.

"Sing me a song," he would say. And I'd grasp the guitar and serenade him with the favorites from camp. Bryan would close his eyes, a certain smile of peace on his lips, and just rest.

"I know that I'm about to die," he would say after a time of repose. "I'm going to die and I'm ready. Jesus is taking care of me." He sounded so certain.

"But Bryan, I know you are hurting. Is there anything I can do?" I must have asked the question a hundred times.

"I'm OK, Shelley," he would say with assurance. And somehow, I began to understand.

Suffering is harder than we can explain or imagine. It comes in various sizes and shapes and it lasts, sometimes, until we're certain we can take no more. Yet we press on.

God uses suffering to grow and to build the very character He has fashioned as you and as me. I'm not sure I can explain what I just wrote, I only know from my experience and from Scripture's teaching that those who know and love our Lord experience the refining of faith at the hand of pain.

Suffering is part of living in this world, and it is not a wasted experience or some ludicrous test. Suffering is allowed and, yes, even designed with true purpose and love in mind.

I can't explain the timing of Bryan's death or the specific purposes for his specific pain. But what I can offer you is testimony after testimony of lives that have been deeply affected and even changed through the love and maturity of this one young man.

Embrace the pain, as strange as that may seem. Please know that your suffering has purpose, and that you are not forgotten by God.

Our suffering is one of God's great packages, wrapped and offered in love and purposed to bring life.

Thank you, Bryan, for offering me the life that is in you. I listened, I learned, and I'm living your example.

THOUGHT FOR THE HEART

I fear these sufferings in my life, but I'm willing to begin to look for God's purpose in their midst.

— *Shelley Chapin*

RHYTHMS OF MY HEART

WORSHIP

CELEBRATION OF THE HEART

"Worship the Lord with gladness; come before Him with joyful songs. Know that the Lord is God. It is He who made us, and we are His; we are His people, the sheep of His pasture." Psalm 100:2-3

I wish you could have known Tom. I wish I had known him longer and better. He was one of those rare individuals who shines with the light of our Lord. He was one who leaves you feeling like you've just been sitting with Jesus.

Lest I deify Tom, let me say that I know he was not perfect or above the soil of this world. Like you and me, Tom was fully human. He simply had an opportunity afforded to only the select few. He was going to be with the Lord, and he had time to put his house in order.

Tom was in his early thirties when we first met. I am a cancer patient myself, and I have the rare privilege of meeting many who suffer from terminal or chronic illness. I made Tom's acquaintance under those conditions.

Tom was in the hospital awaiting surgery for a brain tumor. He was literally scheduled for surgery that day and our meeting was to serve as some kind of encouragement for him. Before entering Tom's room, all I knew about him was a brief history of his illness. He was suffering from a recurrence of cancer, and a wife and two small children were making the journey with him.

For me, there was instant rapport when I entered Tom's room. His eyes were alive with the light and life of Christ and our conversation soared with mutual testimonies of God's goodness. The moments were timeless and the fellowship sweet as we discussed all that God was teaching us in our pain.

I can tell you that it is rare to encounter men and women like Tom. Most are fleeing their suffering; few embrace their pain as a gift of God. Tom and I had been given a similar perspective for our journey, so we had much to offer one another.

After a few minutes, a minister who was with us attempted to bring our time to a close. Acting as he normally would, my friend suggested that we spend some time in fellowship with God. I'll never forget Tom's response.

"What do you think we've been doing!" he laughed with full acceptance and much joy. "We've been worshiping since the moment you entered!" And Tom was right.

Worship can take place in many different places. Though it is difficult for us to allow ourselves the freedom, worship "happens" any time one of God's children gives Him glory. Though formal times together are great, worship is not reserved for a day or a meeting.

Give God glory today! Spend some time focusing on all that He is and ever will be. Spend some time reflecting on all of the ways He cares for you.

And thank you, Tom, for reminding me that worship is a celebration of the heart.

THOUGHT FOR THE HEART

So many times I wait for church or some organized setting to "worship" You. O Lord, help me to offer You my worship each day. Help me to give You my heart full of praise. You alone are worthy.

— Shelley Chapin

•

A CHORUS OF PRAISE

"Worship the Lord in the splendor of His holiness; tremble before Him, all the earth." Psalm 96:9

"Worship the Lord in the beauty of His holiness!" What a tremendous sentiment! My mind wanders when I read those words to every wonderful sight I have seen in my privileged years. Mountains, lakes, seas, sunrises—all have provided me with a picture of His beauty. But nothing reminds me of worship quite like an experience I had many years ago.

I have been a "speaker" for a number of years now (loosely defined as someone who is invited here and there for a variety of reasons). I call myself "an old Bible teacher," because I am most at home teaching God's Word to those who will hear.

Early on in my speaking ministry, I had some wonderful opportunities to travel overseas, and one such trip taught me much about worship.

The scene was set in Ghent, Belgium. I had been speaking through a translator all week long to students who were hungry to hear the Word of God. While they were not persecuted for our involvement, we lived in the midst of those who openly protested our faith.

One day, while walking to the local restaurant where we took our meals, we became aware of a group of loud Marxist protesters. We paid little attention to them until they followed us into the cafeteria and began chanting their disquieting words right in our midst.

The next moment (and from where I still can't recall) a gentle whisper began to resound through the room. And one by one we all joined the chorus.

"He is Lord, He is Lord. He is risen from the dead and He is Lord. Every knee shall bow, every tongue confess that Jesus Christ is Lord."

Such a simple chorus, yet packed with powerful results. The protesters packed their things and disappeared before we could tire of singing our praise.

The spirit of worship is amazing. Where one moment I had been aggravated by the protesters' noise, the next I heard nothing but the unified voice of God's people.

WORSHIP

Worship is not an activity, though activities might be involved. Worship has little to do with a place, though there are places we feel more comfortable than others. And worship is not about a feeling.

Worship is all about a relationship—a relationship that changes lives, moves hearts, unites people who barely know one another, and silences those who cannot hear its music. Worship grows out of our relationship with the very personal, all-loving God of the universe.

Discover the joy of worship today. Open your eyes and ears to see the sights and hear the sounds of God's people lifting their praise. Worship Him in the absolute splendor of His holiness!

THOUGHT FOR THE HEART

I find I most enjoy worship when. . . .

—Phil Hook

●

WEEK-LONG WORSHIP

"God is spirit, and His worshipers must worship in spirit and in truth." John 4:24

For years I thought I knew what worship was all about! It's that activity we practice in church every Sunday, right? Well, if that's been your basic concept of worship as well, stay with me. You may well need to be rescued from "Worship Defrost Syndrome."

No, W.D.S. is not immediately life-threatening. And it does not seriously weaken our spiritual well-being. It is a malady which produces a minimal paralysis of the soul for six days each week, while allowing its victims to attempt spiritual equilibrium on Sundays.

Even the brief weekly cycle of relief contains its problems, though. Like trying to start a car that's been unused through a six-day, sub-zero storm, it can be extremely difficult to get your worship "cranked up" on a given Sunday morning.

Some churches have decided to deal aggressively with the amazing spread of W.D.S. They have now hired worship leaders who recruit worship teams. And the teams join together each Sunday to "get the old heart pumping" and make a dent in the worship flab.

Now, please don't think that I'm saying that such program changes aren't important. Quite the contrary! Such measures provide a spiritual warmth to an otherwise frosty exercise. Church leaders are trying to help, and the help is much appreciated.

But worship is much more than a weekly experience. The joy of worship grows out of our own individual relationships with God and how we live with Him daily. True worship happens in "spirit and truth," and that is what few believers understand or know how to practice.

The spiritual dimension of life and the truth of God's Word go with you wherever you go. Wherever you may be and regardless of the mood you are in, God is there.

This means that you and I can worship the Lord wherever we may be and then come together with one another to share in worship together. It means that God accepts our love and adoration all week long. It means that He does not demand that we look just right or act just right or be in the perfect mood.

What beautiful balance! We live in worship all week long, and then we share that attitude of worship with each other. There is no greater cure for W.D.S. than for you and for me to reach out to our Father. There is no greater cure and no greater privilege.

Talk to God. Share with Him your frustrations and joys. Think about Him throughout the day. And accept the love and support He offers. Once each week simply does not bring us the closeness we desire.

██████████████ **THOUGHT FOR THE HEART**

I will invest my heart with God today. I will reach out to Him in worship and in truth.

—*Boyd Luter*

●

MODERN-DAY IDOLS

"Not to us, O Lord, not to us but to Your name be the glory, because of Your love and faithfulness." Psalm 115:1

We are always tempted to trust in the gods that seem to work. As followers of Christ, we may give lip service to our trust in God, but when our circumstances become thorny, we often trust in our own performance, our own possessions, or the uncertain promises of other people.

Israel experienced many times of weakness and demoralization. As far as we can tell, Psalm 115 was written when the people were beginning to return from the Babylonian Empire. The heathen nations around them were taunting God and challenging the faith of the remnant. Some grew stronger in the face of the opposition, some began to worry.

The psalmist took charge of the situation by contrasting the inanimate idols of the nations with the personal, living God. "Your idols cannot see, hear or walk," he wrote. "And those who trust in them will be like them" (see Psalm 115:5-8). The words made good sense. There was only one problem.

The heathen nations may have worshiped inanimate objects, but God's people had their idols as well. We have our idols. It is chronological snobbery to say we no longer succumb to primitive idolatry. When we look anywhere else but to God as the source of provision and significance, we miss the truth.

We worship God because He is God. We worship God because it is a privilege to open our hearts and our lives to Him. We worship God because He is the only Being worthy of our ultimate allegiance.

God is personal. He cares for you and for me. Because of His love and goodness, He wants what is best for us. And because He is infinite and sovereign, He is able to accomplish His purposes for our lives.

Rejoice! There is only one God! And He is worthy of our worship—not only a formal gathering where we share stories about Him, but a relationship in which He is honored.

Whether in good times or in bad, choose to serve the Lord. Choose to set aside the temporary in favor of the eternal.

THOUGHT FOR THE HEART

I do have a difficult time worshiping You when times are hard. I feel more "in control" when I place my trust in what or who I know. Accept my worship now. Accept my desire to honor You.

—*Ken Boa*

A NEW SONG

"Speak to one another with psalms, hymns, and spiritual songs. Sing and make music in your heart to the Lord." Ephesians 5:19

Have you ever thought about the power of music in our lives? We get in the car, the radio goes on. We enter the elevator and computerized renditions of familiar tunes fill the space between the floors. We go out to jog with a favorite tape popped into the Walkman. We wake to music, sleep to music, and some of us spend hours observing the popular "music videos."

I am astounded by the influence music has on my life. The age-old adage, "Music has charms to soothe a savage beast, to soften rocks or bend a knotted oak" reminds me of the ways that music touches my heart. Soothing harmonies calm me and bring peace. More exciting, harder-edged songs motivate me. Sad, mournful tunes deliver tears, while funny ditties bring laughter. My life is impacted by music every day.

While music plays a critical role in most of our everyday lives, I can't help wondering about the role of music in our worship. How important is music in our adoration of God? Do we know how to "make music in our hearts"? What kind of songs help us to feel worshipful?

I don't know about you, but sometimes when I worship I tend to focus more on the performance of the music than on the worship of God Himself.

"Did I hit all the right notes?" "The organist and pianist aren't really together." "They need to pick up the tempo just a little."

It is easier, at times, to find what is wrong rather than enjoy what is right. I once heard a church vocalist say, "A soloist shouldn't necessarily be chosen because he or she can perform the song well; what's important is how much feeling the soloist puts into the song." I think God would agree. Our vocal range and ability to have perfect pitch pales in comparison to coming before the Lord with "joyful songs." Nothing is as important as the simple act of a child of God worshiping the Father.

We all have the ability to express ourselves through music. Even if we have no natural musical talent, we are still affected by the ebb and flow of melodies and significant lyrics. Why not take a few minutes right now to worship God?

Thumb through a hymnal or songbook and find some lyrics that express how you feel right now. Choose a tune that captures the message you want to offer God. Let the music that plays such an important part in your life be lifted to the Creator of melody itself.

Let's start with the heart and offer a symphony of thanks to the Creator, our Father, the Lord.

███████████ T H O U G H T   F O R   T H E   H E A R T

Please put a new song in my mouth today, Lord; a hymn of praise to You alone.

—*Pam Campbell*

●

ENCOUNTER THE GLORY

"We have seen His glory, the glory of the one and only Son, who came from the Father, full of grace and truth." John 1:14

When you think of Jesus, what comes to mind? Saving grace? Miracles? Compassion? Suffering? After all, what is supposed to stand out about our Lord?

In the first announcement about the Baby Jesus, the heavenly hosts proclaimed, "Glory to God in the highest" (Luke 2:14). The Incarnation began by proclaiming the glory of God.

John points us toward Jesus with another statement, "We have seen His glory, the glory of the one and only Son, who came from the Father, full of grace and truth." Again, the description chosen to reveal our Lord is one of glory and majesty.

Look at Jesus' first miracle. In a Galilean home Jesus attended a wedding, and with some maternal urging, changed six ceremonial pots full of water into wine. The simple statement of John was, "He has revealed His glory." Glory is where the ministry of Jesus all begins.

I remember my first glimpse of this glory. I was attending a mountain retreat for college students and one morning we were asked to spend the day alone with God.

I dutifully set off up the mountain with my Bible and sack lunch in hand. And all was well, I thought, except for the one small detail of weather. It was raining so hard that much of my day was spent trying to stay dry under my raincoat! I read and prayed a lot that day.

I was not prepared for what happened when I read the simple story of the healing of a man's shriveled hand in Mark 3.

"Stretch out your hand," proclaimed our Lord. And the man simply obeyed. He stretched, and before his eyes the hand was completely restored. God chose that simple moment in the rain to reveal a part of His glory to me.

The wonder of a miracle penetrated the stormy weather of that mountain retreat and remains with me almost forty years later. It was as if I were witness to that event — a crippled hand being made straight and useful. I gained a glimpse of what Jesus came to reveal — His glory.

Have you ever interacted with this strong message of Jesus? Have you seen the miracles of Scripture for their glory? Have you seen the baby in the manger as He was announced by the heavenly hosts? Glorious is His name, in every way.

It is an awareness of the glory of Jesus that empowers Paul to sing even though he is a prisoner in Athens. It is an awareness of the glory of Jesus that gives Peter the faith to say, "We believe and know that You are the Holy One of God" (John 6:68).

How do we respond when we experience the glory of God? Isaiah responded with fear and then obedience. Moses responded by hiding his eyes. Peter, James, and John responded by building three shelters to commemorate the event! Different people have responded in different ways throughout the years.

There is no prescribed response that Jesus requires of you and me. There is no correct way to worship as we encounter His glory. Jesus simply asks that we listen as He makes Himself known to us.

The glory of the Lord is there for all to see—glory in great abundance. There is glory enough to fill temples, move kings, fill disciples with fear, and speak powerfully today. Encounter the glory! And allow yourself the privilege of worshiping our Lord as He reveals Himself to you.

▬▬▬▬▬▬ T H O U G H T   F O R   T H E   H E A R T

I am aware of the glory of God in these specific ways in my life right now.

—*Martha Hook*

●

WORSHIP WITHOUT THE TRAPPINGS

"Sing to Him, sing praise to Him; tell all of His wonderful acts. Glory in His holy name." 1 Chronicles 16:9-10

It began to rain as we climbed slowly up the mountainside. The rain was cool on an otherwise hot day, so I was grateful for the diversion. I gazed around and was newly reminded of why I was there. I had been in Haiti for almost a year now, and God had made it abundantly clear why He wanted me to come. His people were in need of an encourager, and I had something to offer.

We had been riding on mules and burros for nearly an hour. Many walked beside us on foot, but the people had insisted that I ride. I have to confess that I think the ride was more draining than the walk, but I could not refuse their wishes. They longed to honor me, and I graciously received their offering.

Finally we crested the mountain and a gasp audibly escaped my lips. I could see for miles and miles—beautiful, rugged country and the ocean not far away. The view was splendid and I was caught up in the joy of the moment. About that time we began to sing.

I dismounted and tried to blend into the crowd (as much as any Englishwoman can blend into a crowd of Haitians!). I wanted, for just a few moments, to be one with all around me. I didn't want to be the physician or the white woman or the teacher or the guest; I wanted to join with my friends in the worship and praise of our Lord. That is why we were there—to love Him, and to express our love in one accord.

I wish my friends at home could learn to worship without all the trappings of schedule, dress, "properness," and the expected. For several hours that Sunday we simply stood outside in the rain and offered praise to our God. We sang, we laughed, we taught one another, we remained silent. We prayed, we cried, we hugged, and we thought.

Together we made a timeless moment and lifted it to God for His enjoyment. Together we said, "Here we are, Lord! We love You!" Together we stood, united in mind and in purpose. Oh, that the feeling could last a lifetime.

THOUGHT FOR THE HEART

I would love to worship You today in spirit and in truth. May my love be lifted high as an offering to You, Lord. You alone are worthy to be praised!

—Pamela M. Reeves

RHYTHMS OF MY HEART